MW00826828

TRUMAN AND THE BOMB

publication supported by a grant from
The Community Foundation for Greater New Haven
as part of the *Urban Haven Project*

Truman

—AND THE—

BOMB

The Untold Story

D. M. GIANGRECO

Foreword by JOHN T. KUEHN

Potomac Books

An imprint of the University of Nebraska Press

An earlier version of chapter 2 previously appeared as "'To Break Japan's
Spine'" in *Hell to Pay: Operation Downfall and the Invasion of Japan,
1945–1947* (Annapolis MD: Naval Institute Press, 2017), 145–60.
Appendix C by Michael Kort originally appeared as "The Historiography
of Hiroshima: The Rise and Fall of Revisionism," *New England Journal of
History* 64, no. 1 (Fall 2007): 31–48. Portions also appeared in *The Columbia
Guide to Hiroshima and the Bomb* (New York: Columbia University Press,
2007). Used by arrangement with Columbia University Press.
Appendix K by D. M. Giangreco is an excerpt from "Casualty
Projections for the U.S. Invasions of Japan, 1945–1946: Planning and
Policy Implications," *Journal of Military History* 61 (July 1997): 521–82.

Library of Congress Cataloging-in-Publication Data
Names: Giangreco, D. M., 1952– author.
Title: Truman and the bomb : the untold story / D.M. Giangreco.
Description: [Lincoln, Nebraska] : Potomac Books, an imprint of
the University of Nebraska Press, [2023] | Includes bibliographical
references and index.
Identifiers: LCCN 2022051869
ISBN 9781640120730 (hardcover)
ISBN 9781640125933 (epub)
ISBN 9781640125940 (pdf)
Subjects: LCSH: Truman, Harry S., 1884–1972. | World War, 1939–1945—
Campaigns—Japan. | Atomic bomb—United States—History—
20th century. | United States—Military policy—Decision making. |
Hiroshima-shi (Japan)—History—Bombardment, 1945. | Nagasaki-
shi (Japan)—History—Bombardment, 1945 | World War, 1939–1945—
United States. | World War, 1939–1945—Soviet Union. | United
States—Foreign relations—1945-1953. | BISAC: HISTORY / Wars &
Conflicts / World War II / General
Classification: LCC E813 G53 2023 | DDC 973.918092—dc23/eng/20230313
LC record available at https://lccn.loc.gov/2022051869

Set in Minion Pro by Mikala R. Kolander.

Cover: President Harry S. Truman presents General of the Army George
C. Marshall with a second oak leaf cluster to the Distinguished Service
Medal he had been awarded in 1919. Marshall, along with Secretary of
War Henry Stimson, was responsible for both the U.S. Army's massive
Manhattan Project to develop atomic bombs and Project Milepost to
secretly prepare the Soviet Union for its coming war with Japan.

CONTENTS

ILLUSTRATIONS

Figures

Table

FOREWORD

JOHN T. KUEHN

The myths of the closing months of World War II in the Pacific still haunt collective memory. Chief among them are those surrounding President Harry S. Truman and the use of two atomic bombs against the Empire of Japan. As Truman famously claimed, "The buck stops here." And he certainly took the credit and the blame for the use of the bombs, despite the incredible institutional momentum already behind using them in an ongoing bombing campaign against Japan under the command of General Curtis LeMay from the Mariana Islands.

D. M. Giangreco explores this issue and far more in this eye-opening account of the endgame planned by the United States, Great Britain, and eventually the Soviet Union against Imperial Japan.

Often the collective memory of America's war in the Far East is clouded by the obsessive focus on the war in Europe. The Pacific appears in popular memory as an inconvenient afterthought. Suddenly, the conflict in Europe is over and Americans realize that a horrendous battle involving suicide bombers and even World War I–style warfare, accompanied by the skyrocketing casualty lists, is taking place at Okinawa. At the same time, Roosevelt's and, beginning in April 1945, Truman's efforts to end the war in the Pacific faced huge odds. The Japanese still had almost three million undefeated troops in mainland Asia, mostly in China. And time was on the side of the Japanese, who had never been conquered on their own territory in three thousand years of recorded history. It was certain that the Japanese Army would fight to the last man, woman, and child to protect the sacred soil of Dai Nippon with the emperor's support or not.

Historians have sometimes been unkind to Harry Truman, portraying him as clueless about the Manhattan Project as vice president. This was not the case, however, and in chapter 2 Giangreco highlights Truman's involvement in the program and his efforts to help keep it secret from as early as 1943. While he feigned ignorance to some degree because of his position in the U.S. Senate, Truman was clearly "in the know." Meanwhile, Japanese diplomats and their allies in the Imperial Army held out a vain hope that Stalin would force the Americans to renounce their demands for unconditional surrender, even after the release of the Potsdam Declaration should have made it clear that Stalin intended no such thing. Giangreco provides abundant evidence of Soviet intentions in the other direction. He takes the issue of both Roosevelt and Truman's desire to bring the Soviet Union into the war head on, illuminating the little known—and even less understood—Project Milepost and Project Hula (chapter 2).

These massive operations aimed to secretly equip and supply the still neutral Soviet Union, which planned to open an Asian front against the Empire of Japan and hasten its defeat. Appendix Q provides previously overlooked information about the actual training of Soviet sailors in Alaska for these purposes. Giangreco also sheds light on how the U.S. Navy planned to keep the Lend-Lease line of supply open to the Soviet Union through the Sea of Japan once it came into the war against Japan in August 1945. He reveals that Admiral King's orders to implement Operation Keel-blocks 4 supporting Soviet operations were sent directly from the Potsdam Conference.

Another area where Giangreco improves our understanding addresses Truman's motivation for working so hard to get the Soviets involved and for using the atomic bombs: saving American lives. Chapter 4 addresses the stumbling block of the disposition of Poland after the victory in Europe and shows that once it was resolved—something that Roosevelt had avoided for political reasons, but that Truman did not shy away from—Soviet participation in combat against Japan was assured. When Truman is examined through the lens of trying to end a brutal war and save lives, these agreements seem far less sinister than later writers have made them out to be.

The suddenness of Truman's accession to power upon Roosevelt's death and how some of Roosevelt's actions had left Truman with the political equivalent of a rudderless ship is addressed in chapter 6. Truman almost immediately applied a firm hand to the tiller. Coming from the Senate, he was, to a degree, more inclined to share and collaborate than his famous predecessor. Chapter 6 addresses his "hardest decision"—to invade Japan—and thus provides the essential context for his decisions in the last months of World War II, including the one to use all means necessary, including invasion, the Soviets, and atomic bombs, to win the war quickly.

Wrapped up in this discussion is the idea that the Japanese were "trying to surrender," which Giangreco shows to be specious nonsense. Japanese leaders, especially the Imperial Japanese Army led by General Anami Korechika, the nation's war minister, had no such intention. When massive Red Army forces invaded Manchuria shortly after the first atomic bomb was dropped on Hiroshima these men finally realized that their hope for a Soviet brokered peace were vain. So much for trying to surrender. Even so, Anami and his army confederates were willing to wait and see until the second bomb at Nagasaki incinerated their hope that the Americans only had one such weapon. They now feared that their plan to turn Kyushu into a bloody killing field for the American invasion (Operation Olympic) had been trumped. If the Americans had more than one of these bombs they could use them tactically to sanitize the beachheads and layered defenses of southern Kyushu.

This brings the casualty issue back into focus. Truman's concerns about casualties were not some postwar invention. He even asked the Quaker former president Herbert Hoover, no warmonger, for his estimates to compare with those of the U.S. Army. For Kyushu alone these estimates ran into the hundreds of thousands, perhaps a half a million to secure all of Kyushu. Purple Heart medal production, which the U.S. Navy had halted, was restarted, since the navy had already run out of these medals due to its unexpectedly high casualties in the last months of the Pacific fighting. These mounting casualties were the numbers in Truman's mind, the frightful numbers he could not escape as Armageddon approached on the mainland of Japan.

Nonetheless, it was, as they say, a "close run thing." Even when the Japanese Imperial Council for the Direction of War decided to accede to the emperor's request to accept the Potsdam Declaration following the twin earthquakes of the bombs and the Soviets' "August Storm" invasion of Manchuria, Anami merely agreed not to contest the decision; he never supported it. At the last minute, mutinous soldiers of the Guards Division in Tokyo tried to seize the emperor Hirohito's surrender recording the night before its broadcast. They failed and were put down by soldiers loyal to the emperor, with their leaders committing ritual suicide. Anami also committed suicide.

There is also the counterfactual argument of Japan's eventual surrender without the atomic bombs due to the effects of the Soviet invasion, a continued (conventional) strategic combing campaign, and naval blockade. This narrative relies on Truman and General George C. Marshall suddenly deciding to cancel Olympic, the invasion of Kyushu. Giangreco shows that this was not in the cards. The blockade proponents, such as Admiral Ernest J. King, had been quieted, although a few of them did believe that the atomic bombs would accelerate the war's end.

Truman's critics forget the thousands of human beings starving and dying of disease every day the war dragged on, not just in Japan but throughout the ruins of Japan's empire in Asia. What happens to the command and control of the empire if the government collapses around Hirohito? This was also something Hirohito himself feared—Japan as a failed state, just as it had been during the 150 years of war, famine, and death that marked the bloody Sengoku period in the fifteenth and sixteenth centuries. The ethics of using starvation and firebombing to obtain a surrender seem little different, in fact bankrupt, when measured against the deaths inflicted by the atomic bombs and in the long run would have been immeasurably worse.

TRUMAN AND THE BOMB

Prologue

The Debate

The decision to use the atomic bomb was a decision that brought
death to over a hundred thousand Japanese. No explanation can
change that fact and I do not wish to gloss it over. But this deliberate,
premeditated destruction was our least abhorrent choice. The
destruction on Hiroshima and Nagasaki put an end to the Japanese
war. It stopped the fire raids, and the strangling blockade; it
ended the ghastly specter of a clash of great land armies.

—SECRETARY OF WAR HENRY L. STIMSON, 1945

Hiroshima. The word conjures up visions of fire. Fire rising up in a towering pillar boiling the very sky as flesh melts from the bones of human bodies far enough from ground zero to have not been vaporized in the initial atomic spark. By the end of September 1945, Japanese authorities had meticulously tallied 70,631 dead and missing–declared dead plus 19,942 "serious" injuries from the August 6 Hiroshima blast.[1] (See appendix A, "Air-Raid Casualties and Property Damage in Japan.") Yet this was only a fraction of the bloodbath taking place along the giant arch of the western Pacific and Asian mainland from Indonesia to northern China and Manchuria during just the last five months of the war.

The number of deaths in 1945 was reaching unimaginable levels, averaging in the range of an incredible four hundred thousand souls per month.[2] These deaths were mostly "invisible" because the vast majority involved civilians, they occurred far from Amer-

1

ican eyes, and they owed principally to starvation, disease, and exposure. Many, however, were the direct result of combat. In February and early March a frenzy of Japanese killing sprees and mass executions (and eventually U.S. artillery fire) in Manila left nearly one hundred thousand dead in the central city.[3] More than eighty-eight thousand died during the Tokyo incendiary bombing on the night of March 8–9, when a cyclone of fire rose from the city's eastern districts and the corpses were stacked four deep in the canals where many had fled to escape the inferno only to be boiled alive.[4] Up to one hundred thousand people died on Okinawa from April through June as the fighting rolled over that island.[5] And China had been experiencing carnage of this sort in bloody peaks for nearly a decade.

Looking ahead to the fighting in Japan itself, a War Department study ordered by Secretary of War Henry L. Stimson concluded that to end the war, "we shall probably have to kill at least 5 to 10 million Japanese."[6] Meanwhile, Imperial General Headquarters in Tokyo made its own clear-eyed assessments. Beyond the dreadful losses suffered in Japan's Okinawa Prefecture and during the Tokyo bombing, nearly ninety thousand more Japanese civilians had lost their lives in recent months—most burned to death or asphyxiated by American incendiary bombs—and eight million had been made homeless even before the atomic bombs were dropped.[7] Based largely on just the Okinawa fighting, a further loss of a remarkable twenty million (represented as total casualties in some records and deaths alone in others) became the figure discussed in Imperial circles.[8]

But it was the ever-growing American casualties in the Pacific that were foremost on the minds of civilian and military leaders in Washington. The dead, wounded, and missing had been climbing steadily throughout the war and were reaching increasingly frightening levels as 1945 ground on: thirty-one thousand on Luzon, twenty-eight thousand on tiny Iwo Jima, followed by brutal all-causes, all-services losses of seventy-two thousand on Okinawa.[9] As General George C. Marshall, the chief of staff of the U.S. Army, lamented to a group of historians in June, "The full impact of the war comes more to me, I think, in some respects than it does to anyone in this country. The daily casualty lists are mine. They arrive in a constant stream, a swelling stream, and I can't get away from them."[10]

Just two days before Harry S. Truman had taken his oath of office as vice president, the *New York Times* printed the warning of General Marshall and chief of naval operations Admiral Ernest J. King that the armed services needed to induct nine hundred thousand men over the next six months to meet the needs of the coming one-front war against Japan.[11] Less than two months later, former president Herbert Hoover's assessment—in a memorandum requested by Truman—spelled out in plain English that the invasion of Japan could cost between five hundred thousand and one million American lives.[12] (See appendix B, "Memorandum on Ending the Japanese War" [memo 4 of 4, May 30, 1945], containing President Harry S. Truman's notation identifying its author and Truman's memorandum to Secretary of War Henry Stimson asking for his opinion.)

This estimate was fully twice of the Pentagon's and Truman had copies of Hoover's memo sent to his most senior civilian advisors on matters pertaining to the war. These men, Secretary Stimson, Undersecretary of State Joseph C. Grew, Director of the Office of War Mobilization and Reconversion Fred M. Vinson, and former secretary of state Cordell Hull, either did not take issue with Hoover's figures or pointedly gave their own grim assessments. Immediately on the heels of the "Truman-Grew-Hull-Stimson-Vinson exchange," Truman called a meeting of the Joint Chiefs of Staff and secretaries of the armed services in order to discuss "the losses in dead and wounded that will result from an invasion of Japan proper." They were informed unequivocally by the White House chief of staff, Admiral William D. Leahy, that "it is [the president's] intention to make his decision on the campaign with the purpose of economizing to the maximum extent possible in the loss of American lives. Economy in the use of time and in money cost is comparatively unimportant."[13]

The fighting on Okinawa was still grinding on when President Truman, a month before the Potsdam Conference, met with these most senior wartime advisors on Monday, June 18, 1945. Nearly all of the casualties, Japanese and American, military and civilian, had taken place at the southern end of the island within an area smaller than that of metropolitan Detroit. Roughly 35 percent of the American soldiers and marines committed to the three-month battle had become casualties and much of the White House meeting centered on the ramifications of that percentage and the likelihood that it would be repeated among the 766,700-man force being committed to Olympic, the first—and smaller—operation of the two-phase invasion of Japan.[14]

All the participants agreed that an invasion of Japan's "home islands" would be extremely costly, but an invasion, in addition to the blockade and bombardment that was already taking place, was essential for the defeat of Imperial Japan. Marshall remarked: "It is a grim fact that there is not an easy, bloodless way to victory." Secretary of War Henry Stimson stated that he "agreed with the plan proposed by the Joint Chiefs of Staff as being the best thing to do, but he still hoped for some fruitful accomplishment through other means." President Truman concluded the conference by stating that the main reason he called them together was "his desire to know definitely how far we could afford to go in the Japanese campaign." Truman stated that he was "clear on the situation now and was quite sure that the Joint Chiefs of Staff should proceed with the Kyushu operation."[15]

In the face of the frightful amount of America casualties expected during the invasion, Truman approved Operation Olympic against Japan's southernmost home island of Kyushu at this meeting and expressed hope that a possibility existed of "preventing an Okinawa from one end of Japan to the other." Like Stimson, he reasoned that there was a chance that "other means" could force Japan's surrender. These included a range of measures, from increased political pressure brought by a display of Allied unanimity at the upcoming conference in Potsdam and the Soviet Union honoring its pledge to enter the war after the defeat of Germany, to the untested atomic weapons that military leaders thought might "shock" the Japanese government into surrender.[16]

For the five million young Americans gathering in the Pacific to take part in the invasion operations of 1945 and 1946, the dropping of atomic bombs felt like nothing short of a miracle. James Jones of the 25th Infantry Division, who would survive his grievous wounding on Guadalcanal to author *From Here to Eternity* and *Some Came Running*, understood as few today could "what it must have been like for some old-timer buck sergeant . . . who had been through Guadalcanal and Bougainville and the Philippines, to stand on some beach and watch this huge war machine beginning to move and stir all around him and know that he very likely had survived this far only to fall dead in the dirt of Japan's Home Islands."[17] As Jones later recalled, "It was known and gossiped about everywhere in the Pacific, and at home among the troops training for the invasion, that the United States expected and was prepared to lose the first three waves, something like one hundred thousand men just getting ashore and in the first few days."[18]

Such loose talk was more than rumor; it was based on hard-learned, brutally cold facts. The commander of the 931st Engineer Construction Group (Aviation), Colonel John H. Dudley, was initially chagrined to find that his engineers were landing with the second invasion echelon, a delay that could have serious repercussions for troops in desperate need of close air support. A close examination of the operational plans, however, quickly revealed that the second landing force was assigned the exact same objectives as the first. "It was clear to me then," Dudley observed. "They expected the first echelon to be wiped out."[19]

Long after the war, a comprehensive U.S. Marine Corps examination of the opposing forces, terrain, and operational plans of the three combat divisions landing on the westernmost beaches came to the conclusion that the "V Amphibious Corps would likely have expended itself trying to reach its two primary objectives, Sendai to the north and Kagoshima to the east."[20] It is likely no accident that the officers who produced the report used of the words "trying to reach" instead of "reaching." Major General Graves B. Erskine, who was to command V Corps's 3rd Marine Division during the invasion, remarked: "Victory was never in doubt. Its cost was. . . . What was in doubt, in all our minds, was whether there would be any of us left to dedicate our cemetery at the end, or whether the last Marine would die knocking out the last Japanese gun and gunner."[21]

Many years later, author James Michener, who was stationed on one of the remote island bases, wrote his friend and fellow vet Martin Allday of the dread eating away at the men of the army's 27th Infantry Division and associated 31st General and 23rd Evacuation Hospitals:

In the summer of 1945 I was stationed on Espiritu Santo close to a big Army field hospital manned by a complete stateside hospital staff from Nebraska and Colorado. I had close relations with the doctors, so I was privy to their thinking about the forthcoming invasion of Japan. They had been alerted to prepare for moving onto the beaches of Kyushu when we invaded there and they were prepared to expect vast numbers of casualties when the Japanese home front defense forces started their suicide attacks.

More important, I was on my own very close to an Army division that was stationed temporarily in a swampy wooded section on our island. They were a disheartened unit for the Japanese had knocked them about a bit in the action on Saipan; their assignment to our swamp was a kind of punishment for their ineffective conduct on Saipan. Now they were informed unofficially that they would be among the first units to hit the beach in our invasion of Kyushu, and they were terrified. In long talks with me, they said that they expected 70 or 80 percent casualties, and they could think of no way to avoid the impending disaster.

So it was with knowledge of what the doctors anticipated and what the Army men felt was inescapable, that I approached the days of early August, and I, too, became a bit shaky because the rumor was that I might be attached to the Army unit because of my expertise in keeping airplanes properly fitted and in the sky. Then came the astounding news that a bomb of a new type had been dropped on Hiroshima, a second one on Nagasaki, and that the Japanese emperor himself had called upon his people to surrender peacefully and await the Allied peace-keeping forces to land and establish the changes required by the recent turn of events.

How did we react? With a gigantic sigh of relief, not exultation because of our victory, but a deep gut-wrenching sigh of deliverance. We had stared into the mouth of Armageddon and suddenly the confrontation was no longer necessary. We had escaped those deadly beaches of Kyushu.

I cannot recall who was the more relieved, the doctors who could foresee the wounded and the dying, or the G.I. grunts who would have done the dying, or the men like me who had sensed the great tragedy that loomed. All I know is that we said prayers of deliverance and kept our mouths shut when arguments began as to whether the bombs needed to be dropped or not. And I have maintained that silence to this moment, when I wanted to have the reactions of the men . . . who had figured to be on the first waves in.

Let's put it simply. Never once in those first days nor in the long reconsiderations later could I possibly have criticized Truman for having dropped that first bomb. True, I see now that the second bomb on Nagasaki might have been redundant and I would have been just as happy if it had not been dropped. And I can understand how some historians can argue that Japan might have surrendered without the Hiroshima bomb, but the evidence from many nations involved at that moment testify to the contrary.

From my experience on Saipan and Okinawa, when I saw how violently the Japanese soldiers defended their caves to the death, I am satisfied that they would have done the same on Kyushu. Also, because I was in aviation and could study battle reports about the effectiveness of airplane bombing, especially with those super-deadly firebombs that ate up the oxygen supply of a great city, I was well aware that the deaths from the fire bombing of Tokyo in early 1945 far exceeded the deaths of Hiroshima.

So I have been able to take refuge in the terrible, time-tested truism that war is war, and if you are unlucky enough to become engaged in one, you better not lose it. The doctrine, cruel and thoughtless as it may sound, governs my thought, my evaluations and my behavior.[22]

A remarkable letter. But what prompted James Michener to write it?

In the mid-1960s, a growing distrust of government and sympathy for the Vietnam protest movement among American intellectuals revitalized the antinuclear "ban the bomb" campaign, which few had taken very seriously before, and spurred criticism of the use of atomic weapons to end World War II. Since then, "enlightened opinion" had been—and continues to be—dominated by a revisionism fueled by seductive tales of conspiracy in high places, unabashed fact-bending, and manipulation of the historical record. The underlying premise behind most, if not all, of the efforts to reexamine the final days of the war against Japan by revisionist historians is the idea that none of the options explored by President Truman and his contemporaries—atom bomb, invasion, or both—was warranted. Rather, they contend that a boisterous but essentially innocent Japan was maneuvered into the war by a cunning and duplicitous United States with ineptitude, chance, miscalculation, and the like figuring only in relatively minor ways, and that the battered and desperate Japanese forces were eager to surrender if only the United States would agree to letting Emperor Hirohito remain on the throne.

Many educators didn't particularly trust the contentions of the revisionists, but their research, thin as it was, became heralded as the "newest scholarship," displayed the right academic architecture, and was gaining acceptability (even among those who should know better) through repetition.

The Japan-as-victim narrative had become embedded by 1994, when the Smithsonian's National Air and Space Museum (NASM) in Washington DC proposed an exhibition to mark the fiftieth anniversary of the end of World War II that would include displaying the Enola Gay, the B-29 Superfortress used to drop the bomb on Hiroshima. A prolonged battle immediately erupted over the exhibition script, which portrayed the Japanese people as "defend[ing] their unique culture against Western imperialism," whereas for the Americans it was simply "a war of vengeance."[23]

In the end there were no winners in that sad affair, which left in its wake tarnished careers, the dismissal of NASM's director,

Martin Harwit, and a torrent of angry words. Harwit, who tried vainly to keep his footing at the center of the melee, wrote after his dismissal from NASM that the controversy was a battle between a "largely fictitious, comforting story" presented by the veterans and the true event "as revealed in trustworthy documents now at hand in the nation's archives," which the veterans "feared . . . could cast into doubt a hallowed, patriotic story."[24]

Veterans' groups during the white-hot debate were routinely dismissed as being overly sensitive to "inconsequential" points in the text that focused almost entirely on the civilian casualties of a single nation, Japan. Yet as geopolitical and national security authority Henry Kissinger used to say, "Even paranoids have real enemies."[25] Martin Allday, wounded on Okinawa and scheduled to head back to the Pacific for the 1946 invasion of the Tokyo area, had been persistent in his efforts to get his author friend, Michener, to weigh in publicly with his knowledge of what the men faced. But this was one battle that Allday could not win.

Michener, like many in the entertainment industry, had already been solicited to make a statement on the "censorship" of NASM and the Smithsonian but had "refused opportunities to testify against the United States in the Hiroshima matter."[26] Although he had attained great stature as an author and become known to millions of Americans through film and television adaptations of his work such as *South Pacific* and *Centennial*, he would only take part in several local commemorative events in Texas. Michener's well-founded fear of the reaction from the literary and Hollywood circles he moved in was so strong that he made Allday promise not to release the letter he'd written until after his death. Said Michener: "I know that if I went public with my views I would be condemned and ridiculed, but I stood there on the lip of the pulsating volcano, and I know that I was terrified at what might happen and damned relieved when the invasion became unnecessary. I accept the military estimates that at least 1 million lives were saved, and mine could have been one of them."[27]

That Michener preferred to keep his opinions to himself, though disappointing, is not particularly surprising when one remembers the derision heaped on veterans at the time from some historians and major institutions. The common refrain, "thank God for the atomic bomb," seemed callous and puzzling to those with little knowledge of the war, and many in the academy supported Martin Harwit's contentions. They maintained that the "contemporary historical scholarship" displayed in the original exhibit script was both sound and authoritative. As far as they were concerned, "A great many U.S. soldiers in the Pacific in 1945 believed the bombs brought the war to a speedy end, but they were not in a position to know."[28]

This presumed, of course, that assumptions based on these "trustworthy" documents were themselves correct and derived from a comprehensive understanding of the material. Yet in the case of NASM, critical decisions about the principal hot-button issue—casualty estimates for the invasion of Japan—were based on highly qualified and limited U.S. Army projections printed in a variety of briefing documents. Scholars involved in the Enola Gay exhibit did not realize that these estimates, derived from standard U.S. Army methodologies for creating such materials, usually represented only the initial thirty days in what was envisioned in 1945 as a series of campaigns extending throughout 1946 and perhaps into 1947.

In effect, it is as if someone during World War II had come across casualty estimates for the invasion of Sicily and then declared that the numbers must represent losses from the entire Italian campaign—and then, having gone that far, announced with complete certitude that the numbers actually depicted likely casualties for the balance of the war with Germany. During the war, such a notion would be dismissed as laughably absurd, and the flow of battle would speedily move beyond the single event that the original estimates—be they good or bad—were for. That, however, was in a long ago war, and historians doing much the same thing decades later have won awards and the plaudits of their peers, received copious grants, and shaped the decisions of major institutions.

In 1945 both the planners creating the documents and the senior officials receiving them— including Secretary Stimson, General Marshall, Admiral Leahy, and President Harry S. Truman himself— understood their contents, as this volume will demonstrate. But institutional memory faded. A half-century and many foggy recollections later, the contentious Enola Gay controversy served to focus attention on the limited nature of the few documents being used by both the critics and supporters of the exhibit, and fresh research beyond the most readily available materials—the "top layer" documents—yielded results that greatly surprised many scholars.

It turned out that President Truman's much-derided accounts of massive casualties projected for the two-phase invasion of Japan were not, as his critics maintained, a "postwar creation" to justify dropping the bombs.[29] Far from fraudulent, they are richly supported by U.S. Army, White House, Selective Service, and War Department documents produced prior to the use of nuclear weapons against Japan and stretching all the way back through the last nine months of the Roosevelt administration. Moreover, the casualty estimates were not secreted away in obscure Pentagon departments to be seen only by the eyes of anonymous junior officers, as the high-level Truman-Grew-Hull-Stimson-Vinson exchange and the subsequent invasion conference at the White House demonstrated.

In truth, military and diplomatic historians had come across and, in some cases published, much of the data before the brawl on the Mall, but its appearance was fragmented and spread over a period of decades. A whole spate of useful works examining various aspects of the end of the war and the atom bomb decision were released around the fiftieth anniversary of the war's end, but although these books were produced by noted scholars, they did not fit into the long-established trend of "Truman bashing." As occurs with so many useful works, they were destined to die the slow death of obscurity, as few of the people who might be able to learn from and use them would ever hear of their release. The ruckus raised by the veterans changed all that, and the books that Robert James Maddox, Robert P. Newman, Norman Polmar with Thomas B. Allen, Edward Drea, Stanley Weintraub, and Alvin D. Coox released around that time received far more visibility than their authors could have dared hope for.[30]

In my own case, and following the books of these scholars, I produced a study in 1997 for the *Journal of Military History* (*JMH*) that examined the methodologies used to produce casualty estimates from the Enlightenment and American Revolution through World War II. "Casualty Projections for the U.S. Invasions of Japan, 1945–1946: Planning and Policy Implications" included precisely what was estimated as the Pacific War came to its bloody conclusion and a sort-of "who knew what-when" for Truman and his senior advisors.[31] Oddly, a comprehensive examination of this sort had not been produced before, apparently because everyone alive when the war ended understood that a land invasion of Japan would have generated enormous losses. No one had suspected that this was something that would later be seriously questioned.

During the war, Dr. Michael DeBakey had produced highly classified Pentagon manpower and casualty data including top-secret analyses of escalating U.S. troop losses that were used by Truman's senior advisors and became a part of their discussions with him. After the war he was the principal proponent behind the development of MASH (Mobile Army Surgical Hospital) units and became well known to the public for his work in the field of heart surgery. DeBakey graciously assigned one of his students at the Baylor University College of Medicine to help me locate certain documents. After fretting over America's deteriorating institutional knowledge of the environment in which all life-and-death decisions had to be made in 1945, DeBakey stated that having to demonstrate that the invasion of Japan would produce "catastrophic casualties" was ridiculous: "It's like having to prove that slamming someone's head with a meat axe will kill him."[32]

The very public Enola Gay mess was like a flashing white light. It was suddenly obvious that you did indeed have to "prove that slamming someone's head with a meat axe will kill him" and that Harry S. Truman well understood the dynamics of a meat cleaver plunging in the direction of that head. The fight at NASM focused critical attention on the problem—indeed, I wouldn't have even known about it, let alone written about it, otherwise—and presidential historian Arthur M. Schlesinger Jr. stated his delight that the JMH "Casualty Projections" study had "demolished the claim that President Truman's high casualty estimates were a postwar invention."[33] Additional research conducted after the exhibit spurred the release of even more books and journal articles by noted scholars such as Richard B. Frank, Sadao Asada, Wilson D. Miscamble, and Michael Kort.

Virtually all of the pillars supporting the revisionist contention that use of the atomic bomb was militarily unjustified were knocked down over a surprisingly short period of time (see appendix C, "The Historiography of Hiroshima" by Michael Kort). For example, the criticism of Truman's decision to drop the bomb almost invariably used the 1946 *Summary Report* of the United States Strategic Bombing Survey (USSBS) report on operations in the Pacific to prop up the line that such a drastic action was unnecessary because the conventional bombing of Japan would have forced its surrender "certainly" before 31 December 1945 and "in all probability" before November 1 "even if Russia had not entered the war, and even if no invasion had been planned or contemplated."[34]

This concluding sliver of the massive, 108-volume Pacific study had no impact at all within military and political circles at the time—and for good reason. While it might not have been so obvious to individuals examining the document when it was resurrected in the 1960s, those reading it in the 1940s recognized that the *Summary Report* was written as a highly political document and treated it as such. One can look at the line of questions in, for example, Senate testimony over proposed roles and missions of the Armed Services or the questions by USSBS interrogators in Japan to see what kind of answers were being shaped to support the long-term objectives of newly established U.S. Air Force.

For researchers looking at the *Summary Report* decades later, the evident case-building was not so evident, and its conclusions were taken at face value. Employing their rigor in the mid-1990s, however, scholars prompted by the work of Robert Newman (including Gian Peri Gentilly and Truman critic Barton J. Bernstein) rediscovered what many in Washington, the media, and the other armed services, through their own rigor and experience, understood in the 1940s. The oft-quoted statement in the final *Summary Report* is soundly refuted by the USSBS's own evidence and most comprehensively in its published interrogations of senior Japanese officials.[35]

Another pillar to fall was the notion that the Japanese forces were itching to surrender as early as the summer of 1945 if the Allies granted terms that would allow them to keep their emperor, and that President Truman and his advisors knew this full well. Through the secret decoding of Japanese military and diplomatic communications, aerial reconnaissance, and other intelligence efforts, American leaders knew differently. Far from being disheartened by the long string of American victories, the Japanese government was committing enormous resources to defend the targeted invasion beaches and crush the Yankee devils. As demonstrated above and confirmed decades later by Ed Drea and Al Coox in separate studies, after three years of the U.S. military's island hopping and end runs in the Pacific, Japanese leaders had gained a clear understanding of the methods and logistic requirements of America's rigidly set-piece amphibious operations, and correctly deduced that southern Japan would be the next stepping stone on the drive toward the heart of their empire.[36]

Related to this was an exchange of diplomatic communications between Japan's foreign minister and its ambassador to the Soviet Union, which some have characterized as evidence that the country was on the brink of calling it quits. In the summer of 1945 Emperor Hirohito requested that the Soviets accept Prince Konoye Fumimaro, a former prime minister and one of his most senior counselors, as a special envoy to discuss the ways in which the war might be "quickly terminated."

The Japanese initiative, however, was not at all what Truman's later critics claimed it to be. While the Americans were focused on "surrender," the Imperial leadership was focused on stringing things out through "mediation" leading to an armistice that would leave not only the emperor on the throne but Japanese forces still in control of an intact empire and the ruling militarists free to pick and choose which underlings would be given up as war criminals.

It was clear from the beginning that, far from a coherent plea to the Soviets to help negotiate a surrender, the proposals were purposely vague. As such they were viewed by both Washington and Moscow as little more than a stalling tactic ahead of the Potsdam Conference to prevent Soviet military intervention, an intervention that Japanese leaders had known was inevitable ever since the Soviets' recent cancellation of their Neutrality Pact with Japan. Herbert Bix, in his Pulitzer-winning *Hirohito and the Making of Modern Japan*, wrote: "The Japanese 'peace' overtures to the Soviets, which had followed Germany's capitulation, were vague, feeble, and counterproductive. They certainly never constituted a serious attempt to negotiate an end to the war."[37]

Some civilian elements within Japan's ruling circle were determined to try to find a way to end the war before the U.S. invasion was launched. Unfortunately, the militarists were in firm control of the government, and Japanese "moderates" had to tread gingerly for fear of arrest or assassination. American officials reading the secretly intercepted messages between Japan's ambassador to the Soviet Union in Moscow and its foreign minister in Tokyo could clearly see that the "defeatist" ideas of the ambassador received nothing more than stinging rebukes from his superior. The fanatical Japanese militarists retained their grip on the decision-making process until the simultaneous shocks of the atom bombs and Soviet entry into the war in August 1945 stampeded Japan's leaders into an early capitulation.[38]

As the pillars underpinning the case against the use of the atomic bombs began to crumble, Truman's critics scrambled to come up with ways to salvage their arguments and explain why leaders on both sides of the conflict made the decisions that they did. This led to some very fancy footwork. For example, the chief proponent of the idea that Truman had made up the massive casualty estimates now turned on a dime, suddenly concluding that the numbers were not only real but so large that Truman would abandon the war. This led Robert Maddox, who had spent decades mincing, slicing, and dicing revisionists over their misuses of the historical record, to wryly comment that this new argument provided the ultimate low American casualty figure to compare against those of Hiroshima and Nagasaki: "zero."[39]

Another contention, which tapped into the urge of many to downplay the critical importance of the atomic bombs in ending the war, was that Tokyo surrendered not because of the atomic attacks on Hiroshima and Nagasaki but because of the Soviet declaration of war. This notion had been in circulation since the earliest days of the atomic debate—indeed even before—with both critics and defenders of the president emphasizing to varying degrees that the "twin shocks" of the bombs and the Soviet invasion of Japanese Manchuria finally forced the Japanese militarists to concede defeat.[40] Now, the final moves in the end game against Japan were recast as a "race" between the United States and Soviet Union. The Americans pushed to use their deadly new weapon to end the war before the Soviets could intervene, while the Soviets moved up their invasion of Manchuria to prevent just such an outcome.[41]

At first this idea was eagerly received and promoted, but it quickly fell apart as a wide range of scholars specializing in the Soviet, Japanese, American historiographies of the endgame and nuclear development pointed out fundamental problems with the theory. For example, the preeminent authority on the decisions of the Japanese war cabinet, Sadao Asada, maintained that Japanese documents from the period clearly demonstrate that the military leaders dominating the government were not ready—or even considering—surrender until receiving the "shock" of the atomic bombs (that's bombs, plural). Leading authorities on Soviet military and nuclear policy such as David Holloway and Jacob Kipp also noted that Soviet documents contradict the idea that the Soviet Union and United States were in such a "race." Meanwhile, a wide variety of American scholars pointed out that both the Roosevelt and Truman administrations labored consistently to get the Red Army *into* the fighting as early as possible (see chapters 3 and 6).

For most Americans, though, such contentions by Truman's critics did not resonate. Though the innerworkings of the Japan's ruling junta, supposed amphibious capabilities of the Soviets in the Pacific, and machinations of U.S. Air Force proponents might prompt a heated debate among some scholars and history wonks, they were far too esoteric to affect how the public at large viewed the use of atomic bombs to end the war.

But while these arguments were not as useful as their proponents had hoped, the original revisionist contentions that the massive casualty estimates for the planned invasion of Japan were a "postwar creation" and that the Japanese forces were trying to surrender still remain a common—and seductive—refrain. Most strikingly, the notion that President Truman dropped the bombs on Japan to intimidate the Russians continues to hold a strong attraction for the simple reason that it offers its own elegantly simple explanation for the Cold War. An explanation, moreover, that presents a political and morality play where a single, recognizable figure—Harry S. Truman—can be used as a proxy for America and its "guilt" for unleashing nuclear weapons upon the world.

Interestingly, this turn of events came as a surprise to some historians who had followed the decades-long rise of atomic bomb revisionism, albeit at a distance. When the deluge of data and contemporaneous documentation supporting the actions of Roosevelt, Truman, and their advisors burst forth on both sides of the Pacific in the aftermath of the Enola Gay fiasco and the death of Emperor Hirohito several years earlier, conscientious scholars such as the de facto editor of Truman's private papers, Robert H. Ferrell, were convinced that the tide had turned. "In long retrospect, now more than half a century," Ferrell observed, "it is safe to say that not merely has Cold War revisionism in general come to an unlamented end, but the single remaining contention of some present-day historians, political scientists, and publicists, over the use of nuclear weapons against wartime Japan, has run its course."[42]

Robert Maddox was not so sure. At the same 1999 conference where Ferrell mused over the "obsequies for nuclear revisionism," he cautioned that his friend "seems too optimistic about the state of scholarship on this subject." Maddox added:

> [Ferrell] cites a number of works that he claims "nearly finished off nuclear revisionism" and states that an article by Sadao Asada provided the "coup de grace." These comments would be warranted if evidence constituted the only criterion. It does not. That the atomic bombs were unnecessary has become the mantra, the bag, the shtick of a number of individuals whose reputations rest on the continued flogging of a dead horse. No amount of documentation will sway them from their task. Unfortunately, the atmosphere in academe and in the media today is much more receptive to their Rube Goldbergish version of events than to

the stodgy view that Truman used the bombs for the reason he said he did: to prevent a bloody war from becoming far bloodier had an invasion of Japan proved necessary.[43]

Afterward, Ferrell confidently maintained that "facts always win out" but soon confided that his comments were "made in hope more than anything else." Within a few years, he would declare that Maddox "couldn't have been more right."[44] Ferrell became particularly disappointed and dismayed by the persistence of the idea—reflexively parroted on the internet, in print, and by many educators in spite of all the documentation to the contrary—that Truman "invented" the five hundred thousand casualty estimate. And he was genuinely surprised by how few in academia were aware of the recently discovered Truman-Grew-Hull-Stimson-Vinson exchange in the Truman Library, which prompted the White House meeting between the president and his most senior advisors on "the losses in dead and wounded that will result from an invasion of Japan."

It became apparent to "optimists" like Ferrell and Schlesinger that there is such a vast amount of material available and continuing to be published in this general subject area that even those with more than a passing interest in the Pacific War will never be able to read it all. They will functionally depend on the widely publicized critics of Truman who are regularly presented to the unwary as unimpeachable experts. And these critics believe—with some justification—that all they have to do is firmly maintain something for it to be accepted at face value and made available to students by likeminded thinkers and the lazy. That is also much of the reason that Truman's critics studiously ignore works that raise troubling questions about their own scholarship.

In spite of the emergent documentation supporting Truman's use of atom bombs, the drum beat of criticism persists. Former Air Force chief historian Stanley Falk expressed his amazement that revisionist historians "keep beating this dead horse."[45] But it must be remembered that Truman's detractors are confident that, except in rare instances, they won't have to address the fact that the horse is dead. They try to deny their foes' visibility in the hope that they will be marginalized and fade from view or, better yet, that their research will not be seen and considered in the first place.

Most gamesmanship by Truman critics is invisible to the public at large because it appears in academic journals and remains functionally "out of sight," only seen when used as the basis for ill-informed decisions like the ones the NASM made during the Smithsonian Institution's Enola Gay fiasco. Yet sometimes their overconfidence leads to so some very public displays of poor scholarship. A typical example is the work of Kai Bird who, with Martin J. Sherwin, won a Pulitzer Prize for *American Prometheus: The Triumph and Tragedy of J. Robert Oppenheimer*. During the Enola Gay mess, Bird firmly maintained in the *New York Times*: "No scholar of the war has ever found archival evidence to substantiate claims that Truman expected anything close to a million casualties, or even that such large numbers were conceivable."[46]

Well, I suppose that it is true that the army chief of staff and the chief of naval operations were not "scholars" in the narrow sense that Bird was using the word. But General George C. Marshall and Fleet Admiral Ernest J. King, looking ahead to the coming "one-front" war against Japan, did inform the public in January 1945, as noted earlier, that the U.S. Army "must provide 600,000 replacements for overseas theaters before June 30, and, together with the Navy, will require a total of 900,000 inductions by June 30 [1945]."[47]

There are countless examples of this sort in the literature and press, but what makes Bird's claim one of my personal favorites is his appeal to authority (himself), the complete certitude that nothing in the historiography contradicts his damning indictment against President Truman, and the fact that the contradiction to his assertion not only exists but that it was part of a front-page article in the very same newspaper in which he would pillory Truman forty-nine years later. But there are no particular consequences to putting nonsense of this sort into print. Indeed, Bird's baseless condemnation preceded his Pulitzer, and he continues to be viewed as an authority today despite a continuing series of ahistorical pronouncements.[48] And who would be the wiser beyond a core of serious educators, young and old and of varying political bents, most of whom were unaware of the extent of the revisionists' shenanigans until the Enola Gay mess and its aftermath?

Did Bird know of the statement made by General Marshall and Admiral King and simply lie to *New York Times* readers and the other American media outlets that follow that paper's lead? I think not. It seems far more likely that he knew nothing at all of it, as the bibliographies and endnotes of his and virtually all of the books critical of the decision to use the atomic bomb give the appearance that their authors stopped doing any serious reading or archival research well before the data deluge following the Enola Gay fiasco and death of Hirohito. At the very least, Bird provides a glimpse at the lack of inquisitiveness by many who have criticized Truman. His and others' pronouncements make it clear that either they are attempting to deceive or that they don't even bother to read the newspapers of the day and are content to view the world of 1945 through a lens fashioned during a completely different Asian war that occurred during their own youth some two decades later.

Americans have not been served well by the skewed interpretations this tendency has wrought and, having closely observed the quality of the scholarship that has helped drive evolving attitudes about the end of the war, the late Larry Bland, editor of the George C. Marshall Papers Project, would periodically quip that I should write an article titled "Everything You Thought You Knew About the End of the War Is Wrong." He was only half joking. Although my Naval Institute Press book *Hell to Pay*—portions of which reappear in this volume—addresses the military factors weighing on the invasion planning for Japan, its length, density, and narrow focus meant that only the bare minimum could be written about the man for whom "the buck stopped" on the decision to use atomic weapons: Harry S. Truman.

This point is important because, for many critics of Truman, the military aspects of the decision are considered purely a sideshow in spite of the fact that it was the crushing weight of the military factors surrounding the planned invasion of Japan that drove all decisions during this period. Similarly, for the increasing number of Americans who might readily mistake Admiral King for a brand of salmon or a *Pirates of the Caribbean* character, the life and death issues swirling around such things as the head counting of casualties and the realities of Pacific theater logistics are utterly incomprehensible. Truman's critics breezily dismiss such matters, examined in depth in *Hell to Pay*, as "arcane historiographical disputes."[49]

Military historians and history buffs aside, many educators are uncomfortable with the revisionist take on the bombings, but they often lack, as Larry Bland put it, "something that they can hang their hats on."[50] Robert Ferrell, who authored, coauthored, or edited innumerable books and articles on Truman, his contemporaries, and the times in which they lived, believed that for most educators—constrained by both time and their own knowledge of the subject—the clearest, most direct way to teach the subject was to focus on the motivations and actions of the one individual that most of their students have at least some familiarity with: Truman. And Bob had an idea.

In 2005 Ferrell, who was already knee deep into producing a hard-hitting series of books examining the U.S. Army in World War I, came up with a simple proposal for something that his "young friend" (me) should undertake. The following is a paraphrase of the gentle prods that would occur two or three times a year for the next decade: "Someone, like yourself for instance, really needs to write a short book that's readily adaptable to classroom use, perhaps thirty-five thousand words. A short and direct account centering on the 'what-did-he-know-and-when-did-he-know-it?' of Truman's decision."

Of course, I had no clue who else might be receiving his pitch, but I liked the idea and steadfastly replied that I would leap to it as soon as I got "just one more" project out of the way. *Truman and the Bomb* is the fulfillment of that promise to Bob Ferrell, who passed away in 2018 and, I hope, an adequate one.

The public's perception today of Truman's decision has been influenced by the vague notion that "the Japanese were trying to surrender" and his critics' focus on limited briefing documents that purportedly "prove" he was lying. The implication is that if Truman exaggerated the number of estimated casualties an invasion would produce then he must have had ulterior motives for using the bomb. And the critics' coy response is that Truman lied in order to hide his monstrous guilt at murdering thousands of Japanese civilians simply to gain a diplomatic advantage over the Soviets in the postwar world. *Truman and the Bomb* makes it clear, however, that nuclear weapons were used for the exact reason Truman said, to prevent a far greater bloodbath "from one end of Japan to the other."[51] This simple fact is fundamental to both understanding why atom bombs were used and, ultimately, how we as a nation view our history and ourselves.

1

The Manhattan Project

What Did Truman Know and When Did He Know It?

Long before the United States entered World War II, the likelihood that it would eventually be dragged into the conflict prompted a mammoth effort to build up its military and defense infrastructure. Senator Harry S. Truman was certain that such an undertaking, if done in great haste, would inevitably entail great waste in both time and resources as the greedy and the incompetent attempted to cash in on the boom. He well remembered the First World War, and as he later remarked: "There'd been a hundred and sixteen investigating committees *after* the fact, and I felt that one committee *before* the fact would prevent a lot of waste and maybe even save some lives."[1]

The Senate Special Committee to Investigate the National Defense Program, popularly known as the Truman Committee, opened its hearings in April 1941, with the senator from Missouri serving as its chairman and driving force until he was nominated for vice president three years later. Truman, in fact, even spent much of January 1941 traveling incognito from defense project to defense project in his old Dodge to get his own firsthand look at the situation, covering states from Florida to Missouri to Michigan in the process.

The senator quickly gained a reputation for fairness—and tenacity. Although his committee did not get involved in military strategy and personnel or the size of the defense effort, it frequently moved beyond its purely "watchdog" role, making positive contributions to the improvement of military equipment such as the B-26 bomber and landing craft for discharging men and materiel directly onto invasion beaches. The public also got into the act as patriotic citizens sent in letters reporting on waste and mismanagement or made their own suggestions for improving the effectiveness of the war effort.[2]

The flood of information coming into his committee necessitated that many avenues of investigation be delayed while others of seemingly more importance took precedence. Initially, references to a project identified only by the codename "Manhattan" were not pursued, but the project's unexplained expenditures and massive land acquisitions began to grow at an alarming rate, prompting Truman to phone Secretary of War Henry Stimson on June 17, 1943. The secretary was regarded as a man of high moral principle who had known or served under every president for the previous forty-five years. Stimson's transcript of the conversation recounts how he told the senator that the facility was part of an "important secret development" which only he and a select "group of two or three men in the whole world know about." Truman immediately began to back off: "You assure that this is for a specific purpose and you think it's all right. That's all I need to know." Stimson hastened to add: "Not only for a specific purpose, but a *unique* purpose."[3]

As chairman of the committee, however, Truman couldn't—or wouldn't—leave it at that. Either his connections or those of Brigadier General Frank Lowe, assigned to his staff by the War Department, allowed him to very quickly find out much more. Less than a month later, he responded to an inquiry by Lewis Schwellenbach, a former Washington senator and good friend concerned about the U.S. Army's enormous land acquisitions around an isolated railroad town called Hanford. Truman wrote that he knew "something about that tremendous land deal" west of Pasco, Washington, and went about as far as he could in his 1943 letter without using words like "atomic" or "nuclear." He told Schwellenbach, who in just a few years would leave his current post as a federal district judge to become now-president Truman's labor secretary, that it was "for the construction of a plant to make a terrific explosi[ve] for a secret weapon that will be a wonder," and added "I hope it works."[4] (See appendix D, "The Manhattan Project: A Chronology of Its Expansion and Subsequent Congressional Investigations.")

The Manhattan Project

Like his "Boss" and the other officer assigned to the committee, Lieutenant Colonel Harry Vaughan, General Lowe had been an artilleryman during the First World War and became a senior reserve officer between the wars. Lowe monitored the Manhattan Project to the best of his abilities, and this closed trio "discussed the fissuring of the atom many times . . . in '42 and '43." Lowe had even touched on the matter as early as 1941 in the report he submitted to Truman after a mission to England. Being an intimate of rocket scientist Robert Goddard who he'd gone to school with, he also mentioned Goddard's views on "this objective."[5]

Years later, Lowe's job as President Truman's eyes and ears in Korea during China's stunning entry into the conflict—perhaps signaling a far larger war to come—freed up both his and Truman's pens to refer back to key pre-Hiroshima-atom-bomb-related matters that otherwise would not have been either verified or even known about by future historians.[6] (See appendix E—Major General Frank Lowe to Brigadier General Harry Vaughn: "Between You, the Boss [Truman], and Me.") And none of this had been shared by Truman and the army liaisons with the civilians on the investigating committee staff who, from their highly constricted vantage point, reported to Truman: "The guise of secrecy is being resorted to by the War Department to cover what may be another socking example [of waste and inefficiency] when the lid is finally taken off."[7]

Truman had once boasted that a single salvo from his wartime battery's 75 mm guns was equivalent to the rifle fire of 862 soldiers, and it seemed to later historians examining his exchange with Schwellenbach that he may simply have assumed that the new weapon was a quantum leap in chemical based explosives technology and not something as unimaginable as the harnessing of the atom to create a blast powerful enough to destroy an entire city. In any case, though Truman had not used the word *atomic* in his message to Schwellenbach, the project's purpose was itself top secret and the future president had clearly risked a serious breach of security in his hasty letter. Truman must have immediately realized his mistake and had the good sense to never again put down on paper what he knew of the Manhattan Project's objective to be—the construction of a "unique" weapon whose "explosion . . . would be a wonder"—and succeeded in keeping it from other members of the Senate while ostensibly working on their behalf to get more information.

Not six months had passed before persistent allegations of waste and inefficiency within the project by Senator Elmer Thomas of Oklahoma—the chairman of the subcommittee on military appropriations—and others prompted fellow committee chairman Truman to break his word to Stimson that he would not pursue the matter.

Truman sent one of the committee's investigators, Fred Canfil, to the now-massive Hanford Engineer Works in December 1943 and, naturally, the man was denied entry. Having put on a proper show for his concerned colleagues, Truman promptly dropped further efforts only to be again roused to action several months later when five members of the Senate, instigated by Washington's Monrad Wallgren, demanded that the Truman Committee "investigate complaints regarding the housing at Pasco."[8] Since these senators, as Truman informed Stimson, were not members of his committee, the actual number of those wanting answers was at least a dozen. Wallgren himself was on the committee and the Hanford plant was located in his home state.

Meanwhile, far more pressure was mounting in the House of Representatives than in the Senate. So much, in fact, that on February 18, 1944, House leaders of both parties held a secret meeting with Secretary Stimson, U.S. Army chief of staff George C. Marshall, and Vannevar Bush, the director of the Office of Scientific Research and Development (OSRD). The hope of Stimson, Marshall, Bush, and Brigadier General Leslie Groves, the director of the Manhattan Project, was that a background briefing with House leaders on the project might serve to better safeguard its secrecy and financial support.[9]

Though the meeting itself was secret, there is reason to believe that Truman learned of it directly or from one of the senators who were pressing him to obtain information relating to the Hanford site. This seemingly opened the door to the Senate officially obtaining more information on the project. On the heels of the meeting with House leadership, the Missouri senator, as chairman of the

Senate Investigating Committee, formulated a careful proposal for the War Department's consideration. It was structured in such a way as to encourage that it would be acted upon by General Marshall instead of being pushed all the way up the chain to Secretary Stimson. Either way, it was going to be rejected and it quickly was.

The rejection owed to the fact that President Franklin D. Roosevelt's 1942 directive to the army and OSRD establishing the Manhattan Project mandated that "extreme secrecy" be exercised in connection with all facets of the operation "particularly with respect to its purpose, the raw materials used to develop the final product, and the manufacturing processes involved." It was "imperative that only those for which knowledge was a vital necessity should be informed" and, even then, "in minimum detail only." It was emphasized that "military security necessitated strict adherence to the restrictive requirements" with the result that a multi-year "determined effort [be] made to withhold the atomic bomb project information from all personnel, including members of Congress" unless they were specifically authorized to receive portions of that knowledge.[10]

Unlike in the House of Representatives, where the persistent and abrasive actions of Congressman Albert J. Engel were viewed as a harbinger of dangers to come, exposure through a formal investigation in the Senate was not judged to be on the immediate horizon.[11] Nevertheless, Truman and other key senators remained under pressure by their colleagues. Chairman Truman's failed request to the War Department had been pushed upstairs all the way to Secretary Stimson's office, and on March 10 he tried again, this time writing directly to the man himself and making note of their conversation ten months earlier. The letter was crafted just as much for the senators demanding action as it was for the War Secretary:

> About June 15, 1943 the Committee requested of the War Department information with respect to the project in the neighborhood of Pasco, Washington, and you will recall that you made a specific request upon me that the Committee not make any investigation whatever as to that project because of your fear that important secrets might become known to the enemy.

Since that time, the Committee has received, both directly and from five members of the Senate, not members of the Committee, suggestions that the undertaking at Pasco is being carried out in a wasteful manner.[12]

Truman then made it clear that he was looking not to gather information on the Manhattan Project itself but on the living conditions of the workers, which were generating complaints. He was also concerned about security and, to that end, was proposing to send only the officers who were assigned to him by the War Department as a further security measure. He wrote:

Bearing in mind your desire for secrecy, the Committee several weeks ago suggested that Brigadier General Frank Lowe and Lieutenant Colonel Harry Vaughan be sent by the Committee to the Pasco project solely for the purpose of investigating questions of waste with respect to the construction of housing roads and other matters not relating to the processes of manufacture or other secrets connected with the project.

This suggestion was made because General Lowe had been assigned by the Chief of Staff of the Army as Executive Officer to the committee for the purpose of carrying out assignments made by the committee in which it was expected that his personal experience and qualifications and his duties in the War Department especially would qualify him. The detail was not sought by General Lowe nor by the Committee but was welcomed by the Committee because the Committee believed that General Lowe could serve a valuable function.[13]

As Truman explained, "In this instance, I thought that General Lowe would be especially valuable." He also wondered if "he could not safely be permitted to examine into the portions of the Pasco project, especially as those portions are being constructed by thousands of civilians who have access thereto." Truman thus put forward an argument that, while unlikely to sway Secretary Stimson, would be well received by the senators at Truman's door:

I understand that Mr. Julius Amberg on your behalf has notified the Committee that you personally oppose any examination into this project, and that you have decided that General Lowe, if sent to the project, would be banned from entering it. I understand further that you suggest that any investigation desired by the Committee be performed by members of the War Department to be chosen by it. If such personnel is limited to those in charge of the construction of the project, it is my opinion that no useful purpose would be served by asking them to investigate themselves. If such investigation is to be conducted by any other personnel, I do not understand why it would be expected that the secrets would be any safer with such other personnel than with General Lowe, in whom the Committee has the utmost confidence.

If General Lowe is not to be permitted to serve the functions for which he was detailed, a serious question arises as to whether his detail should not be reviewed by the War Department insofar as his duties with this Committee affect the War Department.

The decision which has been made by the War Department with respect to the Pasco project, if it has been made as indicated above, is a serious one. It may be necessary for the Committee to consider the appointment of a subcommittee to investigate the project. On your urgent request, that usual procedure will not be adopted at this time. The responsibility therefore and for any waste or improper action which might otherwise be avoided rests squarely upon the War Department.[14]

Since Truman stated only that it *might* be necessary to *consider* an investigation of the Manhattan Project, Stimson simply ignored his arguments. He wrote back on March 14: "I am declining to take into my confidence any further persons, whether Army officers or civilians, I am merely carrying out the express directions of the President of the United States."[15] General Groves's impression was that Truman "accepted the Secretary's decision in good grace."[16]

This answer, while less than satisfactory to the senators, was enough to demonstrate to them that the door was closed "until the project had served its war purpose or until the then existing security restrictions could be lifted."[17] Truman had been caught in the middle between angry senatorial colleagues, to whom he had to feign ignorance, and a secretary of war who he had personally promised would see no inquiries from his committee. To all appearances, Truman had worked diligently on the senators' behest and there is nothing to suggest they had a clue that Chairman Truman, who knew full well of about the development of a "unique" weapon whose "explosion . . . would be a wonder," was not being completely forthcoming with them. Thomas, in fact, would officially be let in on Manhattan's secrets in June 1944, but as late as 1951 he would write: "In so far as I can learn, neither the members of the Truman investigating committee nor Congressman Engel ever received or secured any information whatever respecting the attempted development of the super-explosive atomic energy."[18]

As far as Truman was concerned, this was just fine. But the Senate Investigating Committee chair, who had twice been instrumental in deflecting potentially disruptive inquiries into the Manhattan Project, would have been shocked to know what Secretary Stimson had written in his diary the very night of the March 13 response to the senator. Said Stimson: "He threatened me with dire consequences. I told him I had to do just what I did. Truman is a nuisance and a pretty untrustworthy man. He talks smoothly but he acts meanly."[19]

As had happened with Truman, who clearly said more than he should have in his July 15, 1943, letter to Lewis Schwellenbach, Stimson would not likely have characterized his most recent dealings with the senator from Missouri in this way if he had reflected on the matter. Truman's few box-check efforts to "investigate" the secret project following the Schwellenbach letter, spread many months apart and prompted solely by other senators with knit brows knocking on his door, were far more restrained than the systematic pounding and threats from Michigan's Engel that spanned 1941 to 1945 (see appendix D).

But a diary is only a diary, and Stimson's complaints, whether representing a firm belief or simple venting, have been an oft-repeated nugget used to support all matter of claims regarding Truman's integrity, demeanor, or lack of knowledge of the Manhattan Project ever since it was made widely available to public institutions in the 1970s. Some authors have also speculated that Stimson's supposed animosity toward Truman lay behind the senator not being among the chosen few in Congress to officially be let in on the atomic secret. In fact, the three House and four Senate members given an overview of Manhattan before Truman became president were the Speaker of the House along with the rest of either the majority and minority leaders or select members of the relevant appropriations committees. Truman held no purse strings and colleagues far more senior than he were likewise never briefed.

The death of Roosevelt on April 12, 1945, thrust Truman—who had become vice president just three months earlier—into the role of commander in chief. It is here that the story of what Truman did or did not know about the atomic bomb became very complicated for historians trying to make sense of conflicting statements. By the time that nuclear weapons were used in August, the year since he had left the chairmanship of his investigating committee must have seemed like a century. The senators interested in this matter assumed, as did Senator Thomas, that Truman had known little more than the rest of them about the industrial sites associated with the mysterious Manhattan Project and it would seem only natural that after becoming vice president that Truman would now be made privy to far more information since he was first in line to succeed the visibly ailing Roosevelt.

This proved not to be the case. And as far as Secretary Stimson and James F. Byrnes—soon to be Truman's secretary of state—knew, Truman had little or no knowledge at all of the project, let alone its details. The same was apparently believed by the previous vice president, Henry A. Wallace, who Truman had asked to stay on as his secretary of commerce.

Office of Scientific Research and Development director Vannevar Bush's meeting with Roosevelt and Wallace on October 9, 1941, had led directly to the atomic bomb project's approval, and Roosevelt subsequently created the Top Policy Group—consisting of himself (though he never attended any of its meetings), Wallace, Stimson, and General Marshall—to control the program.[20] Wallace was thus one of the select few kept fully apprised of the project, and he received Bush's top secret Manhattan District reports, which covered the status of the project. It is unclear, however, if he continued to receive status reports after he moved out of the vice president's office to make way for Truman. In any event, Truman was not receiving those reports and Wallace, whose knowledge was extensive but nevertheless second hand, left the matter of briefing him to those more directly involved in Manhattan—Stimson and Marshall.[21]

Immediately after Truman's swearing in and impromptu first cabinet meeting, Stimson approached his new boss about the project he had codenamed "s-1" in his diary and personal communications. A meeting with the new president was set up (see appendix F—Stimson to Truman on atom bomb development) and decades later after leaving office, Truman wrote:

> He asked to speak to me about a most urgent matter. Stimson told me that he wanted me to know about an immense project that was under way—a project looking to the development of a new explosive of almost unbelievable destructive power. That was all he felt free to say at the time, and his statement left me puzzled. It was the first bit of information that had come to me about the atomic bomb, but he gave me no details. It was not until the next day that I was told enough to give me some understanding of the almost incredible developments that were under way and the awful power that might soon be placed in our hands.[22]

Truman recalled in his memoirs how he, at Secretary Stimson's request, had earlier refrained from investigating certain "top secret" facilities involved in what Stimson described as "the greatest project in the history of the world." Truman stated that he "was not to learn anything whatever as to what that secret was until the Secretary spoke to me after that first Cabinet meeting. The next day Jimmy Byrnes, who until shortly before had been Director of War Mobilization for President Roosevelt, came to see me, and even he told me few details."[23]

Appearing as this did in Truman's own memoirs—and fitting nicely into Roosevelt's well-known method of managing and manipulating friends and foes alike—Truman's claim of ignorance seemed perfectly plausible and became a fundamental element in the atomic bomb story, setting the tone for much of the subsequent analysis of how the unprepared "accidental president" dealt with the crushing responsibilities of his new office. It was only a matter of time, however, before scholars delving deeply into his papers, as well as the memoirs and papers of his colleagues, found it to be increasingly evident that Truman knew somewhat more than he let on; he certainly knew far more than Stimson believed he did.

While Truman was in office, he is reputed to have told presidential assistant Clark Clifford "on many occasions" that Stimson's comments were the first he'd heard of the bomb.[24] Yet he would tell his good friend and close confidant Admiral Leahy that during his August 18, 1944, luncheon with the president, "FDR had told him much about the situation but not the details."[25] This statement to Leahy, of course, does not address whether or not Truman knew of the "situation" and "details" beforehand.

When later interviewed for a book by his former press secretary Joseph Daniels, Truman said that the first word he heard about a nuclear bomb came from his investigator, Canfil, after trips to Hanford and the facility at Oak Ridge, Tennessee.[26] But he also "cautioned [Daniels] not to trust his memory but to check the facts where they were recorded."[27] The extent of Truman's knowledge of the "fissuring of the atom" in connection to the Manhattan Project as early as 1942, which appears in one of General Lowe's "Only between you, the Boss & me" letters to Vaughan in 1950, did not become public until publication of this volume.[28]

So why did Truman, when it came time to write his memoirs, maintain the fiction that he'd known nothing until after the death of Roosevelt? Hiding his knowledge of the Manhattan Project as he went through the motions of acting on the persistent demands of his fellow senators had its utility when he was the chairman of an investigating committee. Rather than say that he'd been in on the secret for years and couldn't tell them, Truman took the far less troublesome tack of implying that he was in the same boat. Likewise, he kept his cards close to his chest when he suddenly became president.

There is no hint in the writings of the individuals who briefed the new president that he expressed any special knowledge of what was going on, only that he listened attentively and apparently asked good questions. Byrnes, Stimson, and Groves worked for him—not the other way around—and for Truman it may simply have been a matter of seeing who would say what to their new boss. The editor of Truman's private papers, Robert H. Ferrell, noted that the Schwellenbach letter of July 15, 1943, demonstrated that Truman "had to have known what was going on . . . and at such a huge cost!"[29] Truman knew Byrnes quite well but knew Stimson and Groves only through their government service and reputations. Said Ferrell: "I suspect he didn't know everything and might therefore be doing the Callieres exercise, whereby if you have ten dollars (guineas) you say you have one."[30]

But again it was Truman's memoirs that fixed the understanding among historians and the public alike of what he suddenly faced. Although Truman had a deep knowledge of both military affairs—particularly those of the U.S. Army—and the prosecution of the war on the home front, he had almost no knowledge at all of foreign affairs beyond what he avidly read in the newspapers. Roosevelt had shared little if anything with him regarding his foreign policy goals and their relationship to military policy. Similarly, Truman had only the vaguest familiarity with the relations between the "Big Three" powers: Great Britain, the United States, and Soviet Union.

The newly minted commander in chief was up to the task ahead and immediately initiated a crash course on the current state of U.S. foreign policy. A hand-picked selection of Roosevelt's top civilian and military lieutenants tutored him. Always a voracious reader, Truman plowed through memoranda and reports. He even implored Harry Hopkins, one of Roosevelt's closest confidants, stating plainly: "I need to know everything you can tell me about our relations with Russia all that you know about Stalin and Churchill and the conferences at Cairo, Casablanca, Teheran, Yalta."[31]

Truman's statements about his knowledge—or reputedly the lack of it regarding the atomic bomb—was in line with the facts of the overall situation that he found himself in during his first month in office and presented a clear, uncomplicated story. Truman could have mentioned in his published memoirs, as Byrnes later carefully noted, that "he knew of the project generally through his Senate Committee work."[32] Yet Ferrell suggested that the president may have felt that, after more than a decade of maintaining that he knew absolutely nothing of the project, "he was in a box of his own making" and the best thing to do was "elaborate no further," especially since his prior knowledge of the atom bomb's development "had no impact at all on the decision to use it against Japan."[33]

2

Projects Milepost and Hula

America's Hidden Role in the Soviet Invasion of Manchuria

[President Truman said] the Russian situation was causing him a

lot of concern . . . [but] that all of his wires to Stalin had been

couched in the most friendly language. . . . The President said the

Russians were like people from across the tracks whose manners

were very bad. He said, however, that his one objective was to be

sure to get the Russians into the Japanese war so as to save

the lives of 100,000 American boys.

—DIARY ENTRY OF COMMERCE SECRETARY AND FORMER

VICE PRESIDENT HENRY A. WALLACE AFTER

THE MAY 18, 1945, CABINET MEETING

Before, during, and after the Potsdam Conference, President Truman made it clear that his "chief interest" was "to see the Soviet Union participate in the Far Eastern War in sufficient time to be of help in shortening the war."[1]

The president conveyed this message in explicit language to the Joint Chiefs of Staff as a group and discussed it individually with at least two of them, as well as the secretary of war, secretary of the navy, and the assistant secretary of war. Truman also discussed it with his commerce secretary, who preceded him as vice president, and innumerable others, including the White House chief of staff, the U.S. ambassador to the Soviet Union, the former U.S. ambassador to the Soviet Union, the secretary of state, the undersecretary of state, his—and previously Roosevelt's—emissary to Soviet leader Joseph Stalin, and his emissary to British prime minister

Winston Churchill. He even personally broke the news to the Chinese foreign minister.

The day before leaving Washington for the Potsdam Conference, Truman reviewed a memorandum of his final meeting with his senior civilian advisors listing "the entry of Russia into the Japanese War" as his first priority.[2] After the conference he told at least two White House staffers in separate remarks that he'd gone to Potsdam "entirely for the purpose of making sure that Stalin would come in."[3] Truman penned this in his diary and even wrote his wife after his key meeting with Stalin: "I've gotten what I came for—Stalin goes to war August 15th with no strings on it . . . I'll say that we'll end the war a year sooner now, and think of the kids who won't be killed! That is the important thing."[4] He echoed this in his diary the following day.

One might think that such a degree of documented specificity before, during, and after Potsdam on the part of the president would encourage historians, be they critics or defenders of Truman, to closely examine why he was focused so single mindedly on "get[ting] from Russia all the assistance in the war that was possible."[5] Instead, this objective is usually given only a cursory acknowledgment before the focus shifts to areas more in line with the comfort zones of those interested in "atomic diplomacy" and the coming Cold War than the fundamental need to bring the current war to a victorious conclusion with the least possible cost in American lives. To a very real degree, however, historians have been only partially to blame on this matter because Americans, allies, and enemies alike were kept in the dark on Projects Milepost and Hula, both of which supplied massive amounts of U.S. aid in support of the Soviet invasion of Manchuria.

The enormity of this U.S. assistance never became a part of World War II historiography, unlike the use of Lend-Lease in the battle against the Nazis, which was trumpeted throughout the war. Convoys above the Arctic Circle valiantly fighting their way to Murmansk, trains festooned with American and Soviet flags rumbling across Iran to the Caucasus, and other such events had great visibility. Yet the deployment of Lend-Lease aid on reflagged Liberty ships to prepare the Russians for their coming war with

Japan was a closely guarded secret because of the extreme vulnerability of Russia's lines of land and sea communication to the key Soviet port of Vladivostok in the Far East to preemptive action from even a weakened Japan.

Immediately after war, the secrecy surrounding the Americans' part in the Manchurian operation retained its own momentum. And besides, the United States had plenty to crow about that wasn't secret. The Soviets themselves made absolutely zero mention of it, as they wanted nothing to distract from the image of a magnificent achievement of Soviet arms. Yet, within a relatively short period of time, knowledge of the massive American effort would have grown on its own. For example, the book by the U.S. military mission chief to Moscow, Major General John R. Deane's *The Strange Alliance: The Story of Our Efforts at Wartime Cooperation with Russia*, was cleared for public release in 1946 and published the following year.[6] But increasing tensions with the Soviets were already giving more and more credence to the criticism of Yalta and Potsdam, which had begun in earnest as soon as the shooting stopped. Even before the communist victory in China and tensions between the former allies had developed into a full-blown Cold War, and long before the "hot war" of Korea, the United States government's direct aid in the seizure of Manchuria by the Red Army was not something that anyone in either government, each for their own reasons, wanted to draw any attention to.

Down the "memory hole" it went, skewing what historians thought they knew about Truman's actions in the final months of the war. By the time that details of the projects began to emerge a decade later, their official release was given little visibility and the narrative on the war had already been well-established.[7] The resultant void in the historiography even contributed to the final moves in the end game against Japan being recast as a "race" between the United States and Soviet Union; ostensibly, the Americans sought to use the deadly new atomic bomb to end the war before the Soviets could intervene, while the Soviets moved up their invasion of Manchuria to prevent just such an outcome. In fact, Roosevelt and Truman went to great lengths to ensure Stalin fulfilled his pledge to enter the war against Imperial Japan.

Projects Milepost and Hula

Projects Milepost and Hula, and how they came about, are essential to understanding Truman's dealings with Stalin during the early months of his presidency and the U.S.-Soviet military agreements at Potsdam that historians have essentially ignored. The strenuous efforts of Roosevelt and his successor, who held fast in the face of persistent opposition, fly in the face of the notion that Truman engaged in a so-called race to drop atomic bombs on Japan before Stalin could enter the Pacific War. Yet there really was a race of sorts involving the United States and Soviet Union in the Far East. It was a race by both allies to get the Red Army *into* the war against Japan as quickly as possible.

The wreckage was still smoldering at Pearl Harbor when President Roosevelt and Secretary of State Cordell Hull suggested to Soviet ambassador Maxim Litvinov that his country join forces with the United States in a war against Japan. Litvinov replied on December 11 that the Soviet Union "was not then in a position to cooperate with U.S. against Japan." "Russia," he said, "was fighting on a huge scale against Germany and could not risk an attack by Japan."[8]

As this exchange was taking place, General Douglas MacArthur in the Pacific raised the issue with General George C. Marshall in Washington: "The mass of enemy air and naval strength committed in the theater from Singapore to the Philippines and eastward established his weakness in Japan proper." U.S. airpower in the Philippines had been destroyed by the Japanese military, leaving the islands open to invasion, and it was a desperate MacArthur who pressed Marshall to make the case for Soviet intervention: "Entry of Russia is enemy's greatest fear. Most favorable opportunity now exists and immediate attack on Japan from north would not only inflict heavy punishment but would at once relieve pressure from objectives of Jap drive to southward."[9]

Although the Soviets had firmly closed the door on Roosevelt's request, it was also clear to them that entry of the United States and Japan into the now truly global conflict might well be the opening that they needed to rise from the humiliation of the Russo-Japanese War and undo the 1905 Treaty of Portsmouth. On December 26, 1941, Solomon Lozovsky, deputy commissar of the People's Commissariat of International Affairs, directed a memorandum on the need to begin postwar planning to Stalin and his immediate boss, Vyacheslav Molotov, who served as both deputy premier and minister of foreign affairs.[10] With Hitler's armies now thrown back from the gates of Moscow and the United States in the war, Lozovsky reasoned that victory over Germany, Japan, and their allies was inevitable.

Anglo-American war aims had recently been publicly articulated in the Atlantic Charter and it was time for the Soviet Union to do their own planning. Among the nation's goals, which included reducing the long-term power of postwar Germany through various means, Lozovsky stated that the territorial gains achieved as a result of the Nazi-Soviet Pact (eastern Poland and the Baltic states) must be guaranteed. The pact had greatly enhanced Soviet access to the Atlantic, and the Soviets believed that other maritime frontiers must also be made more secure. Said Lozovsky: "We can no longer tolerate the fact that Japanese warships could at any moment cut us off from the Pacific Ocean and from our ports and close La Perouse, Kuril, Songar and Tushima Straits. We cannot accept the old situation in the Baltic and Black Sea. The issue of our land and maritime communications must be reconsidered from the point of view of security and freedom of communications."[11]

But standing in the way of Soviet designs in the Far East was the Kwantung Army, the collective name for a group of powerful Japanese armies in Manchuria. Ever since the largely independent Kwantung consolidated its control of Manchuria in late 1931 and established the puppet state of Manchukuo with the assistance of the ascendant radical faction within the Imperial Army, the forces of Japan and the Soviet Union had maintained a precarious balance of power.[12] Each side escalated and re-escalated their force structures to the point where nearly one million troops were poised nose-to-nose along the Amur and Ussuri Rivers by 1940.[13] Holding the firm belief that Japan would not enjoy complete strategic security until eastern Siberia was under Imperial control, the Kwantung Army actively engaged in offensive war planning designed to destroy all Soviet forces in the region throughout the 1930s. As for the Soviets, they were "determined to hold that region," and though their posture was fundamentally defensive, they realized that "the strategic security of the region requires the ultimate expulsion of Japan from the mainland of Asia and from Southern Sakhalin."[14]

But the Soviets were not—and likely never would be—in a position to do this. Much like the U.S. outpost in the Philippines, the Red Army in the Far East was situated at the extreme end of a tenuous and highly vulnerable supply line that Japan could sever with ease at the very hint of hostilities. Though Soviet forces in the Far East were generally more numerous and decidedly more mobile than the Kwantung, any new Russo-Japanese war would see them quickly cut off and forced into a prolonged defensive campaign with only the men and supplies on hand. Rescue would only come if the Soviet armies west of the Urals laboriously moved along a single rail line through Siberia to amass near Lake Baikal and then fought their way a further thousand miles east (roughly equivalent to the distance between Lake Superior and the Gulf of Mexico) before their embattled comrades in the Maritime Provinces and the port of Vladivostok finally ran out of bullets, borscht, and men. And the Japanese forces planned for such a move when updating their strategy throughout the 1930s and reexamined it again when the main Soviet Armies became bogged down in a series of massive land battles with Nazi Germany.[15]

Luckily for Mother Russia, the Imperial Navy's desperate need for oil and other raw materials in 1941 tipped the scales in favor of those who advocated seizing the "southern resource region"— modern-day Indonesia, covered by a strike at Pearl Harbor—instead of one on the Asian mainland.[16] With the threat of an all-out war between Japan and the Soviet Union now removed for the time being, the Japanese Army began a steady withdrawal of the Kwantung's most experienced formations to shore up a quickly deteriorating situation in the Pacific. This, however, did not change things a whit for the Soviet position in the Far East, as they too had been syphoning off forces for their battles with the Nazis. The Maritime Provinces remained as vulnerable as before and now the situation was even more dangerous because the rail line from Vladivostok had also become a key conduit for Lend-Lease supplies flowing from the United States.

The lifeline that so much depended on was the Trans-Siberian Railroad, and Major General Deane, head of the U.S. military mission in Moscow, did not mince words when describing the situation that its limitations put the Soviets in:

> The Trans-Siberian railroad constitutes the bottleneck in the support of military operations in Siberia. It is now double-tracked for most of its ten thousand miles, but there are still enough stretches of single track to reduce its capacity considerably. On its eastern end the roadbed is within a few miles of the northern and eastern borders of Manchuria, and it was therefore quite vulnerable to Japanese land and air attack. It has a number of bridges and tunnels the destruction of which would have indefinitely interrupted traffic between western Russia and the Maritime Provinces. The only other source of supply was from across the Pacific, and it was reasonable to suppose that Japan would be able to blockade that route.[17]

It is important to add that the Japanese forces did not have to limit their attacks to the most apparent spots and, as postwar studies demonstrated, they didn't plan to.[18] The rail line follows the giant arc of the Amur River, which forms the northern border of Manchuria, more than 1,200 miles. For most of this distance the tracks run a bare thirty to thirty-five miles from the river and as little as ten to fifteen along numerous stretches. Bridges and tunnels abound. Turning south, the railroad follows the river valley of the Ussuri for 250 miles toward Lake Khanka near Vladivostok, all the while under easy observation—and reach—of the Kwantung Army on the west bank.

The Soviets were painfully aware of all these factors. Further, despite great efforts, the line's capacity in relation to the Maritime Provinces' increased needs had changed only marginally in the decades since the Russo-Japanese War, when it was blamed as a principal reason for the Russian defeat. Throughout the long U.S. effort to bring the Soviet Union into the war against Japan (discussed in chapter 4), as well as by the detailed planning on what to supply them for offensive rather than fundamentally defensive operations, the Soviets repeatedly stressed the need for absolute secrecy lest the Japanese military preempt everything by simply striking the rail line. U.S. ambassador to the Soviet Union Averell Harriman diplomatically reported to President Roosevelt that at one point during an October 17, 1944, meeting in Moscow, when rumors of the negotiations appeared in American newspapers, Stalin personally expressed his concern—General Deane said he "berated" them—over the matter: "The need for utmost secrecy must be observed. The Marshal stated that he wished to explain why he was so insistent on security and caution. If there is any indiscretion he feared that information might leak out to the press which would cause the Japanese military to embark on premature adventures as a result of which the valuable Vladivostok area might be lost. If Vladivostok were lost before major operations commenced, it would be extremely unfortunate for both countries." Perhaps to soften the pummeling, he added, "I am a cautious old man."[19]

Almost a year before at Tehran, Stalin had surprised his Western allies by opening the conference by stating that the Soviet Union would join them in their war against Japan after Germany's capitulation. He now reiterated that his Tehran pledge was "not empty words" and remarked that the U.S. and Soviet strategic plans "were in coordination." The United States would strike at "the industrial heart of Japan" while the Soviet Union would "break the Japanese spine."[20]

Imperial forces in Manchuria, Korea, and northern China, according to contemporary estimates, totaled 1,200,000 men. General Marshall had recently been briefed by Lieutenant General Stanley C. Embick, the Joint Strategic Survey chief, that if the United States invaded Japan before a Soviet declaration of war, "a considerable part" of the Kwantung's 800,000-man army would be transferred to the Home Islands and concentrated against the Americans.[21] For obvious reasons, General Marshall was anxious to have the Soviets tie down the Kwantung before the launch of Operation Downfall. He must have been relieved when informed of Stalin's belief "that as soon as the Russians struck in the Manchurian-Mongolian regions, the Japanese would attempt to move troops [back] to Korea" and determination that this retreat "must be cut off." Stalin added that if Imperial forces were also "cut off in China, the Allied task would be greatly facilitated."[22]

Cutting off instead of pushing back Japanese forces was an extremely important point because a quick, total victory over the Kwantung Army would prevent elements of that force from being withdrawn to Japan and subsequently employed against the American invasion of Honshu designated Operation Coronet. U.S. submarines and army air power operating out of the recently invaded Philippines would soon provide an effective blockade between China and Japan in the East China Sea. Above Korea's Tsushima Strait, however, shipping across the Sea of Japan from the puppet state of Manchukuo (Manchuria) would remain largely unmolested until U.S. air bases were established on the Home Island of Kyushu during Olympic. (See appendix Q, "Planned U.S. Naval and Air Operations in Support of the Soviet Invasion of Manchuria," "For the benefit of our forces as well as for the benefit to the Russians.") The Soviets annihilating the Kwantung would remove that threat altogether.

In a conference held the previous day, Stalin maintained that "if stores could be built up now the attack could be made 2 or 3 months after Germany's collapse" and stated that "planning should begin at once." Throughout the Yalta and Potsdam Conferences as well as all the Moscow negotiations before and between them, the Soviets never deviated from this timetable, which would serve as the basis for all military-to-military coordination between the two powers and an immediate jump in Lend-Lease deliveries to the Soviet Union, even though it would not be formally codified until months later at the Yalta Conference the following year.[23]

To launch an offensive of this type so quickly after their forces defeated the Nazis in Europe, the Red Army would have to depend on the Americans to secretly supply much of the food, fuel, war supplies, and even the trucks to move them both before and during the offensive.[24] At the October 17 meeting, Harriman and Deane were presented with a breathtakingly huge wish list, which the United States moved immediately to fill under a secret expansion of the Lend-Lease program codenamed "Milepost." And this was only the U.S. down payment on the Soviet offensive.

By this point in the war, material destined for the final battles with the Nazis and to support the Russian population was already ordered or in the pipeline. Jacob W. Kipp and General Makhmut Akhmetevich Gareev outline the opening request to support operations specifically against Japan:

> The General Staff was particularly concerned with building up sufficient stockpiles to sustain combat operations in the Far East should the Maritime Provinces be cut off by Japanese surface, air, and submarine operations against the sea lines of communications with Vladivostok or by ground and air operations against the Trans-Siberian Railroad. To this end General [and Chief of Staff Alexei E.] Antonov handed to Deane a list of supplies and equipment that the Soviet Union wished to receive from the United States in order to support a theater offensive of 1,500,000 men, 3,000 tanks, 75,000 motor vehicles and 5,000 aircraft. The list was impressive and included:
>
>> 230,000 tons of petroleum products (major items: 120,000 tons of aviation gasoline, 70,000 tons of automobile fuel),
>>
>> 186,000 tons of food and fodder (major items: 60,000 tons of flour, 20,000 tons of beans or macaroni, 25,000 tons of canned meat, and 50,000 tons of oats or barley), 14,580 tons of clothing material and hospital supplies (major items: 3 million meters of overcoat cloth, 4.5 million meters of uniform cloth, 12 million meters of underwear cloth, and 2 million pair of shoes),
>>
>> 296,385 tons of automobiles, road machines and airdrome equipment (major items: 30,000 trucks, 1,000 DUKWS [amphibious trucks], 2,000 oil and gas tank trucks, and two truck assembly plants),
>>
>> 306,500 tons of railroad equipment (major items: 500 steam locomotives, 3,000 box cars, 2,000 flat cars, 1,000 tank cars, 800 kilometers of rails and 500 switches),
>>
>> 20,175 tons of engineering and signal corps gear (major items: 5,000 tons of barbed wire, 200 radio sets, 200 radar sets and 10,000 kilometers of field telephone cable),

A flotilla of small ships and craft (major items: 10 frigates, 20 corvettes, 30 minesweepers, 50 large subchasers, 20 large troop landing craft), Medical supplies worth $3 million. The Soviet General Staff placed the total tonnage to be moved by sea at 1,056,410 tons (860,410 tons of dry cargo and 206,000 tons of liquid cargo), which would require a sea lift of ninety-six merchant freighters (9,000 tons cargo per ship) and fourteen tankers (15,000 tons of liquid cargo per tanker).[25]

Soviet participation in the war was now linked to the Western Allies' vision of the end game's attrition phase, and the first ships with Milepost cargos arrived at Soviet ports in the Far East before the end of 1944.[26] Soviet requirements escalated over the next few months, and the United States put as much into motion as it could without compromising its own Pacific operations. Of inestimable value during the multifront offensive into Manchuria were the 42,599 trucks (including DUKWs), 1,119 tractor prime movers, 89 field repair trucks, 2,426 jeeps, 1,115 motorcycles, 336 C-47s, and 50 PBY Catalina flying boats. American tanks also played a prominent role in the offensive, and 92 of them were shipped directly to Vladivostok aboard Liberty ships—reflagged with Soviet colors to protect the fig leaf of continued Soviet neutrality—to supplement the M4A2 Shermans that arrived on flatcar loads from the west. As Kipp explained:

> Lend-Lease deliveries to the Far East after the end of the war in Europe continued and even accelerated. They were on such a scale so as to shift radically the balance of forces in the theater. In the period May 12 to September 2, 1945, these deliveries amounted to 1,252,385 long tons on 171 sailings. Indeed, May 12–31 saw the largest number of sailings to the Far East (51) of any period of the entire war. Among the deliveries over the four-month period, May 12–2 September were 744 aircraft, including 316 locomotives, 50,509 tons of explosives, 371,670 tons of petroleum products, and 235,607 tons of food.
>
> These deliveries were the result of intense negotiations in which Stalin sought to guarantee the success of Soviet arms and the political recognition of his intended gains in the Far East.

For the Americans these negotiations were matters of changing military priorities dominated by the military demands of prosecuting the war against Japan to a speedy and less costly conclusion. Japanese intelligence, while aware of the trans-Pacific ship bridge to the Soviet Far East, did not note the increased volume of those ships in the last month of the war in Europe or in the months following the end of the war.[27]

Japanese observers could not miss, however, the buildup of forces flowing from across the Urals. On April 5, 1945, the Imperial leadership was shaken by the Soviet announcement that they would be withdrawing from the Japanese-Soviet Neutrality Pact signed in 1941. Though the statement would have been equally true if issued any time after Pearl Harbor, the Soviets now declared: "Germany attacked the USSR, and Japan, an ally of Germany, helps the latter in its war against the USSR. Moreover, Japan is at war with the U.S. and England, who are allies of the USSR. Under these circumstances, the Neutrality Pact between Japan and the USSR has lost its meaning, and the extension of the Pact has become impossible." An uptick in eastbound military shipments that had become apparent and after the defeat of Nazi Germany became an alarming torrent a month later.[28]

On June 6, 1945, the chief of the Imperial Army's General Staff, Umezu Yoshijirō, was conducting an "urgent meeting" with senior commanders from northern China and Manchuria at Dairen (previously Port Arthur, today Dalian), and in his stead Deputy Chief of Staff Kawabe Torashirō explained the situation to a session of the Supreme War Direction Council: "While pushing operations preparations against the Soviet Union, the Army is endeavoring to avoid instigating Soviet entry into the war, but in the final analysis, the most effective way to discourage Soviet entry is to deal a heavy blow against the American forces in their impending invasion of our Homeland." This presumed that a war with the Soviets was not in the immediate offing and that it might in fact be avoided altogether.

The chief of the Imperial Navy General Staff, Toyoda Soemu, followed Kawabe and was a little more blunt regarding the likelihood of war: "Enemy efforts against the Kuril Islands and Hokkaido will most likely be diversionary in scope, but caution must be exercised, as the Americans may invade these areas if the situation permits in view of American relations with the Soviet Union, especially when the Soviet Union enters the war."[29]

Japanese intelligence specialists, working from essentially the same logistic tables and assumptions used by their American and Soviet counterparts, examined the readily visible eastbound rail traffic and concluded as late as the July Imperial General Headquarters strategic assessment that the Soviets could theoretically be ready to launch a limited offensive as early as August if they felt that they could achieve a swift victory. They also reasoned, from what their own eyes told them, that their longtime enemy would not have amassed enough power to do this—let alone land the massive killing blow that Stalin envisioned—before winter.[30] Since this train-by-train-by-train movement was observed and analyzed in complete isolation from the Milepost deliveries, it became the general consensus within Japanese intelligence and higher command that the coming war with the Soviet Union (see chapter 3) was unlikely to erupt before the spring of 1946. "They were convinced that the USSR would attack Japan eventually," said Edward Drea, "but only when the Soviets found it to their greatest advantage." Drea adds:

> The cardinal assessment that the USSR would await the opportunity to attack a near-prostrate Japan in conjunction with American landings in Japan or on the Asian mainland was really a political interpretation. It presumed that the Soviets were so weakened by the German war that they would be content to pick at the leavings of the Americans. It also leaned on the fragile reed of the Neutrality Pact which, although abrogated, had a one year's grace period, i.e., April 1946. Together with the military difficulty of winter operations in Manchuria, these factors spelled Soviet inaction until 1946.[31]

Similarly, as early as November 1944, Pentagon planners made much the same point—that the Soviets might just let the American and Imperial armies fight it out—and implied that they could then simply reap the desired rewards at their leisure. Later, between the Yalta and Potsdam Conferences when Milepost sailings were scheduled to reach record levels, this was restated with more specificity in the U.S. Army's principal planning document for the endgame against Japan, JCS 924.[32] Secretary Stimson provided this summary to acting secretary of state Joseph Grew:

> The concessions to Russia on Far Eastern matters which were made at Yalta are generally matters which are within the military power of Russia to obtain regardless of U.S. military action short of war. The War Department believes that Russia is militarily capable of defeating the Japanese and occupying Karafuto [the southern half of Sakhalin island], Manchuria, Korea and Northern China before it would be possible for the U.S. military forces to occupy these areas. Only in the Kurils is the United States in a position to circumvent Russian initiative. If the United States were to occupy these islands to forestall Russian designs, it would be at the direct expense of the campaign to defeat Japan and would involve an unacceptable cost in American lives.

The secretary of war closed out this portion of the May 12 memo with his own succinct view of the situation: "Furthermore, the Russians can, if they choose, await the time when U.S. efforts will have practically completed the destruction of Japanese military power and then seize the objectives they desire at a cost to them relatively much less than would be occasioned by their entry into the war at an early date."[33]

On the other hand, the army planning staff also issued variations on a boilerplate proviso covering the necessity of weighing Soviet needs versus our own requirements and stating that the United States didn't need Russian hordes to defeat Japan. Joint Planning Staff (JPS) papers approved by the Joint Chiefs of Staff as early as November 1944 and as late as two weeks into the Truman presidency noted that among war planners "there is implicit conviction that the defeat of Japan may be accomplished without Russian participation in the war." And subsequently, "Because of our estimated ability to interdict Japanese movement between the Asiatic mainland and Japan proper"—a supposition that American war leaders would learn in July had been disastrously wrong—"early

Russian entry into the war against Japan and attendant containing of the Kwantung army is no longer necessary."[34] Others in the Pentagon disagreed. Brigadier General George A. Lincoln's Strategy and Policy Group firmly maintained that Allied support was of major importance, "particularly Russia['s], whose aid we need to press the war to the quickest possible conclusion."[35]

As the army hierarchy in Washington and Manila would soon learn through intercepts made through the top secret cryptanalysis project known as MAGIC, the last of the Kwantung divisions that it had known and feared had already arrived in Japan as a "shield for the Emperor." The Japanese military made no effort to send them through the thoroughly blockaded East China Sea, and they instead had flowed freely across the Sea of Japan from Korean ports that remained largely beyond American reach. And despite the effectiveness of U.S. minelaying efforts, the new Kwantung divisions being raised in Manchuria could and would follow if there was no Soviet intervention until the Neutrality Pact was officially dead in April 1946.

Throughout this entire period General Marshal was determined to smooth the way for Soviet entry into the fray and not do anything that might prompt fears of Yankee duplicity. For example, in October 1944 the U.S. Army chief of staff rejected General Embick's proposal to adopt an attrition strategy in the Pacific and slow down operations while awaiting a Russian declaration of war. Marshall believed that following this path would arouse Stalin's suspicions that "we are maneuvering to get them into the fight in such a manner that they will suffer the major losses."[36] In such a case, might not the Soviets feel free to pull their punches or find an excuse to suddenly stop their offensive altogether, as they had recently done on the outskirts of Warsaw? That decision had disastrous consequences for the Polish underground, which had emerged and seized most of the city only to be slaughtered by the Nazis as Soviet forces sat and watched. In the final battles against Imperial Japan, both sides must be able to fully trust that their ally's offensive would be carried out in the timeframe and manner agreed upon.

What both Marshall and his Pacific commander MacArthur desired was a one-two punch: a Soviet invasion of Manchuria

Projects Milepost and Hula

against the massive Kwantung Army on the Asian mainland followed by the beginning of U.S. operations in the Home Islands in the fall of the following year, 1945. And this had always been the Americans' intent, for as Harriman recapped in a 1943 message to Marshall, the instructions when he and General Deane were sent to Moscow were "not only to obtain Russian participation but [also] to have them give U.S. the right kind of help and enough time to prepare to make their help effective."[37] Stalin's scheme of operations fit perfectly with the strategic thinking of the Joint Chiefs of Staff, which desired the maximum disruption of Japanese communications between Manchuria and Japan. MacArthur, in accord with Joint Chiefs' earlier thinking, preferred that they attack soon with the forces already on hand because "it was only necessary for action to commence in Manchuria to contain that force (the Kwantung Army)."[38]

For Stalin, a hasty assault like MacArthur preferred was not a matter he would give the slightest consideration, for even if the Kwantung didn't get wind of it and strike first to cut off Soviet forces in the Far East, a less than "full blood" offensive might still provide the Japanese forces with the ability to interdict, or even break, the rail link at numerous locations and entailed a much longer, costlier campaign. This was of no particular concern to MacArthur, who said it was "only right that they should share the cost in blood of defeating Japan" and that they must "pay their way" for the territorial gains they would inevitably achieve.[39] MacArthur apparently did not view the possibility that the Japanese military might take advantage of a stalled Soviet offensive to send reinforcements to Japan as a credible scenario.

Stimson, for his part, had brought up the matter of the Kurils to Grew on his own initiative. This was done because—unlike the Soviet foot-dragging and evasions that characterized the long, frustrating, and ultimately futile negotiations regarding the basing of U.S. strategic bombers on Soviet territory and the establishment of a Russo-American coordinating staff—the Soviets had on multiple occasions expressed interest in the U.S. initiating operations in the Kurils. Such operations would remove—at no cost to themselves—the imminent threat to their vital Pacific sea lines of communication when war was declared as well as achieve the cherished goal of permanently ending that threat, since the Soviet annexation of those islands was to be assured at the Yalta Conference.

Though it still had some advocates, principally among desk-bound army planners in Washington, adoption of a northern route of approach against Japan was a dead issue that virtually none of the Joint Chiefs were interested in revisiting. A report on the third phase of a well-prepared, weeklong Far East war game conducted by the Military Mission in Moscow only reinforced this and revealed the limitations of the U.S. position in the Pacific.

The game operated from the premise that if the Japanese military struck first they would be able to quickly cut the rail line at numerous vulnerable points and interdict Lend-Lease shipping through the Sea of Okhosk. Admiral Nimitz had informed Deane that one of the war games' conclusions—that Lend-Lease shipping ships would need to be gathered into convoys at Petropavlovsk on the Kamchatka Peninsula, from which they would fight their way through to the mainland ports—would be unnecessary.[40] Nevertheless, American forces already stretched to the max by their own offensives far to the south and with limited assistance from the Soviets would have to overcome Japanese naval and air elements in the Kurils and on Hokkaido attacking and closing the various straits. In order to fully secure the sea lanes, a major campaign would then have to be mounted to seize the key Japanese bases on the adjoining islands of Paramushiro and Shumshu across the Pervyy Kurilskiy Strait from the Kamchatka Peninsula.[41]

General Deane did not believe that this could be done without making critical sacrifices elsewhere. In his memorandum enclosed with the report, he concluded: "Objectives in the northern Kurils or Kamchatka are not suitable as positions from which to provide contributory support, commensurate with costs, to our over-all objective in the war against Japan. Furthermore, examination so far has indicated that there will be deficiencies in forces and resources, particularly in service support units, required for a major operation in the north Pacific on the scale of a Paramushiro-Shimushu [sic] operation."[42]

The Joint Chiefs agreed with Deane. The January 22, 1945, briefing paper produced for the Combined (British and American) Chiefs of Staff before the coming three-power meeting stated that because of the "cost of operations to maintain and defend a sea route to the Sea of Okhotsk," the possibility of seizing and maintaining a position in the Kurils was "remote due to lack of sufficient resources."[43]

Although the U.S. military explored the matter in great detail, the Soviets were given no encouragement to believe that amphibious operations would be launched in the Kurils. On the third day of deliberations, Admiral King recited almost verbatim from the briefing paper. When the Soviet Navy's commander in chief, Admiral Nikolay Kuznetsov, then asked directly "if the capture of an island in the Kurils was planned for 1945," King reiterated that the "means were not available to undertake it as well as the other operations which had been planned." But King left the door at least partially ajar in case the enemy inflicted some catastrophe on the Soviet supply lines when he added, "However, as always, it [is] a question of the relative importance of the various operations under consideration."[44]

Several days later, Marshall and the Red Army's chief of staff, General Alexei E. Antonov, briefly discussed the virtual certainty that the Kwantung would attack first "if the Japanese obtained any intimation of the Russian concentration and intention." And, with Soviet honor on the line, Antonov stated that the Soviets would take responsibility for keeping open the La Pérouse Strait along the northernmost Japanese Home Island of Hokkaido.[45]

Thanks to Milepost, the increased speed, weight, and violence of the Soviet offensive could reasonably be expected to render Kwantung plans against the rail line useless, but the importance of securing the sea lanes remained as critical as ever. Kuznetsov was apparently not fully confident that his forces were up to the task of keeping them open and maintained some hope that American warships would defend the shipping. Kipp notes that during conversations with his American counterpart, "Kuznetsov asked about U.S. escorts for the convoys to the Soviet Far East after the Soviet Union entered the war, but King said that the Navy would be concentrated in the south in the Sea of Japan and that the Soviets could expect no escorts."[46]

The American position remained that the Soviets themselves would need to undertake the anti-air, anti-mine, and anti-submarine effort in the La Pérouse Strait between Sakhalin and Hokkaido once hostilities began and until its waters turned to ice sometime in October. From that point on, Vladivostok would be closed until American warships and airpower forced open the Tsushima Strait. (See chapter 6, "'I've Gotten What I Came For': Potsdam, the Bomb, and Soviet Entry into the War," and appendix Q, "Planned U.S. Naval and Air Operations in Support of the Soviet Invasion of Manchuria.")

Discussions were already in the works to establish a training regime for the Soviet sailors who would man the vessels supplied under Milepost. The U.S. alternative to a direct commitment in the Kurils was to ramp up the naval side of the Lend-Lease expansion by helping the Soviets establish a modest amphibious capability before they entered the war. This was to be done by setting up a secret base at an existing facility—Fort Randall at Cold Bay, Alaska—where Soviet sailors could quickly learn to operate the hundreds of combat ships coming to them under Milepost.

Though the Soviets originally preferred Dutch Harbor or Kodiak Island, Admiral Kuznetsov was presented with the Cold Bay location on February 8 and found it to his liking. Kuznetsov readily agreed on his own authority and the first wave of 2,300 Project Hula sailors arrived before the end of March. Ultimately, some 15,000 Soviet naval personnel were trained at Fort Randall and manned the 149 American-made minesweepers, sub chasers, frigates, LCI assault craft, and LSM-sized floating workshops turned over by the end of August 1945.[47] (See appendix G—U.S. Navy combatant ships transferred to the USSR under Project Hula, May–September 1945.) Unanticipated at the time, however, was that the American *nyet* to even supply convoy protection would set in motion Soviet contingency planning for an invasion of Hokkaido itself. Deemed impractical with the limited amphibious resources available to them, the invasion was never carried out. After the Japanese surrender announcement, it was scaled back to a much smaller administrative landing that was similarly canceled.[48]

3

Roosevelt, Stalin, and Poland

The Tehran, Moscow, and Yalta Conferences

December 1, 1943, 3:20 p.m. SECRET

[Roosevelt] added that there were in the United States from six to
seven million Americans of Polish extraction, and as a practical
man, he did not wish to lose their vote. He said personally he agreed
with the views of Marshal Stalin as to the necessity of the restoration
of a Polish state but would like to see the Eastern border [with
Russia] moved further to the west and the Western border moved
even to the River Oder [in Germany]. He hoped, however, that the
Marshal would understand that for political reasons outlined above,
he could not participate in any decision here in Tehran or even next
winter [Yalta] on this subject and that he could not publicly take
part in any such arrangement at the present time.

Marshal Stalin replied that now the President
explained, he had understood.

—MINUTES OF PRESIDENT ROOSEVELT'S MEETING
WITH JOSEPH STALIN, TEHRAN CONFERENCE

The key agreement at Potsdam, which cleared the way
for the U.S. and Soviet chiefs of staff to hammer out the
direct coordination of combat operations in the coming
months, was obtained the afternoon of July 17, 1945, the day before
the proceedings opened. Greatly relieved, Truman wrote his wife:
"I've gotten what I came for—Stalin goes to war August 15 with no
strings on it. He wanted a Chinese settlement [treaty with China

granting territorial and other concessions]—and it is practically made—in a better form than I expected. [Chinese foreign minister] Soong did better than I asked him. I'll say that we'll end the war a year sooner now, and think of the kids who won't be killed! That is the important thing."[1]

The rest of the conference centered on a range of other important matters that related to the nature of the postwar world. All were of great concern to the United States—and Secretary of State Jimmy Byrnes in particular—such as reparations and postwar Europe's economic stabilization as part of the "sphere of influence" peace that Byrnes and Truman negotiated there. Truman, however, could no more announce the secret U.S.-Soviet agreements at Potsdam than his predecessor could announce those made with Stalin at Tehran and Yalta. This chapter will discuss these earlier agreements in light of the military plans that underlay all the key decisions of the period, including use of the atomic bomb.

The settlement of important but nevertheless secondary issues at Potsdam were presented in the most grandiose terms possible for public consumption and a fine gloss laid over continuing disagreements concerning Poland, which had long bedeviled Truman's predecessor as well. Consequently, to better understand Truman and the atomic bomb decision we must look at Roosevelt's handling of the Polish question within the wider sphere of U.S.-Soviet relations.

President Roosevelt had little interest in Central Europe beyond its effect on domestic political alignments and its seemingly perpetual role as a powder keg waiting for any spark that would set off a bloody conflict between the great powers. As early as March 1943 Roosevelt told British foreign secretary Anthony Eden that he "did not intend to go to the Peace Conference and bargain with Poland or the other small states; as far as Poland is concerned, the important thing is to set it up in a way that will help maintain the peace of the world." Only a year and a half earlier in the Atlantic Charter, the United States and Great Britain had resoundingly committed themselves to supporting the restoration of self-government for all countries occupied during the war and allowing all peoples to choose their own form of government. Now Roosevelt declared

Roosevelt, Stalin, and Poland

that "the big powers would have to decide what Poland should have" and stated flatly that "the Russian armies would be in the Baltic States at the time of the downfall of Germany and none of us can force them to get out."[2]

Poland's government in exile, headquartered in London, was energetically publicizing its great expectations of the country's role in Europe after the defeat of Germany. This resonated with Polish Catholics who made up solid voting blocks in various key states, and the president carefully moved to dampen any overblown expectations before attending the Tehran Conference with Churchill and Stalin. Roosevelt explained to the influential Roman Catholic archbishop of New York (later cardinal), Francis Spellman, that the administration "planned to make an agreement among the Big Four. Accordingly, the world would be divided into spheres of influence." Moreover, the formerly Russian lands making up "the Eastern half of Poland"—as well as the Baltic states, northeastern Romania, and, thought Roosevelt, Finland—would be directly incorporated into the Soviet Union.

"There is no point to oppose these desires of Stalin," said Roosevelt, "because he has the power to get them anyhow. So better give them gracefully. . . . It is natural that the European countries will have to undergo tremendous changes in order to adapt to Russia, but he hopes that in ten or twenty years the European influences would bring the Russians to become less barbarian." In the meantime, he stressed, "The European people will simply have to endure Russian domination."[3]

At the conference, Roosevelt elaborated on the domestic realities he must deal with if he ran for reelection the following year. In a private meeting with Stalin, Roosevelt explained, according to the conference minutes: "There were in the United States from six to seven million Americans of Polish extraction, and as a practical man, he did not wish to lose their vote. He said he personally agreed with the views of Marshal Stalin (on Poland) . . . He hoped, however, that the Marshal would understand that for political reasons outlined above, he could not participate in any decision here at Teheran or even next winter [Yalta] on this subject and that he could not publicly take part in any such arrangement at the present time."[4]

Stalin replied that he understood the president's concerns, but Roosevelt's problem extended beyond just Polish Americans, as the Baltic states created with the Treaty of Versailles—and now destined for extinction—were also predominately Catholic. "There were a number of persons of Lithuanian, Latvian and Estonian origin . . . in the United States," Roosevelt noted, before quickly clarifying "that he fully realized the three Baltic Republics had in history and again more recently been part of Russia and jokingly added, that when the Soviet armies re-occupied these areas, he did not intend to go to war with the Soviet Union on this point."[5]

Roosevelt had accepted the Democratic nomination for vice president to run with Governor James Cox of Ohio in 1920 only to be solidly trounced by the Republican ticket headed by Warren G. Harding. Moreover, Roosevelt had energetically campaigned in support of the ailing Woodrow Wilson's unpopular effort to obtain American membership in the League of Nations and remembered well the mass desertion of Irish Catholics from the Democratic Party that resulted from Wilson's pro-British stance during the crushing of the "Easter Rebellion" in Ireland.[6]

Now, in 1943, the winning of a fourth term was not at all seen as a foregone conclusion by the once-stung Roosevelt for, as coreligionists of the Poles, temperamental Irish Catholics could well join them and bolt again with disastrous consequences. Whether or not he knew of Roosevelt's dilemma, a certain junior senator from Missouri who'd commanded an artillery battery of tough Irish cannoneers during the brutal fighting of World War I would have certainly understood what the president was having to contend with. Moreover, this unease extended well beyond Catholic voters. Public opinion polling throughout 1943 and 1944 consistently showed that the country took the Atlantic Charter seriously and that Americans "would not look favorably upon Soviet violations of self-determination in Eastern Europe."[7]

There could be no hint whatsoever of U.S. involvement in the imminent Soviet expansion into Central Europe through both direct annexations and establishment of satellites. But there was a way that Stalin could ease Roosevelt's—and later Truman's—burden of making such realities palatable to the American electorate that Roosevelt must placate, said Ambassador Harriman: plebiscites "which would give a color of decency to the operation."[8]

Before Tehran the president optimistically maintained to Archbishop Spellman that "one should not overlook the magnificent economic achievements of Russia" and that Europeans "will be able to live well with the Russians."[9] He now told Stalin that "the big issue in the United States, insofar as public opinion went, would be the question of referendum and the right of self-determination. He said he thought world opinion would want some expression of the will of the people, perhaps not immediately after their reoccupation by Soviet forces, but some day, and that he personally was confident that the people would vote to join the Soviet Union."[10]

Roosevelt's talk of "public opinion" prompted Stalin to remark that "he did not quite see why it was being raised." The president explained "that the truth of the matter was that the public neither knew nor understood" that within recent living memory the lands had belonged to Russia. Stalin found all this a little tiresome and he responded that Americans "should be informed and some propaganda work should be done," adding "as to the expression of the will of the people, there would be lots of opportunities for that to be done in accordance with the Soviet constitution." Roosevelt continued to press Stalin, bluntly stating, "It would be helpful for him personally if some public declaration in regard to the future elections to which the Marshal had referred, could be made." But Stalin would only reiterate that there would be "plenty of opportunities for such an expression of the will of the people."[11]

Though Roosevelt was unable to coax out of Stalin the kind of statement that he desired on self-determination for the peoples of Eastern Europe, he had at minimum impressed upon him the importance of not making statements that might put Roosevelt's reelection in jeopardy. Roosevelt's view was commonly held throughout the U.S. government at the time, and Averell Harriman, who shared it, later noted that until Stalin's refusal to give timely assistance to the Polish resistance fighters who had captured much of Warsaw, Secretary of State Cordell Hull "had not been overly concerned with Soviet behavior in Poland." At the same time, "What troubled [Harriman] more was Russia's position on . . . the proposed United Nations Organization," which both Roosevelt and his successor saw as the key to future world peace.[12]

As 1943 moved inexorably into 1944 and military planning for the endgame against both Germany and Japan ramped up, the need for coordination of combat operations became paramount. It had long been understood by the Roosevelt administration and the U.S. military that the Soviet Union, once freed from the war with Germany, would eventually have the means available to do almost anything it wanted against a now badly overstretched Japan, but that the critical vulnerabilities to its position in the Far East for now still remained (see chapter 3). Equally well understood was that the United States was engaging only a small fraction of Japan's land forces at vulnerable spots around the periphery of the empire's lunge outward at the beginning of the war.[13]

As Americans drove deeper into the core of Japan's Pacific defenses, the priceless ability to island-hop and bypass Japanese defenses steadily diminished and would disappear completely once on Japanese soil. Meaningful operational maneuvers would become a thing of the past on the narrow Japanese plains, which were defended by an intact, cohesive army of at least 3,500,000 men and sandwiched between rugged mountains and the sea. This ground could only be bought through a relentless adherence to grinding attritional warfare dependent on massive firepower and the bravery of U.S. Army and Marine infantrymen.

Army planners ran their comparison of American and Japanese losses during the fierce fighting on Saipan against the Japanese force they believed that they were likely to confront during the invasion: "It cost approximately one American killed and several wounded to exterminate seven Japanese soldiers. On this basis it might cost us half a million American lives and many times that number wounded . . . in the home islands." This "Saipan ratio" set the grim standard for strategic-level casualty projections in the Pacific. Together with the experience of combat attrition of line infantry units in Europe, plus the assumption that fighting in Japan could stretch nearly as far as 1947, it provided the basis for the U.S. Army and War Department manpower policy for 1945, and, thus, the pace for the big jump in Selective Service inductions and expansion of the training base even as the war in Europe was winding down.[14]

But this was not the end of the terrible calculus of defeating the Japanese Empire on its own soil. More than a million Imperial troops were stationed nearby on the Asian mainland with fully three-quarters of them not engaged in combat operations at all and thus available for the defense of the Home Islands.

With the Chinese military largely ineffectual when engaged in offensive operations—and likely to stay that way no matter how much U.S. aid was lavished upon it—only the Red Army offered the prospect of quickly neutralizing this massive force by either destroying it outright or, at minimum, tying it down on the Asian mainland. Thus the timing and scope of any future Soviet operations were of critical importance. What both U.S. Army chief of staff George C. Marshall and his Pacific commander, General Douglas MacArthur, desired was a one-two punch, a Soviet invasion of Manchuria against the massive Kwantung Army on the Asian mainland followed by the launch of U.S. operations in the Home Islands. And this had been the Americans' intent from the beginning. When Harriman and General Deane were sent to Moscow in 1943, General Marshall stated that they were "not only to obtain Russian participation but [also] to have them give U.S. the right kind of help and enough time to prepare to make their help effective."[15]

During the long run-up to the Yalta Conference, Harriman and Deane believed that they were finally making progress toward this end when their "faith in the possibility of cooperation with Stalin was badly shaken."[16] Stalin had halted the Soviet offensive into Poland at the outskirts of its capitol, Warsaw, in early August when local underground forces associated with the exiled government in England had risen and seized much of the city. It was the Soviet-controlled Lublin Provisional Government in Moscow, unencumbered by any noncommunist elements, that Stalin wanted to see installed in the capitol. Desperate fighting ensued and the Germans were able to substantially reinforce their garrison while the Soviets sat by and even refused to let British supply aircraft use their nearby airfields.

Churchill's direct entreaties to Stalin on August 20 that the Russians at least airdrop supplies and munitions to the embattled Poles or "agree to help our planes in doing it very quickly" were sternly rebuffed.[17] Churchill turned to Roosevelt for assistance. Five days later he proposed that they dispatch a joint message stating their intent to send planes, "Unless you [Stalin] directly forbid it."[18]

Throughout the Warsaw crisis, however, Harriman had repeatedly found that "Washington"—Roosevelt, Secretary Hull, and the army—showed "real apprehension that too much aggressiveness in behalf of the Warsaw insurgents might jeopardize the prospect of further Soviet military collaboration."[19] Though Britain had gone to war over the German invasion of Poland and hosted the country's government in exile, the United States was additionally committed to a long bloody struggle against Japan that would continue well after the Nazis were crushed. President Roosevelt bluntly informed Churchill on August 26 that while he had "no objection" to the Prime Minister sending the cable under his own name, "I do not consider it advantageous to the long-range general war prospect for me to join with you in the proposed message to U.J. [Uncle Joe Stalin]."[20]

The Soviets had publicly called for the Poles to rise up against their Nazi occupiers but then refused to come to their aid once they had exposed themselves. Such grotesque, overt duplicity prompted Harriman to write, "I can only draw the conclusion that this action [was taken out of] ruthless political considerations."[21] The situation of the Poles in Warsaw inexorably deteriorated, and Harriman later described himself as "torn between frustration and hope" when he wrote Harry Hopkins on September 10 that Soviet actions had called into question that the United States would receive "the kind of cooperation we expect." Harriman lamented that their "policy appears to be crystallizing to force us and the British to accept all Soviet policies, backed by the strength and prestige of the Red Army." Nevertheless, Harriman observed: "I am disappointed but not discouraged. . . . I am not going to propose any drastic action but a firm but friendly *quid pro quo* attitude."[22]

Roosevelt, Stalin, and Poland

As far as Eastern Europe was concerned, the United States had neither the means nor desire to materially influence events. However, a confluence of interests in the Far East would very soon enable Harriman to get his wish in one very specific area of America and Russia's complex relationship as both countries needs for the endgame against Imperial Japan would soon precipitate a classic quid pro quo that was both massive in scale and highly secret. The Roosevelt and Truman administrations would labor diligently to keep up America's end of the bargain and ensure at Potsdam that Stalin did the same.

As the Warsaw uprising entered its final bloody death throws, Stalin began to profess sympathy for the Warsaw Poles and made some halfhearted gestures to ease their situation, presumably to soften Churchill's anger and blunt the growing American distrust. Then, two weeks after Harriman's anguished memo to Hopkins, a seeming reversal in the Soviets' attitude toward cooperation in the war against Japan came out of the blue from Stalin himself.

During a briefing by Harriman and his British counterpart, Sir Archibald Clark-Kerr, on the results of the Second Quebec Conference between Roosevelt, Churchill, and their military staffs, the Soviet premier appeared genuinely surprised that, considering the discussion he'd had with Roosevelt at Tehran, there was no mention of any Russian participation in the war against Japan. In a message marked "For the eyes of the President only," Harriman reported: "Stalin inquired whether we wished to bring Japan to her knees without Russian assistance or whether you wished, as you suggested in Teheran, Russian participation. The British Ambassador and I both assured him that Russian participation was desired but that no plans could be made for the use of Soviet resources until Marshal Stalin was ready to initiate discussions. He then stated that there was no change in his attitude as he had expressed it to you at Teheran. Russia is ready to participate in the war against Japan after German is defeated."[23]

After a year of delays, evasions, and false starts—all punctuated by extended periods of studied silence—this seeming change in attitude appeared to finally open the door to Soviet-American collaboration in the war against Japan detailed in the previous chapter.[24] Harriman continued:

> [Stalin] gave every indication of being ready and willing to cooperate but did not want to be an uninvited participant. It seems clear that we will get greater cooperation from him if we will suggest the operations that we would like the Russians to undertake, rather than wait their proposals. Because of this new aspect General Deane is cabling the Joint Chiefs of Staff for more detailed instructions than he has previously received.
>
> I strongly recommend that we follow the course Stalin has indicated and that General Deane be authorized to discuss with the Red Army staff, in broad outlines at least, our Pacific strategy and to propose the full measure of Russian participation desired.[25]

Harriman, according to Deane, was "filled with enthusiasm" and fully convinced that "this time Stalin meant business." Deane, however, was "a bit more pessimistic."[26] Fearing a loss of momentum if Stalin called for discussions before any instructions were received from Washington, he cabled General Marshall with his own suggestions on what role the United States might want the Russians to play.

Deane's suggestions were quickly approved then supplemented by additional instructions. The talks held with Stalin and his chief of staff, General Alexei E. Antonov, in Moscow on October 14–17, 1944, resulted in a far-reaching, though little known, agreement ahead of the Yalta Conference. The United States would strike at "the industrial heart of Japan" by seizing the Tokyo Plain while the Soviet Union, as Stalin succinctly put it, would "break the Japanese spine" with an invasion of Manchuria.[27] Stalin declared that "if stores could be built up now the attack could be made two or three months after Germany's collapse." "Planning," he added, "should begin at once."[28]

This was to be no simple "spoiling attack" to simply hold down the powerful Japanese armies in Manchuria collectively called the Kwantung, but a massive, multipronged offensive intended to cut off and annihilate it that would require the Russians "to move

Roosevelt, Stalin, and Poland

some twenty-five to thirty divisions to the Far East before they could play their part against the Japanese," according to Stalin.[29] To launch an operation of this size and scope so quickly after the Nazis were defeated in Europe, however, the Red Army would be dependent on the Americans to secretly supply nearly everything that the gathering force would need, from food and fuel to war supplies of all description, and even the tens of thousands of American-made trucks to move it all both before and during the offensive. As Deane explained:

> We were given a list of the needs of the Soviet Union for a two months' supply of food, fuel, transport equipment, and other supplies, calculated on the requirements of a force of 1,500,000 men, 3,000 tanks, 75,000 motor vehicles, and 5,000 airplanes. The total tonnage involved was 860,410 tons of dry cargo and 206,000 tons of liquid cargo. It was considered necessary to have the deliveries completed by June 30, 1945, and it was all in addition to the program under the current Fourth Protocol [of Lend-Lease]. It was a neat little chore which the Soviet Union presented to the United States. In view of the time limit imposed, I could not help feeling resentful of the time that had been wasted the preceding year.[30]

What did Stalin want for entering the war? Most fundamentally, a reversal of the territorial losses Russia had suffered in the Russo-Japanese War forty years earlier and an end to Japan's threats to the nation's rail and sea communications with the far eastern port of Vladivostok in the Soviet Union's Maritime Provinces. Any additional influence, perhaps even direct control, that Stalin could leverage over a weakened Japan in the postwar world would be gladly accepted.

Harriman later wrote that "there was little disposition in Washington to pick quarrels with the Russians" over this. He also stated: "The fact that Stalin was now asking for both supplies and territory did not visibly disturb the President or the Joint Chiefs when [my] report of the conversation reached Washington. Stalin had promised to fight the Japanese armies, not only in Manchuria but also in North China, and Washington seemed well satisfied with the bargain."[31]

As outlined in the previous chapter, the United States moved immediately to fill its end of the "bargain" by embarking on a huge—and highly secret—expansion of the Lend-Lease program, codenamed "Milepost," long before Roosevelt, Churchill, and Stalin met again at the Yalta Conference. Moreover, Stalin's October 16 list was only the U.S. government's down payment on the Soviet offensive. Harriman returned to Washington to brief the president on the meetings with Stalin and stressed that the supplies "had to be delivered across the Pacific by June 30." Harriman conceded to Roosevelt and Harry Hopkins at their November 18 meeting that "shipping was still in short supply" but "urged that additional ships be made available somehow, warning that if they were not, Stalin might delay joining the war against Japan."[32]

Roosevelt promised to do all he could. "The defeat of Japan without the aid of Russia," he noted, "would be extremely difficult and costly and we should do everything to support Stalin's plans."[33] As for the U.S. Army and War Department, General Dean in Moscow, the Joint Chiefs of Staff in Washington, and Roosevelt himself now had reason to believe that they were finally on the road to meaningful joint planning with the Russians against Imperial Japan. Deane, assisted by Harriman, had labored diligently for more than a year to encourage Soviet agreement to that end—a working relationship along the lines of what existed with the British—and also that the United States might finally begin the construction of bomber bases on Soviet territory from which strikes could be conducted against Japan.

It was not to be. The all-too-typical delays in setting up a joint planning staff continued, and the few times when designated officers from both countries did get together before Yalta the proceedings quickly became meetings to set up additional meetings because the Red Army contingent was not authorized to make any decisions. Then, on December 16, as the organization for Milepost's massive surge of supplies was being completed, Deane was summarily informed by General Antonov that "after careful calculations" the Soviets had decided that the United States could not operate from Soviet territory after all. Keeping his composure, Deane reminded him that this contradicted assurances that Stalin had personally given on six separate occasions and that America was carrying out its commitments on the expectation that the Soviets would carry out theirs. The response was less than satisfactory:

> Antonov replied that in view of the fact that I had raised the matter of promises made by Stalin, he would take the matter up with him and let me have a decision in a few days. Three days later he sent word to me that the decision against the project would stand. I was amazed at Antonov's bland renunciation of a firm agreement, and especially at the way in which the decision had been withheld until our [Milepost] supply program had gained a momentum which would be difficult if not impossible to stop.[34]

Stalin's "about face" on the long-sought goal of establishing bomber bases in the Maritime Provinces came as "a shock" in Washington, said Elliot Richardson who added that it reinforced the belief of "many at State and War that the Russians could not be depended upon to uphold their agreements."[35] Roosevelt and his senior advisors were, however, willing to look past this setback. On January 5, 1945, he issued a directive to the new Secretary of State, Edward R. Stettinius Jr., for distribution to all departments and agencies engaged in fulfilling the current congressionally approved fourth protocol of the Lend-Lease Program as well as the secret Milepost expansion, to prepare Soviet armies for the coming war with Japan. It began: "Russia continues to be a major factor in achieving the defeat of Germany. We must, therefore, continue to support the U.S.S.R. by providing the maximum amount of supplies which can be delivered to her ports. I consider this a matter of utmost Importance, second only to the operational requirements in the Pacific and the Atlantic."[36]

Similar statements had been issued before. But although it was clear, in spite of the recent German counterattack in the Ardennes, that the end of the war in Europe was near, Roosevelt added: "The USSR has been requested to state requirements for a Fifth Protocol to cover the period July 1, 1945, to June 30, 1946. It is desired that, within the limitations of available resources, every effort be made to meet these requirements. Pending the formulation of the Fifth Protocol, it is my desire that every effort be made to continue a full and uninterrupted flow of supplies to the USSR."[37]

With Milepost a deep and well-kept secret and the Soviet Union in a nonaggression pact with Japan, this may have been disseminated as much for the prying eyes of Soviet intelligence gatherers as those of the American administrators. It clearly demonstrated—ahead of the Yalta Conference—the Americans' commitment and sincerity in directly supporting the Soviet Union in what could well develop into a lengthy struggle against the Japanese military on the Asian mainland.

The Roosevelt administration was confident that in the wartime environment Milepost deliveries—despite their raw volume—would be mistaken by Japanese intelligence as regular Lend-Lease shipments for the final battles against the Nazis. Congressional and public interest, however, insured the opposite for the administration's policy toward Eastern Europe.

Roosevelt's tacit approval of Soviet territorial claims at Tehran had essentially removed boundary issues as a problem before Yalta, but how disclosure of those agreements and the issue of self-determination in Eastern Europe might affect public opinion remained as vexing as ever. Polish Americans—and to a wider extent, the massive body of Catholic voters—had not been aroused before the November elections, and Democrats won handily with their standard-bearer easily obtaining an unprecedented fourth term. Now, however, the concern of Roosevelt and his administration shifted to ensuring that any erosion of support over developments in Poland did not precipitate enough discord in the Senate to block the establishment of the United Nations, much as it had prevented U.S. participation in the League of Nations after the previous world war.[38]

This had been a major concern of Secretary of State Hull and remained so for his successor. Two years earlier, John D. Hickerson of the State Department's Division of European Affairs had reminded Hull that the notion that the Soviets could somehow be induced to not seize the territory they lost after World War I was

Roosevelt, Stalin, and Poland

"sheer military fantasy."[39] Now, in 1945, the Red Army had indeed evicted the Nazis from this land, and Hickerson told his new boss that the United States should not fritter away its limited bargaining power by opposing the Soviets. His advice to Secretary Stettinius centered on two points: the United States must work carefully to gain Soviet cooperation in establishing the United Nations and not lose sight of the fact that they "sorely need the Soviet Union in the war against Japan when the war in Europe is over."[40]

This view was commonly held among the U.S. leadership, who believed that there was little that could be done for the peoples of Eastern Europe. Remarked Hickerson:

> There are certain things in connection with the foregoing proposals which are repugnant to me personally, but I am prepared to urge their adoption to obtain the cooperation of the Soviet Union in winning the war and organizing the peace. By acting on these things, we may be able to work out a regime which will obtain the cooperation of the Soviet Union for the rest of Europe and the rest of the world. There are good arguments from the Soviet point of view in favor of all of these proposals. I am willing to sponsor and support the Soviet arguments if it will save American lives in winning the war.[41]

Hickerson, who would later play a key role in the formation of the North Atlantic Treaty Organization (NATO), believed that Soviet domination in Eastern Europe would have to be the price paid "if it will save the rest of Europe from the diplomacy of the jungle which is almost certain to ensue otherwise." This would be a bitter pill for Polish Americans and as well as those who had been inspired by the Atlantic Charter. Consequently, Hickerson advised: "If the proposals set forth in the foregoing paragraphs should be adopted as the policy of the United States Government, a program should be undertaken immediately to prepare public opinion for them. This would involve off-the-record discussions with Congress, with outstanding newspaper editors and writers, columnists and radio commentators."[42]

At a preliminary meeting to the Yalta Conference, Secretary Stettinius told his British counterpart, Foreign Secretary Anthony

Eden, "that from the point of view of American public opinion it was extremely important that some equitable solution should be reached." Stettinius explained: "It was impossible for the United States Government simply to recognize the Lublin Provisional Government. What seemed to be required was some kind of Council including all the relevant parties including [Stanisław] Mikolajczyk [the exiled prime minister of the Polish government]. Failure to reach a satisfactory solution of this question at the forthcoming meeting would greatly disturb public opinion in America especially among the Catholics and might prejudice the whole question of American participation in the post war world organization."[43]

At the Yalta Conference, Roosevelt again reminded Stalin that he had to consider "six to seven million" Polish Americans. "It would make it easier for me at home if the Soviet Government could give [back some territory] to Poland" along the new boarder as a "gesture" of goodwill.[44] Stalin refused, and the matter was dropped, but he did agree to sign a "Declaration of Liberated Europe." Released with great fanfare, the declaration reaffirmed the principles of the Atlantic Charter and called for the establishment of provisional governments "broadly representative of all democratic elements in the population and pledged to the earliest possible establishment through free elections of governments responsive to the will of the people."[45] As hoped, this was hailed as a magnificent accomplishment and, together with future secretary of state James F. "Jimmy" Byrnes's deft handling of the press upon his return from the conference, set the tone for how Americans initially viewed Yalta.[46]

The pledge to hold free elections throughout Eastern Europe was not, however, what it appeared to be, as there was absolutely no enforcement machinery built into the agreement. Instead of occurring under the direct supervision of the Big Three, they would merely "consult together on the measures necessary to discharge the joint responsibilities set forth" in the declaration.[47] The agreement was "so elastic" that Admiral Leahy, the White House chief of staff, warned, "The Russians could stretch it all the way from Yalta to Washington without technically breaking it." Roosevelt wearily replied, "I know, Bill, I know it. But it's the best I can do for Poland at this time."[48]

Roosevelt, Stalin, and Poland

The principal matter at hand, beyond a show of Allied unity in defeating the Nazis, was gaining direct Soviet participation in a war against a country that it had pledged not to attack—Japan. As for the agreement itself, Joint Chiefs Marshall, King, and Leahy raised no objections whatsoever when Harriman showed them a draft copy of the agreement and asked for their comments. Each of these men believed that the United States could and would, if necessary, defeat Imperial Japan on its own. Victory was not in question. But the cost of going it alone was. "This makes the trip worthwhile," Leahy remarked to Harriman after reading the agreement. As the curmudgeonly old admiral later wrote, "No one was more surprised than I to see these conditions agreed to at Yalta labeled as some horrendous concessions made by Roosevelt to an enemy."[49] (See appendix H, "Agreement regarding the Entry of the Soviet Union into the War against Japan.")

The conference protocol made no mention of this secret accord, which would be quietly released after a year had passed from its signing.

4

A New President

"The Storm Broke Almost at Once"

Before Hopkins left for Moscow, I had impressed upon him the need

for getting as early a date as possible on Russia's entry into the war

against Japan. Hopkins had been with Roosevelt at Yalta and knew

of Russia's commitment there to move against Japan after the war

in Europe was ended. On May 28 Hopkins and Harriman got from

Stalin a very important declaration which Hopkins cabled me.

"Harriman and I saw Stalin and Molotov for the third time last

night," Hopkins said. "Following are the important results:

The Soviet Army will be properly deployed on the

Manchurian positions by August 8th."

—PRESIDENT HARRY S. TRUMAN

Upon Roosevelt's death on April 12, 1945, President Truman immediately sought foreign policy information and advice from those State Department officials in his administration who he naturally assumed would have the most comprehensive knowledge of the subtleties of the Soviet-American relationship. Early briefings by Under Secretary Joseph Grew, a firm advocate of a "tough stance" approach to negotiations with the Soviet Union, guided Truman's thinking and were strongly reinforced by the returning Harriman. The new president believed that the best course to follow was one of strict adherence by both sides to agreements already negotiated. But just as Admiral Leahy had warned Roosevelt at Yalta about the "elasticity" of Stalin's agreement to hold free elections throughout Eastern Europe, principally made for public consumption in the United States, he made it clear to Truman that the Declaration of Liberated Europe "could be read two ways and it would be a serious matter to break with the Russians."[1]

Unfortunately for Truman, it wasn't immediately clear to him that Roosevelt, painfully familiar with State Department leaking and evasions of his intent, had chosen to be his own State Department when it came to matters concerning the other two-thirds of the "The Big Three," Stalin and Churchill. One very noticeable result of this was that, until Yalta, no secretary of state had even been part of the U.S. delegation at these bipartite or tripartite conferences. Even then, Secretary Stettinius was denied knowledge of Stalin's pledge to go to war against Japan.

In a private conversation with Roosevelt, Stettinius asked "whether there was some aspect of the Far East negotiations that the State Department ought to know about." Military considerations, however, remained paramount, and it was critical that Stalin's agreement to enter the Pacific War remain a closely held secret if the Soviet's vulnerable buildup in the Far East was to proceed unmolested. "[Roosevelt's] reply," according to Stettinius, "was that Harriman alone had handled that matter, which was primarily military in any case, and that it had best remain that way."[2] Admiral Leahy retained possession of the signed document, and upon his return to Washington he locked it in the president's personal safe. (See appendix H, "Agreement regarding the Entry of the Soviet Union into the War against Japan.") The document was made available to Truman after Roosevelt's death and to incoming Secretary of State Jimmy Byrnes ahead of the Potsdam Conference, but its actual text was not released to the press until February 11, 1946, one year after it was signed by Roosevelt, Churchill, and Stalin.[3]

Harriman, who had worked long and hard to develop a more quid pro quo approach to U.S.-Soviet negotiations, returned to Washington after Roosevelt's death to be at the disposal of his new boss. His unique experience as ambassador to Moscow understandably positioned him as the new president's preeminent advisor on the Soviet Union. Not yet fully understood by Truman was the role of Harry Hopkins. Officially, he was the U.S. chairman of the Combined Chiefs of Staff (British and American) Munitions Assignment Board. In fact, Hopkins was Roosevelt's closest advisor on foreign affairs and a personal envoy to both Churchill and Stalin. He and his wife lived in the residential area of the White House, and he was the sole civilian, other than the president himself, to have access to the secret "Map Room" communications center. From there, he acted as the conduit through which the center's most relevant products were hand-delivered to the president.

While Harriman was a hardliner, alarmed and angered by Soviet's reneging on the spirit of Yalta's Declaration of Liberated Europe almost before the ink was dry as well as the treatment of downed American fliers under Soviet control, Hopkins was convinced that full and immediate no-strings-attached cooperation in all matters relating to prosecution of the war was in the best interest of the United States. But Harriman's advice to the new president that the United States take a firm quid pro quo approach in his dealings with the Soviet Union fit well with Truman's own tendencies and what Harriman and others in the administration claimed was Roosevelt's growing frustration with Stalin in the weeks before his death.[4]

Secretary of War Stimson and General Marshall greatly desired Soviet participation in what was envisioned to be a prolonged and frightfully costly endgame in the Pacific, but their stated reservations to the resulting "tough stance" approach were initially ignored as Truman followed the council of his State Department advisors.[5] The result was a steady deterioration in U.S.-Soviet relations beginning on April 23, barely ten days into Truman's presidency, when he sharply demanded of Foreign Minister Vyacheslav Molotov that the Soviet government live up to its commitments and culminating with an "accidental" cutoff of Lend-Lease shipments almost three weeks later on May 11—just four days after the German surrender and right in the middle of the Milepost buildup.

Truman, rightly or wrongly, later laid the blame squarely on Grew. After the May 8 cabinet meeting, he and Foreign Economic Administrator Leo Crowley brought to Truman's attention "an important order in connection with Lend-Lease which President

Roosevelt had approved but not signed" that directed that the volume of aid sent to the Allies be lowered once Germany had been defeated. "I reached for my pen," Truman recalled, "and, without reading the document, I signed it. The storm broke almost at once."[6]

Instead of a gradual lessening of aid as Stettinius and Harriman had discussed—with the secretary pointedly directing that aid supporting Russia's coming war with Japan "should continue to be energetically pressed"—a literal interpretation of the order was executed. The secret, separately administered Milepost Program was included in the order and virtually all Lend-Lease operations were completely shut down, with even ships at sea being ordered to turn about mid-ocean.[7] The president immediately rescinded the order, but the damage was already done. Recalled Truman: "Stalin at Potsdam would bring it up every chance he had, that we cut off Lend-Lease while he was still getting ready to go to war with Japan. . . . I think Crowley and Grew put it over on me that morning. That taught me a lesson early in the game— that I should always know what was in those documents myself, personally, and I had to read all night some nights to do that."[8]

In the meantime, Truman finally received a detailed formal briefing on the Manhattan Project, though he already knew, through the efforts of Truman Committee military liaison General Frank Lowe, far more than either his contemporaries or scholars today would ever imagine (see chapter 2). On April 25, two days after the president's run-in with Molotov, project director General Leslie R. Groves and Secretary Stimson described the yet-to-be-produced atomic bomb as "the most terrible weapon ever known in human history" and stated that the special techniques used in its manufacture would not remain a secret forever. Moreover, Stimson was deeply worried over what this might portend for mankind itself: "The world in its present state of moral advancement, compared with its technical development, would be eventually at the mercy of such a weapon. In other words, modern civilization might be completely destroyed."[9]

Stimson shared more details of the plan with the president : "Steps are under way [to establish] a select committee of particular qualifications for recommending action to the executive and legislative branches of our government when secrecy is no longer in full effect. The committee would also recommend the actions to be taken by the War Department prior to that time in anticipation of the postwar problems. All recommendations would of course be first submitted to the President."[10]

The Interim Committee referred to by Stimson—who served as its chair—had a completely civilian makeup. It included Byrnes, acting as Truman's personal representative; Dr. Vannevar Bush, serving as director of the Office of Scientific Research and Development; several prominent government and industrial figures; and a scientific panel made up of Manhattan Project physicists that included Enrico Fermi and J. Robert Oppenheimer. On May 9, with the VE-Day festivities still ringing in their ears, Stimson opened the Interim Committee's first meeting: "Gentlemen, it is our responsibility to recommend action that may turn the course of civilization." The session covered, according to Stimson, "the whole field of atomic energy, in its political, military and scientific aspects."[11]

After the use of nuclear weapons against Japan, these proceedings and virtually everything related to the massive Manhattan Project became the subject of intense scrutiny and debate. At this point in the war, however, it was not known if the secret project would indeed produce functioning atomic bombs or even if such weapons would perform as expected. It was also unclear how the military junta controlling the Imperial government in Japan would actually react to their use. The first test of a nuclear device at the Trinity test site in the New Mexico desert was still more than two months away.

While the Manhattan Project moved toward its questionable future, other highly secret—and ostensibly more tangible—operations reached their respective peaks as the countdown in the Pacific ground on: reflagged American Liberty and other cargo ships flying the Soviet hammer and sickle from their masts sailed nervously through Japanese straits with supplies for the invasion of Manchuria (Project Milepost, see chapter 3); Russian sailors by the tens of thousands passed in the opposite direction to Cold Bay, Alaska, to be secretly trained to operate American-made warships when the Soviets went to war (Project Hula); and in San Francisco Bay, construction of prefabricated components for a massive artificial harbor to be assembled near Tokyo during the invasion of Japan (codenamed Ironhorse) carried a priority second only to the Manhattan Project.[12]

British and American leaders had expressed the need for a swift and decisive victory against Japan after the defeat of Germany as early as the Casablanca Conference (ANFA) in January 1943. They codified that idea at the Quebec Conference (QUADRANT) that August and reaffirmed it at the end of 1943 during the Cairo Conference (SEXTANT). Subsequently, the September 1944 conference at Quebec (OCTAGON) involved a considerable amount of planning for the endgame, as the main elements of Britain's Royal Navy began their shift to the Pacific. Finally, at Yalta (ARGONAUT), the Soviet Union formally—and secretly—agreed to take on Imperial forces in the western half of the Japanese Empire, Manchuria, while the United States proceeded with the invasions of Kyushu followed by the Tokyo Plain on Honshu.[13]

Operation Downfall, the massive, two-phase invasion of Japan in 1945 and 1946 would ultimately require more than 3,500,000 soldiers, sailors, and Marines taking part in combat operations plus another 1,500,000 more young Americans providing direct support in the western Pacific. Much of this force was not yet in the Pacific. The U.S. First Army, which had pummeled its way from Normandy to the heart of Germany, and the Eighth Air Force, based in England, were on the way as well. The complex, minutely planned redeployment to the Pacific saw the first of a planned twenty American combat divisions pulled from the line in March. One of the formations, the 95th Infantry Division, received its marching orders for an "about face" west on Truman's second day in office.[14]

The large combat divisions would start shipping out in June, but hundreds of smaller non-divisional engineer and support elements were critically needed in the Pacific, and the invasion schedule—with "little margin of error"—required that many of them begin the process of leaving directly for the Pacific, where they would be immediately absorbed into General Douglas MacArthur's rapidly expanding forces.[15] Time was tight; shipping for moving the men and material was tight, and Winston Churchill was worried. But not about the final battles with Japan.

No sooner than the Soviets and many in Washington had exploded in anger over the brief cutoff of Lend-Lease aid to Russia, the prime minister made his presence felt. Still smarting over his inability to prod President Roosevelt and the U.S. command into seizing Berlin—or even the former Czech capital of Prague—just weeks earlier, Churchill now began to bombard President Truman with lengthy and dire warnings over the U.S. redeployment and events unfolding in Eastern Europe:

British Prime Minister Churchill to President Truman—
Personal and Top Secret

11 May 1945, [Message] Number 41,

The allies ought not to retreat from their present positions to the occupational line until we are satisfied about Poland and also about the temporary character of the Russian occupation of Germany, . . . If [matters] are not settled before the United States armies withdraw from Europe and the Western world folds up its war machines, there are no prospects of a satisfactory solution and very little of preventing a third world war.[16]

This was but the first of four lengthy cables Churchill sent to Truman over the next few days that pressed the issue. Other messages expressed similar sentiments:

12th May 1945, Number 44,

1. I am profoundly concerned about the European situation as outlined in my number 41. I learn that half the American air force in Europe has already begun to move to the Pacific Theatre. The newspapers are full of the great movements of the American armies out of Europe. . . .

2. Meanwhile, what is to happen about Russia? . . . An iron curtain is drawn down upon their front. There seems little doubt that the whole of the regions east of the line Lubeck-Trieste-Corfu will soon be completely in their hands.[17]

A New President

12th May 1945, Number 45,

1. If ["the situation"] is handled firmly before our strength is dispersed, Europe may be saved another blood bath. Otherwise the whole fruits of our victory may be cast away and none of the purposes of world organization to prevent territorial aggression and future wars will be attained.

2. I trust that a standstill order can be given on the movements of the American armies and air forces from Europe, at any rate for a few weeks.[18]

13th May 1945, Number 46,

Time is on [Stalin's] side if he digs in while we melt away.[19]

Truman fully appreciated that Britain had literally gone to war with Nazi Germany over its invasion of Poland and would have to live with the consequences of "the tide of Russian domination sweeping forward 120 miles on a front of 300 or 400 miles" long after the Americans had gone home.[20] Like Roosevelt, however, he strongly believed "that there was no fundamental conflict of interest between the United States and the Soviet Union; that both nations could rely on the United Nations to guarantee their postwar security."[21] In the meantime, U.S. forces in Europe had accomplished their part in the defeat of Germany, and a sizeable portion of that force had other things to do on the opposite side of the globe.[22] Truman issued the following response to Churchill's vigorous proposals:

President Truman to British Prime Minister Churchill

14 May 1945, [no.] 39 [responding to] Your numbers 44 and 46.

Thank you for your estimate of the future situation in Europe as outlined in your No. 44. From the present point of view it is impossible to make a conjecture as to what the Soviet may do when Germany is under the small forces of occupation and the great part of such armies as we can maintain our fighting in the Orient against Japan.[23]

It was at this point that the question of American casualties was elevated to the level of those already at the forefront of Truman's attention.

The United States had entered the war "late," and because of its sheer distance from Europe and the western Pacific it did not begin to experience grinding day-in, day-out casualties comparable to those of the other belligerents until the conflict's final year. The U.S. Army alone during that period was losing soldiers at a rate that Americans today would find astounding, suffering an average of sixty-five thousand killed, wounded, and missing each and every month during the "casualty surge" of June 1944 to June 1945, with the November, December, and January figures standing at seventy-two thousand, eighty-eight thousand, and seventy-nine thousand respectively in postwar tabulations.[24]

Most of these young men were lost battling the Nazis. But Americans from Waukegan to Washington believed that the United States had only reached the midpoint of the war, and the frightful casualties then emerging from the fighting on Iwo Jima and Okinawa suggested that once Japan itself was invaded, the second half of the war would certainly be no less bloody than the first. Even before Truman was sworn in as vice president, manpower requirements for that operation were moving to the front burner. Stimson called a press conference on January 11, 1945, where he announced that the U.S. Army's monthly Selective Service call up, which had already been increased from sixty thousand to eighty thousand in January 1945, was going to be ratcheted up yet again in March to one hundred thousand men per month in anticipation of the invasion.[25]

One week later, letters outlining the military's critical manpower needs were sent from Roosevelt, Marshall, and Chief of Naval Operations Ernest J. King to the House Military Affairs Committee and released to the *New York Times* and other newspapers on January 17, 1945. The public was informed in front-page articles that the army "must provide 600,000 replacements for overseas theaters by June 30, and, together with the Navy, will require a total of 900,000 inductions."[26] To handle the influx of draftees, the army also planned to increase of the number of training regiments to thirty-four in order to form a ready pool of replacements. Replacement training centers were expanded to a wartime peak of four hundred thousand in June, long after U.S. combat divisions had pulled to a halt along Germany's Elbe River.[27]

Essentially, this near doubling of draft quotas meant—in terms of the planned invasions of Japan—that starting in March 1945, when levies were increased to one hundred thousand per month for the U.S. Army and Army Air Force and forty thousand for the navy and marines, nearly every man inducted would enter a "replacement stream" that was now oriented for a one-front war against Japan. The army did not sugarcoat the prospect of a long, bloody war for the soldiers in the field and new inductees and warned that various "major factors—none of them predictable at this stage of the game—will decide whether it will take 1 year, 2 years or longer to win the Far East war."[28]

By the time of Germany's surrender and Churchill's onslaught of dire warnings, the United States was already several months along a Selective Service track to support roughly the same quantity of casualties over the one-year period starting with Downfall's initial invasion operation, OLYMPIC in the fall of 1945, as it had during the one-year "casualty surge" that began in June 1944. At this point, however, two disturbing things happened: First, the United States discovered that the Imperial Army on Japan itself was gearing up to be nearly twice as large as the estimated 3,500,000 that the army's original manpower requirements were based on.[29] Second, the ongoing battle on and around Okinawa demonstrated that the Japanese forces were capable of inflicting casualties at a far higher rate than anticipated.

The clock was ticking. And the crux of the problem facing Stimson and the rest of the senior leadership had to do with the casualty ratios emerging from Okinawa, which, if duplicated in Japan's Home Islands, threatened to outstrip the carefully constructed replacement stream for troop losses projected through the end of 1946. More than a military problem, it was also a political problem.

The newspapers of the day told the story. Young soldiers taking part in specialized training to fill the military's critical need for men with engineering and other demanding skills were being yanked from college to shore up the ground-pounding infantry's grim combat losses. Readers, appalled by the rapidly escalating casualties, demanded that eighteen-year-old draftees be given more training before being shipped oversea. Church groups and individual citizens expressed outrage that the House of Representatives had passed a bill authorizing the drafting of women nurses.[30] Wives demanded to know why husbands with small children who had been drafted a year before Pearl Harbor could not be sent home now that there were "so many men in uniform." This could all be found on the pages of daily newspapers as well as the periodic lists of local dead and wounded.[31] Moreover, the rallies and marches by the gaggle of organizations making up the isolationist America First movement, some huge by standards of the day, were hardly a distant memory.[32]

As military intelligence officers in the Pentagon were beginning the process of crunching the new—and far larger—Japanese force structure figures and coming up with decidedly unsettling results, Stimson reached outside the administration of the newly sworn-in Truman for additional perspectives on the costs of the war and its aftermath. In secret from the cabinet and all but perhaps one or two members of the White House staff, Stimson was working—unsuccessfully—to arrange a meeting between Truman and that incurable number-cruncher Herbert Hoover, Stimson's old boss when he was secretary of state in the early 1930s. Hoover was being regularly briefed by Pentagon officers and had been testifying before congressional committees on some of the troublesome aspects of America's mobilization.[33]

On May 15, two days after a lunch and afternoon meeting at Stimson's Long Island estate, Hoover provided him with a memorandum outlining his thoughts on ending the war with Japan that took a wider view of the fighting ahead. In this document and another prepared for Truman later that month, Hoover suggested that the invasion could ultimately cost "500,000 to 1,000,000 lives," an estimate that pointedly warned of up to twice as many deaths as then postulated by the army in its principal planning document for the endgame in the Pacific, JCS 924. Stimson sent Hoover's memorandum to General Marshall's staff for comment and hid its origins by stating only that it had been authored by "an economist."[34]

Hoover's maximum figure of up to one million American dead

was fully double the mortality figure used in JCS 924, the key strategic planning document for the invasion of Japan, and far beyond the cumulative total of the army's 100,000-men-per-month replacement stream that was, by now, several months into its implementation. Marshall's staff maintained that Hoover's casualty estimate was "entirely too high." Yet the pointed disclaimer that immediately followed their assessment—"under the present plan of campaign"—is regularly omitted from accounts of critics' analyses of Truman's atomic bomb decision even though, excluding headlines, it is literally the only portion of the 550-word response with a typed underline.[35] This emphatic qualifier would soon turn out to be highly perceptive. Just two months later, it was discovered that the Japanese army was rapidly reinforcing the very areas where the invasion was to be launched.[36]

Marshall and Stimson understood the grim possibilities well. On May 16 Marshall wasn't able to attend an important meeting with Stimson and senior army leaders on issues relating to the redeployment of U.S. forces from Europe to the Pacific and the "converting of men from the Service Corps and other places into Infantrymen" because of the severe combat losses being suffered among their ranks. Instead, Marshall met with Truman, after which Stimson had his own meeting with the president. Meanwhile, Churchill was unrelenting in his efforts to convince Tuman of the need to slow up the Pacific redeployment.

The new president, however, was by now thoroughly versed in the Yalta and earlier Moscow agreements covering both the Soviets' entry into the war against Japan and the massive Projects Milepost and Hula, which aimed to ensure a speedy—and complete—victory within their sphere of operations. Whatever the president was told on May 16 by Marshall, Stimson, or both about the absolute need to get the Red Army into the fight, he needed little convincing. Indeed, as a not-so-young doughboy preparing to ship out to the battlefields of France nearly thirty years earlier, he wrote to his future bride, "If we are ordered to go to Berlin, go we must—or be buried on the way. I hope, Russia saves us the trip."[37]

Following the meetings with Marshall and Stimson, Truman flatly stated to commerce secretary and former vice president Henry Wallace on May 18 "that his one objective was to be sure to get the

Russians into the Japanese war so as to save the lives of 100,000 American boys."[38] Truman had also finally had enough from Churchill on the subject, and two days later he bluntly informed the prime minister, "I must not have any avoidable interference with the redeployment of American forces to the Pacific."[39]

Stimson, meanwhile, was still angling to put presidents Truman and Hoover together. Two days after his May 13 meeting with Hoover, Stimson again failed to persuade him to visit Truman without a specific invitation. He did, however, finally succeed in convincing Truman of the need for a meeting. Against the pointed advice of some of the political staff that he inherited upon the death of Roosevelt, on May 24 Truman invited Hoover to the White House. A meeting was arranged for May 28.[40] In the meantime, Churchill remained almost frantic over the redeployment of U.S. forces to the Pacific. Worse yet, with U.S.-Soviet relations unexpectedly becoming visibly strained almost overnight—just within the few weeks after Roosevelt's death—the American public was caught completely off guard.[41]

Truman dispatched Hopkins and Harriman to meet with Stalin and, in what Harriman described as a particularly "gauche" move, Joseph E. Davies, the prewar U.S. ambassador to the Soviet Union—and unabashed Russophile—was sent to London "to persuade Churchill that he was being too hard on the Russians."[42] The resultant series of heated discussions changed neither man's mind, but they did appear to have finally brought home to Churchill that only the bare minimum of U.S. occupation forces would remain in Europe.[43]

Though Stalin was still rankled over the abrupt cutoff of Lend-Lease aid, Hopkins's simultaneous meetings in Moscow to discuss the full range of U.S.-Soviet issues went considerably smoother. Beyond setting up a meeting of the Big Three, "Hopkins hoped," wrote Harriman, "for solid results and, above all, an agreement on Poland." Harriman, however, "had been over that boggy ground too many times to look for miracles."[44]

What Harriman may not have fully understood at the time was that the special envoy he accompanied had received instructions from the president to accept whatever could reasonably be presented to the American electorate as diplomatic success and smoothed U.S.-Soviet relations. In a May 23 memo, Truman instructed Hopkins to:

> Make it clear to Uncle Joe Stalin that I knew what I wanted—and that I intended to get it—peace for the world for at least 90 years. That Poland, Rumania, Bulgaria, Czeckoslovakia [*sic*], Austria, Yugo-Slavia, Latvia, Lithuania, Estonia, et al. made no difference to U.S. interests [and were relevant] only so far as World Peace is concerned. That Poland ought to have "free elections" at least as free as [American political bosses Frank] Hague, Tom Pendergast, Joe Martin or [Robert] Taft would allow in their respective bailiwicks. . . . and Uncle Joe should make some sort of gesture—whether he means it or not—to keep before our public that he intends to keep his word. Any smart political boss will do that.[45]

Many historians have focused on Truman likening the Soviet dictator to just another "political boss" no different than his mentor Tom Pendergast as an example of the new president's naivete. However, Truman's instructions to Hopkins to elicit "some sort of gesture—whether he means it or not—to keep before our public" was completely in line with Roosevelt's own actions toward Poland and Eastern Europe (see chapter 4). As with Roosevelt before him, Truman believed in the critical importance of ensuring that any erosion of support over developments in Poland did not precipitate enough discord in the Senate to block the establishment of the United Nations, much as it had prevented American participation in the League of Nations after the previous world war.[46]

Polling showed that, as recently as the Yalta conference, Americans dissatisfied with the degree of cooperation among the "Big Three" powers tended to focus blame on Great Britain. By mid-May, with Soviet intransigence over the structure of its representation in the proposed United Nations and the arrest of London-backed Polish resistance leaders by the Soviets, this had completely flipped. The situation could, with further deterioration, prove disastrous when it came time for Senate ratification of the UN Charter, which was still being negotiated.[47]

Before he and Hopkins met with the Soviet premier, Harriman

also consulted with the new president's closest advisors: "Stalin in their last conversation had asked him whether Truman was prepared to honor the Yalta agreement assigning to Russia the Manchurian ports and railroads, South Sakhalin and the Kuriles. 'Since Stalin appeared to think that the question was open,' Harriman recalled, 'I thought we might as well look at it again. I found that nobody had any serious objection to going through with the agreement Roosevelt had made.'"

Harriman found that Stimson's opinion had not changed at all and that the war secretary held fast to the opinion that Pentagon planners had stated the previous November—that the Soviets might just let the American and Imperial armies fight it out. He also implied that the Soviets could then simply reap the desired rewards at their leisure. Now, between the Yalta and Potsdam Conferences, the secret Milepost sailings to support the Soviet's coming war with Japan were reaching record levels, and this point was restated with more specificity in JCS 924.[48] Harriman explained:

> Stimson continued to believe, as he wrote in a letter from San Francisco to Grew [now acting secretary of state] on May 21, that "Russian entry will have a profound military effect in that almost certainly it will materially shorten the war and thus save American lives." He did not see that much good would come of trying to revise the Yalta accords. Stimson felt that Russia had the power to occupy Manchuria, Korea, Sakhalin and North China at will, whatever the United States might do. Only in the Kuriles could the United States hope to forestall Soviet designs and he advised against such a course. Even Forrestal, who had told Harriman that he believed Russian intervention would not be necessary because the war was pretty much won, saw no reason to set aside Roosevelt's secret agreement with Stalin.[49]

Upon arriving in Moscow, Hopkins, who had worked closely with Stalin during the darkest days of the Nazi invasion, immediately leveled with the Soviet premier:

> The real reason Truman had sent him, Hopkins said, was that so many Americans were disturbed or alarmed over the trend

of relations with Russia. . . . The crucial point was that Truman would find it difficult to carry forward Roosevelt's policies of cooperation with Russia without the support of public opinion. And the deterioration in popular support, as he saw it, arose from "a sense of bewilderment at our inability to solve the Polish question." Unless the Polish matter was cleared up promptly, Hopkins said, the situation would get rapidly worse.[50]

In negotiations extending over a period of two weeks, Stalin refused to budge on key issues relating to Poland even though, according to Harriman, "Hopkins repeatedly stressed that Poland was important chiefly 'as a symbol of our ability to work out problems with the Soviet Union.'"[51] Minor concessions on the composition of the Polish provisional government together with a major agreement over voting procedures within the UN Security Council ultimately provided the Truman administration what it needed to soothe public opinion toward the Soviet Union, but some, Truman noted, "thought we should have a war to keep Poland free."[52]

What Americans did not know was that very early in the negotiations President Truman was greatly relieved to receive the "important results" of the diplomats' third session with Stalin: "Before Hopkins left for Moscow, I had impressed upon him the need for getting as early a date as possible on Russia's entry into the war against Japan. Hopkins had been with Roosevelt at Yalta and knew of Russia's commitment there to move against Japan after the war in Europe was ended. On May 28 Hopkins and Harriman got from Stalin a very important declaration which Hopkins cabled me. . . . The Soviet Army will be properly deployed on the Manchurian positions by August 8th."[53]

Ironically, even as Stalin was sharing the Soviets' invasion plans with Hopkins and Harriman in their third evening session, eight time zones and half a world away Truman was finally sitting down for a friendly—and informative—chat with former president Hoover. The meeting would quickly prompt a chain of events that would lead to Truman summoning the Joint Chiefs and the armed service secretaries to a war council in the White House ahead of the Potsdam Conference.

5

Truman's White House Meeting

"My Hardest Decision"

I have to decide Japanese strategy—shall we invade Japan proper or
shall we bomb and blockade? That is my hardest decision to date.
But I'll make it when I have all the facts.

—President Harry S. Truman, the night before
his June 18 White House meeting with the
Joint Chiefs and service secretaries

Two days after their meeting, Secretary Stimson again failed
to persuade Hoover to visit Truman without a specific
invitation, but he finally succeeded in convincing Truman of the need for a meeting. Despite the warnings of some of
his political staff from the Roosevelt administration, Truman, on
May 24, invited Hoover to the White House. He wrote the invitation in longhand, placed a three-cent stamp on the envelope, and
mailed it himself in order to ensure that it did not become "accidentally" mislaid.[1] This was apparently his staff's first—and far
from the last—experience with Truman's propensity to use the
U.S. Postal Service to circumvent their better judgment.[2]

The two finally met on May 28, Monday of the following week,
and discussed Hoover's opinion that the army should administer food relief in Europe in addition to a wide variety of international issues. Truman was impressed with the depth of Hoover's
knowledge and genuine willingness to be of service and recorded
in his diary that he "had a pleasant and constructive conversation
on food and the general troubles of U.S. Presidents—two in par-

ticular." Before they parted, Truman requested that Hoover prepare memoranda on the issues discussed.[3]

Upon his return home to New York, Hoover prepared extensive notes on the meeting. He then produced four memoranda on "1. The European Food Organization; 2. The Domestic Food Organization; 3. The Creation of a War Economic Council; [and] 4. The Japanese Situation." In memo 4, a brief work less than seven hundred words in length, Hoover stated twice that the cost to America from an invasion of Japan could run from "500,000 to 1,000,000 lives," and thus implied total casualties far beyond the acceptable all-causes losses represented by the current induction rate of one hundred thousand men per month.[4] This memo and the others were sent to Truman via Press Secretary Charley Ross, the president's longtime friend, in order to avoid possible mischief from the Roosevelt holdovers. Hoover's letter left New York on either May 30 or 31.

The existence of Hoover's May 15 and May 30 memos, as well as the two subsequent Pentagon analyses of memo 4 requested by Stimson, are well known, and all have been noted in a wide variety of books and articles.[5] What has virtually never been discussed, however, is Truman's reaction to the memos. Recently discovered documents at the Harry S. Truman Presidential Library shed light on this question.

Truman acknowledged the receipt of Hoover's memos on June 1, yet the existence of this material is hardly the same as evidence that the president actually read them. But, in fact, Truman seized upon memo 4 and ordered each of his senior advisers to prepare a written analysis before coming in to discuss it face to face. (See appendix B, "Memorandum on Ending the Japanese War" [memo 4 of 4, May 30, 1945], containing President Harry S. Truman's notation identifying its author and Truman's memorandum to Secretary of War Henry Stimson asking for his opinion.)

Truman received the material from Ross and, after writing "From Herbert Hoover" across the top, forwarded the original of memo 4, "Memorandum on Ending the Japanese War," to Fred M. Vinson, the new director of the Office of War Mobilization and Reconversion, on or about June 4. Truman's manpower chief did not bat an eye over the casualty estimate when he responded on June 7. Vinson suggested that Hoover's paper be sent to Stimson, acting secretary of state Joseph C. Grew, and former secretary of state Cordell Hull. Truman agreed and had his staff type up additional copies of memo 4 on June 9 and send them to all three men. Truman asked each for a written analysis of the memo and told Grew and Stimson that he wished to discuss their individual analyses personally after they submitted their papers. The request for a meeting was not made of Hull, who was then hospitalized at the Bethesda Naval Medical Center.[6]

Grew immediately initiated an oral and written exchange on the memo with Judge Samuel L. Rosenman, a longtime Roosevelt adviser and speechwriter who was then serving as Truman's special counsel.[7] Stimson, meanwhile, sent his copy to the army's deputy chief of staff, Lieutenant General Thomas J. Handy, because he wanted to get "the reaction of the [Operations Division] Staff to it." Stimson also mentioned in his diary that he "had a talk both with Handy and with Marshall on the subject." Subsequently, Grew sent Stimson a carbon copy of his memo to Rosenman.[8]

Cordell Hull responded first. He branded memo 4 Hoover's "appeasement proposal" in his June 12 letter and did not take issue with the casualty estimate. Grew, in his June 13 memorandum to Truman, confirmed that the Japanese people "are prepared for prolonged resistance," adding that "prolongation of the war [will] cost a large number of human lives."[9] It should also be noted that Grew had earlier "received competent military opinion to the effect that the military operations in Japan cannot be anything but costly in terms of human lives," and that his answer would not have come as any surprise to the president.[10] Grew had told both Truman and Rosenman (ironically just hours after the meeting with Hoover), "The Japanese are a fanatical people capable of fighting to the last man. If they do this, the cost in American lives will be unpredictable."[11] One can readily surmise that Hoover's and Grew's statements, hitting virtually back-to-back, were not of much comfort to the new commander in chief.

Grew's memorandum and Cordell Hull's letter both arrived on June 13, and Truman subsequently met with Admiral Leahy on the matter.[12] In addition to serving as the president's White House chief of staff, the admiral was also his personal representative on the Joint Chiefs and acted as an unofficial chairman at their meetings. The morning after the Hull and Grew messages arrived, Leahy sent a memorandum stamped "URGENT" to the other JCS members as well as to Stimson and Secretary of the Navy James Forrestal. The president wanted a meeting the following Monday afternoon, June 18, where he would be, in effect, "reopen[ing] the question of whether or not to proceed with plans and preparation with Olympic . . . a campaign that was certain to take a large price in American lives and treasure."[13] Leahy informed them that the commander in chief wanted answers on three very specific questions:

> He desires an estimate of the time required and an estimate of the losses in killed and wounded that will result from an invasion of Japan proper.

> He desires an estimate of the time and losses that will result from an effort to defeat Japan by isolation, blockade, and bombardment by sea and air forces.

> He desires to be informed exactly what we want the Russians to do.[14]

Leahy's memo stated unequivocally: "It is his intention to make his decision on the campaign with the purpose of economizing to the maximum extent possible in the loss of American lives. Economy in the use of time and in money cost is comparatively unimportant."[15]

This directive to the Joint Chiefs and relevant members of Truman's cabinet was issued before the president received Stimson's written response to Hoover's memo 4, although the secretary had spoken with Marshall about it on June 11 and received a carbon copy of Grew's June 16 memo to Rosenman. Stimson apparently made no written statement on the casualties question until after the June 18 meeting with Truman.[16] He did, however, receive the "staff opinion" he had requested from General Handy.

As noted earlier, the upper end of Hoover's estimate of 500,000 to 1 million U.S. dead was fully double the mortality figure used in

JCS 924 and far beyond the cumulative—and acceptable—total of the army's 100,000-men-per-month replacement stream that was, by now, several months into its implementation. Consequently, Marshall endorsed the comments by the staff officer, who said that the estimate "appears to deserve little consideration." The previous week Marshall also received an apparently different officer's comments on the same estimate when it appeared in Hoover's earlier May 15 memorandum, which had been submitted directly to Stimson after their Long Island meeting. The two analyses displayed varied approaches to Hoover's points. From Marshall's perspective, each was a sound analysis, completely in line with army doctrine yet carrying different interpretations. He signed off on both.[17]

The May 15 memorandum traveled the same path as the May 30 memorandum requested by Truman: Lieutenant General Handy passed it down to Brigadier General George A. Lincoln's Strategy and Policy Group, who then sent it back up the chain with its accompanying commentary to Stimson, who forwarded neither set of documents to Truman. As noted in the previous chapter, the staff officer responding to the May 15 memorandum agreed that Hoover's casualty estimate was "entirely too high," yet the pointed disclaimer that immediately follows—"under the present plan of campaign"—is regularly missing from the accounts of Truman critics.[18]

This highly visible qualifier emphasized the very basic point made clear by Iwo Jima and the battle then raging on Okinawa. After three years of fighting, the Japanese forces had a clear understanding of the U.S. military's methods and logistical requirements.[19] They correctly inferred that southern Kyushu would likely be the next invasion target and were moving quickly and decisively to reinforce Kyushu with a massive number of troops before it could be cut off by U.S. air and seapower.[20]

Stimson was willing to expose others' thoughts to the president, unfiltered by his own analysis, as he did when he forwarded a letter from Manhattan Project engineer Oswald C. Brewster to Truman. But he apparently saw nothing in the staff comments that warranted the chief executive's direct examination, and neither document was sent to the president.[21]

Other than Stimson's oral statements during the June 18 meeting with the Joint Chiefs of Staff, Navy Secretary Forrestal, and Truman, there is no record that he directly addressed the question of casualties to the president until his memorandum of July 2, 1945, a report that became well known largely because it was later published in a high-profile article in *Harper's Magazine*. In it he maintained that U.S. forces will face "a more bitter finish fight than in Germany [and] we shall incur the losses incident to such a war."[22] With American casualties directly related to combat then topping 1.25 million, the bulk of which had been suffered during the war against Germany in just the previous year, Truman would not have found such an unambiguous statement from his secretary of war encouraging.[23] (See appendix I—Secretary Stimson's "Proposed Program for Japan" and cover letter handed to President Truman on July 2, 1945. See also appendix J—William B. Shockley to Edward L. Bowles, expert assistant to the secretary of war, "Proposal for Increasing the Scope of Casualties Studies," with attached paper "Historical Study of Casualties," by Quincy Wright, July 21, 1945.)

This discussion of army staff comments *not* shown to President Truman may appear out of place in a chapter discussing his knowledge of U.S. casualty estimates for the planned invasion of Japan. But unlike the Truman-Grew-Hull-Stimson-Vinson exchange in the aftermath of Hoover's memo 4, which remained unknown to historians until it was discovered after the controversial Enola Gay exhibit at the National Air and Space Museum four decades later, the "staff opinions" supplied to Secretary Stimson on Hoover's memorandums continue to figure heavily in the discourses of both critics and defenders of Truman's decisions. As a result, they cannot be ignored. Indeed, these documents provide a window to the thinking of strategic planners in General Lincoln's Strategy and Policy Group. But it must be noted that the views were not shared by all strategic planners, the Pentagon's logistic and medical planners, or by the relevant echelons within MacArthur's headquarters. In fact, these officers' opinions and the plethora of informal exercises conducted in the spring of 1945 by other planning elements in the Pentagon had no impact at all within the army hierarchy and the War Department's already-implemented manpower policy for that year—nor were they intended to do so.[24]

There are other U.S. Army documents about possible casualties during the invasion that the president never saw. Produced exclusively as possible briefing papers during the frenzy of activity preceding the June 18 meeting, virtually all of the briefing papers were either superfluous, technically flawed, or contained portions structured in a form that was contrary to army doctrine, which rendered them ambiguous and thus unusable. Consequently, Marshall, who personally pieced together and read the meeting's opening statement, did not include them in either his opening remarks or the detailed outline of invasion plans then being produced for use at the upcoming Potsdam Conference.[25] The briefing papers also did not have any effect on the army's complex manpower policy for 1945. Stimson and Marshall had long since moved on by the summer of 1945, by which point they were in the midst of examining manpower needs for the following year's invasion near Tokyo, Operation Coronet, and explaining those needs to the relevant congressional committees.[26] Nevertheless, the documents must also be briefly discussed since, just like the staff comments to Stimson, they have been featured prominently in previous works as proof that Truman's "high" casualty figures were a "postwar creation."[27]

The first of these is Joint War Plan Committee (JWPC) 369. Leahy's memo about the June 18 meeting had stressed that Truman's first priority was to minimize the loss of American lives.[28] The night before that momentous meeting, Truman wrote in his diary that the decision whether to "invade Japan [or] bomb and blockade" would be his "hardest decision to date."[29]

In compliance with the president's request, Marshall and Admiral King asked for additional information from their immediate staffs and from subordinate commands in the Pacific in order to obtain the most current data. Marshall received papers submitted by the Joint Planning Staff and several other staffs, including the Strategy and Policy Group's Joint War Plan's Committee headed by Brigadier General William W. Bessell Jr. The JWPC paper, "Details of the Campaign Against Japan," supplied much of the language and analysis that would go into Marshall's opening remarks and the accompanying "Memorandum for the President."[30]

While such estimates were not out of the ordinary for logistical and medical planners, these strategic staffs were suddenly required to quickly produce hard, specific numbers for the meeting. This was a highly unusual task for these officers, but they did their best. The JWPC's paper, edited by Lincoln, stated that it would be "difficult to predict whether Jap resistance on Kyushu would more closely resemble the fighting on Okinawa or whether it would parallel the Battle of Leyte." They placed quotation marks around the term "educated guess" when they presented "best estimate" hard numbers for battle casualties from several possible sequences of operations—extending out for ninety days—in the Home Islands.[31]

The JWPC's figures were based primarily on the ratio of American-to-Japanese losses from Leyte. This choice resulted in lower casualty estimates than those produced by navy planners, who had selected Okinawa as their model.[32] Yet another element within the Strategy and Policy Group, probably Colonel Max S. Johnson's Strategy Section, also produced "an involved calculation based primarily on Okinawa."[33] But while Marshall used much of the JWPC's language, he discarded its hard-number figures. This had less to do with the probability that the navy's estimate was more likely to be appropriate (in light of the terrain and recent experience) than that "prediction of battle casualties is hazardous at best."[34]

Marshall, Lincoln, and Bessell's JWPC were all opposed to presenting hard numbers that could be rendered worthless by any number of factors, such as unforeseen weather or terrain conditions, or even modest changes in the force structures of the opposing armies. Instead, they preferred to stick to standard army doctrine and present ratios to predict a range that could be modified to account for changing circumstances, such as the extensive Japanese reinforcement of Kyushu, which would not become clear for more a month.

In fact, the JWPC paper specifically advised against using any hard-number strategic estimates, which obviously included the very material it was ordered to create. Marshall didn't need much convincing. He deleted their hard-number estimates without further comment. Instead, he used a second, more standard JWPC table of medical staff origins that presented known casualties from recent operations as a baseline from which a series of ratios was applied.[35]

In addition to JWPC 369's hard-number tables, Marshall also discarded casualty projections from MacArthur's headquarters in Manila; consequently, Truman never saw them. The rushed nature of Marshall's request for estimates and a series of misunderstandings and miscommunications resulted in figures that were based on medical staff planning being sent to the Pentagon. While correct for the specific aspect of the Operation Olympic casualty evacuation program that they dealt with, the data's structure clearly indicated that the estimates were generated too far down the chain of command to be appropriate for the upcoming meeting with the president. In fact, they were just as ambiguous as earlier material from MacArthur's headquarters, which had prompted Lincoln to complain that the Strategy and Policy Group "cannot, from the data I have seen, deduce his estimated battle casualties."[36]

When it came time for the meeting with Truman, Marshall distributed copies of the JWPC's briefing paper—minus the number estimates. The only table included with the paper was the aforementioned standard ratio table displaying known casualties from recent, large-scale operations used as baselines.[37] The text of the paper was presented orally by Marshall himself, who began by stressing the importance of Russian participation in the war: "With references to clean up of the Asiatic mainland, our objective should be to get the Russians to deal with the Japs in Manchuria (and Korea if necessary) and to vitalize the Chinese to a point where, with assistance of American air power and some supplies, they can mop out their own country." He continued:

> *Casualties.* Our experience in the Pacific war is so diverse as to casualties that it is considered wrong to give any estimate in numbers. Using various combinations of Pacific experience, the War Department staff reaches the conclusion that the cost of securing a worthwhile position in Korea would almost certainly be greater than the cost of the Kyushu operation. Points

on the optimistic side of the Kyushu operation are that: General MacArthur has not yet accepted responsibility for going ashore where there would be disproportionate casualties. The nature of the objective area gives room for maneuver, both on the land and by sea. As to any discussion of specific operations, the following data are pertinent: [See table 1.]

Table 1: General MacArthur's Operations 1 March 1944–1 May 1945

Campaign	U.S. Casualties Killed, Wounded, Missing	Jap Casualties Killed and Prisoners (not inc. wounded)	Ratio U.S. to Jap
Leyte	17,000	78,000	1:4.6
Luzon	31,000	156,000	1:5
Iwo Jima	20.000	25,000	1:1.25
Okinawa	34,000 (Ground) 7,700 (Navy)	81,000 (incomplete count)	1:2
Normandy (1st 30 days)	42,000	[—]	[—]

Notes: The record of General MacArthur's operations from 1 March 1944 through 1 May 1945 [northwestern New Guinea and the Philippines] shows 13,742 U.S. soldiers killed compared to 310,165 Japanese soldiers killed, or a ratio of 1 to 22.

It is at this point in the discussion that historians—military and civilian alike—invariably lose track of exactly what the meeting's participants were saying to each other. The table's numbers, representing American and Japanese casualties during the most recent campaigns, were used solely as a base to establish ratios that might be applicable to the fighting ahead. Ratios from recent campaigns comparing U.S. battle casualties with the number of enemies killed were presented for comparative purposes. So was a U.S. casualty total for the first third of the fighting in the Normandy campaign, with no ratios given because of uncertainties in the corresponding number of German casualties.

Throughout the meeting, participants made references to operations or portions of operations. These do not refer to the baseline figures, which are frequently quoted by authors and historians, but to the ratios they spawned, which only suggest how battle casualties from the much larger Japanese and U.S. forces involved in the first of Operation Downfall's two lengthy invasion operations, Olympic and Coronet, might play out. Lincoln explicitly stated this in a memo to his chief, Lieutenant General John E. Hull, during the formulation of the JWPC paper: "About 30,000 for the first 30 days (which are the casualties we have experienced in Luzon to date [160 days]) is about a balanced estimate."[38] The one exception to this came when Admiral Leahy questioned the baseline figure for Okinawa, which he believed to be incomplete. The intensity of the fighting and prolonged length of time that units were required to stay in combat had resulted in roughly as many nonbattle casualties as direct battle casualties, primarily because of psychiatric breakdowns (commonly, and euphemistically, referred to as "battle fatigue").[39] Leahy believed that not including nonbattle casualties had made the baseline figure for Okinawa artificially low, thus skewing the ratio.

Marshall continued: "There is reason to believe that the first 30 days in Kyushu should not exceed the price we have paid for Luzon [160 days]. It is a grim fact that there is not an easy, bloodless way to victory in war and it is the thankless task of the leaders to maintain their firm outward front which holds the resolution of their subordinates. Any irresolution in the leaders may result in costly weakening and indecision in the subordinates."[40]

Marshall's "price," one American battle casualty for every five Japanese, represents only a fraction of the casualties accrued during the smaller operation on Luzon. The limitation of the estimate to the "first 30 days" of the planned ninety-day drive to a "stop line" one-third of the way up the island was made because the ratio could very easily change as U.S. soldiers and marines started to fight their way into the mountains against additional Japanese divisions moving down from northern Kyushu. Detailed speculation beyond thirty days could come back to haunt Marshall, and even the first thirty-day projection was hedged by the qualifier "there is reason to believe." As the minutes describe, Marshall's opening remarks ended with the following conclusions, which again stressed the importance of the Soviet Union joining the fight in order to shorten the war and save American lives:

GENERAL MARSHALL said that he had asked General MacArthur's opinion on the proposed operation and had received from him the following telegram, which General Marshall then read:

"I believe the operation presents less hazards of excessive loss than any other that has been suggested and that its decisive effect will eventually save lives by eliminating wasteful operations of nondecisive character. I regard the operation as the most economical one in effort and lives that is possible. In this respect it must be remembered that the several preceding months will involve practically no losses in ground troops and that sooner or later a decisive ground attack must be made. The hazard and loss will be greatly lessened if an attack [by Russia] is launched from Siberia sufficiently ahead of our target date to commit the enemy to major combat. . . ."

GENERAL MARSHALL said that it was his personal view that the operation against Kyushu was the only course to pursue. He felt that air power alone was not sufficient to put the Japanese out of the war. It was unable alone to put the Germans out. General [Ira C.] Eaker and General [Dwight D.] Eisenhower both agreed to this. Against the Japanese, scattered throughout mountainous country, the problem would be much more difficult than it had been in Germany. He felt that this plan offered the only way the Japanese could be forced into a feeling of utter helplessness. The operation would be difficult but no more so than the assault in Normandy. He was convinced that every individual moving to the Pacific should be indoctrinated with a firm determination to see it through.

ADMIRAL KING agreed with General Marshall's views and said that the more he studied the matter, the more he was impressed with the strategic location of Kyushu, which he considered the key to the success of any siege operations. He pointed out that within three months the effects of air power based on Okinawa will begin to be felt strongly in Japan. It seemed to him that Kyushu followed logically after Okinawa. It was a natural setup.[41]

Navy Secretary Forrestal, when later asked by Truman for his views, seconded King and "pointed out that even if we wished to besiege Japan for a year or a year and a half, the capture of Kyushu would still be essential." Discussion of the tactical and operational aspects surrounding the opening invasion of Kyushu, the southernmost of Japan's Home Islands, followed with emphasis on their effects on U.S. casualties. One portion of that discussion would have a great impact on the Enola Gay debate many decades later.

The president inquired if a later decision would not depend on what the Russians agreed to do. It was agreed that this would have considerable influence. The president then asked Admiral Leahy for his views of the situation. Leahy recalled that the president had been interested in knowing what the price in casualties for Kyushu would be and whether or not that price could be paid. He pointed out that 35 percent of the troops on Okinawa had been casualties. If this percentage were applied to the number of troops to be employed in Kyushu, where he expected the fighting to be similar, it would give a good estimate of the casualties to be expected. He was interested, therefore, in finding out how many troops would be used in Kyushu.[42]

Leahy did not believe that the figure of 34,000 ground-force battle casualties offered a true picture of losses on Okinawa. In fact, depending on the accounting method used those numbers ran from 65,631 to 72,000, largely due to psychiatric breakdowns.[43] He used the total number of casualties to formulate the 35 percent figure. Since Leahy, as well as the other participants, including Truman, already knew that ground-force casualties on Okinawa were far higher than 34,000 and approximately how many men were to be committed to the Kyushu fight, he was obviously attempting—as was common in such meetings—to focus attention on the statistical consequences of the disparity. Fifty years later, Leahy's use of the 35 percent figure from Okinawa to gain a better understanding of potential casualties during Olympic would become controversial.[44]

Truman's White House Meeting

The table of organization strength (TOE) of strictly ground-force combat units at the commencement of Operation Olympic was 190,000 troops. Dividing the TOE by one-third results in a thumbnail casualty estimate of approximately 63,000 for the first month. Indeed, Leahy noted in both his diary and autobiography his impression that Marshall was "of the opinion" that this same number represented likely casualties from some undefined portion of the invasion.[45] However, even though 63,000 is in line with a one-month estimate derived from the TOE, one can only guess at what the number actually represents. Because it does not appear in the meeting transcript—and Leahy attached no parameters to the estimate—it has been discarded by military historians who have instead used more properly documented estimates.

None of the meeting's participants found Leahy's approach unusual or took issue with his statement that the 35 percent number "would give a good estimate of the casualties to be expected." Indeed, Marshall had the data at hand and answered Leahy's question by presenting the most recent figure for the troop commitment forty-five days into the invasion: 766,700.[46] He then allowed those around the table, including Leahy, to draw their own conclusions as to the long-term implications. The meeting's participants also understood that Marshall's figure did not include replacements for losses, who would themselves become part of the equation and subject to the ratios because of the extended length of Operation Olympic.

The participants then discussed the sizes of the opposing Japanese and American forces, which was fundamental to understanding how the ratios might play out. Finally, Truman, who had been monitoring the rising casualty figures from Okinawa on a daily basis, frequently with Leahy at his side, cut to the bottom line: "The President expressed the view that it was practically creating another Okinawa closer to Japan [Tokyo], to which the Chiefs of Staff agreed."[47]

More discussion ensued. Truman asked "if the invasion of Japan by white men would not have the effect of more closely uniting the Japanese." Stimson answered that there was "every prospect" such an outcome could take place. He added that he "agreed with the plan proposed by the Joint Chiefs of Staff as being the best thing to do, but he still hoped for some fruitful accomplishment through other means." The other means included a range of measures, from increased political pressure—brought to bear through a display of Allied unanimity at the upcoming conference in Potsdam—to the untested atomic weapons that some hoped would "shock" the Japanese military into surrender.

Continued discussion touched on military considerations and the merits of unconditional surrender. The minutes show that the meeting ended as follows: "The President reiterated that his main reason for this conference with the Chiefs of Staff was his desire to know definitely how far we could afford to go in the Japanese campaign. He had hoped that there was a possibility of preventing an Okinawa from one end of Japan to the other. He was clear on the situation now and was quite sure that the Joint Chiefs of Staff should proceed with the Kyushu operation."[48]

Throughout the meeting Truman also kept coming back to the third question he posed when calling them all together: "Exactly what [do we] we want the Russians to do?" General Marshall had stressed: "An important point about Russian participation in the war is that the impact of Russian entry on the already hopeless Japanese may well be the decisive action levering them into capitulation at that time or shortly thereafter if we land in Japan."

In his concluding remarks, "the President stated that one of his objectives in connection with the coming conference would be to get from Russia all the assistance in the war that was possible. To this end he wanted to know all the decisions that he would have to make in advance in order to occupy the strongest possible position in the discussions."

FIG. 1. LCI(L) 551, redesignated DS-48 by the Soviets, and with its American-trained crew, was one of the thirty large infantry landing craft provided to the Soviet Navy specifically for the coming war with Imperial Japan. It was returned to the United States under Lend-Lease provisions in 1955. National Archives.

FIG. 2. Soviet and American sailors aboard an *Admirable*-class minesweeper are addressed by Soviet rear admiral Boris D. Popov during a May 20, 1945, transfer ceremony at the secret Cold Bay, Alaska, training base. Fourteen *Admirable*-class minesweepers were provided to the Soviet Union for the coming operations against Imperial Japan. National Archives.

FIG. 3. Antiaircraft gunners aboard the light cruiser USS *Phoenix* look anxiously to the sky as the sailor in the foreground points to an unidentified aircraft directly above their ship, December 18, 1944. Naval Historical Center, U.S. Navy.

FIG. 4. Japanese pray over the charred remains found in the rubble of central Tokyo shortly after the war's end in 1945. U.S. Army Signal Corps.

FIG. 5. After breaking into Manila's Rizal Stadium, 1st Cavalry Division troops move cautiously across right field. An important Japanese supply dump was located under the bleachers, and a deep, fifteen-foot-wide drainage ditch on the other side of the facility limited tank access to the area, which had held out for two days. These soldiers are attempting to attack the "back door" of the fortified ballpark, but Imperial Marines had fortified the infield and waited until troops had entered the enclosed space before firing from the dugouts-turned-bunkers and concrete-lined stairwells in the bleachers. The 1st Cavalry used tanks, satchel charges, and flamethrowers to reduce the defenses on February 16, 1945. After the Japanese had taken control of Manila in the waning days of 1941, American civilians and foreign nationals had been processed for internment at the stadium, and it was used as a U.S. supply dump after its costly seizure. U.S. Army Military History Institute.

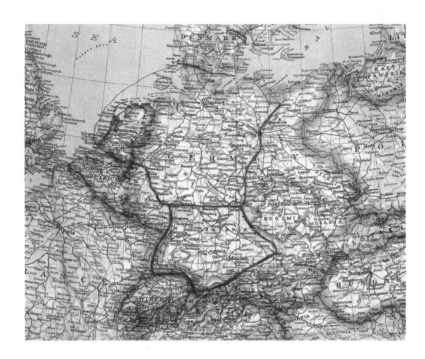

FIG. 6. President Franklin D. Roosevelt penciled his view of the postwar Soviet occupation zone stretching all the way to Berlin on a *National Geographic* map while enroute to the December 1943 Cairo Conference. He told the U.S. Joint Chiefs of Staff that he believed "Marshal Stalin might 'okay' such a division." (Quote: *Department of State, Cairo and Tehran*, in "Foreign Relations" series, 253–55.) U.S. Army Center of Military History.

FIG. 7. (*opposite top*) *Left to right* at the Yalta Conference, February 1945, British prime minister Winston Churchill, U.S. president Franklin D. Roosevelt, Soviet premier Joseph Stalin, and their military staffs. White House chief of staff and member of the Joint Chiefs admiral William D. Leahy stands behind Roosevelt and Soviet chief of staff Alexei E. Antonov behind Stalin. Also present are Joint Chiefs member fleet admiral Ernest J. King (*in white scarf*) and on the opposite side of the column is General George C. Marshall (*obscured by Leahy*). U.S. Army.

FIG. 8. (*opposite bottom*) (*Left to right*) Future secretary of state James F. "Jimmy" Byrnes, Truman, and Henry A. Wallace attending the funeral of President Franklin D. Roosevelt. All three men knew of the secret Manhattan Project to create an atomic bomb, particularly Wallace who was Roosevelt's representative in the Top Police Group overseeing the bombs development. At this time, neither Wallace nor Byrnes were aware that Truman knew any details of the project. Harry S. Truman Library and Museum.

FIG. 9. President Truman, Secretary of War Henry Stimson (*left*), and General George C. Marshall with the original surrender documents signed by the Japanese dignitaries aboard the USS *Missouri* in Tokyo Bay on September 2, 1945. U.S. Navy, Harry S. Truman Library and Museum.

FIG. 10. Special envoys Joseph E. Davies (*left*) and Harry Hopkins (*right*) meet with Truman and Admiral William D. Leahy after their discussions with, respectively, Prime Minister Winston Churchill and Premier Joseph Stalin, June 13, 1945. Harry S. Truman Library and Museum.

FIG. 11. Soviet fleet admiral Nikolai Gerasimovich Kuznetsov greets U.S. fleet admiral Ernest J. King upon his arrival at the Yalta Conference, February 1945. U.S. Navy photo from Russian Archives.

FIG. 12. Major General John R. Deane, chief of the U.S. Military Mission to Moscow, and his deputy rear admiral Clarence E. Olsen. Deane and U.S. ambassador to the Soviet Union Averell Harriman carried out the negotiation with Soviet premier Joseph Stalin and Soviet chief of staff Alexei E. Antonov that launched the massive Milepost Project to prepare the Soviet Union for its coming war with Imperial Japan. Olsen Papers, Naval History Center.

FIG. 13. Soviet premier Joseph Stalin and President Harry S. Truman at the Potsdam Conference, July 1945. In the background is Charles "Chip" Bohlen, Truman's interpreter at the conference, who would later serve as the U.S. ambassador to the Soviet Union. Harry S. Truman Library and Museum.

FIG. 14. Soviet foreign minister Vyacheslav Molotov speaking with Premier Joseph Stalin at the Potsdam Conference, July 1945. To Stalin's right, U.S. ambassador to the Soviet Union Averell Harriman carries on a different conversation with someone obscured by Molotov. National Archives.

FIG. 15. Vice Admiral Jack Fletcher, victor at the Battle of Midway and now commander of the North Pacific Force (*second from right*), and Soviet rear admiral Boris D. Popov (*left*) confer at Fletcher's headquarters at Adak, Alaska. In the midst of the Potsdam Conference, Fleet Admiral Ernest J. King ordered six CVE aircraft carriers and supporting elements to reinforce Fletcher whose job it would be to keep open the sea lanes for Milepost supplies to Soviet Vladivostok after hostilities erupted between Imperial Japan and the Soviet Union. National Archives.

6

"I've Gotten What I Came For"

Potsdam, the Bomb, and Soviet Entry into the War

The President reiterated that his main reason for this conference with the Chiefs of Staff was his desire to know definitely how far we could afford to go in the Japanese campaign. He had hoped that there was a possibility of preventing an Okinawa from one end of Japan to the other. He was clear on the situation now and was quite sure that the Joint Chiefs of Staff should proceed with the Kyushu operation.

—From the minutes of President Truman's June 18, 1945,
meeting with the Joint Chiefs of Staff,
secretary of war, and secretary of the Navy

Dawn had not yet arrived in New Mexico on the morning of July 16, 1945, when suddenly, "The whole country was lighted by a searing light with the intensity many times that of the midday sun. . . . With the light came a sensation of heat that persisted even as a huge ball of fire—like a rising sun—took shape, then transformed quickly into a moving orange and red column. Out of this broad spectrum of colors rose a narrower column that rapidly spilled over to form a giant white mushroom cloud surrounded by a blue glow."[1] All this occurred in dead silence.

From his observation bunker ten thousand yards from "ground zero," Brigadier General Thomas Farrell described how the event "lighted every peak, crevasse and ridge of the nearby mountain range with a clarity and beauty . . . the great poets dream about." The awed observer noted that "thirty seconds after the explosion came, first, the air blast," pressing hard against people and things, "to be followed almost immediately by the strong, sustained, awesome roar that warned of doomsday."[2]

At Potsdam, on the outskirts of the conquered Nazi capital of Berlin, it was already early evening when War Secretary Stimson handed President Truman and Jimmy Byrnes, his recently appointed secretary of state, a carefully worded message announcing the successful test. Stimson found Truman to be "greatly interested" in the result. Increasingly detailed information would arrive in each of the next two days. What was Truman's reaction to learning that the test, codenamed Trinity, confirmed that a single nuclear device could consume an entire city in an instant?

> "Most of the big points are settled," Truman noted, adding that Soviet leader Joseph Stalin would "be in the Jap War on August 15th. Fini Japs when that comes about."[3]
>
> "I've gotten what I came for—Stalin goes to war August 15 with no strings on it. . . . We'll end the war a year sooner now, and think of the kids who won't be killed! That is the important thing."[4]

Truman's focus on the Russians instead of the reality of the bomb should not be surprising. When Truman had written in his diary shortly before Potsdam Conference about his "hardest decision to date," that decision had nothing to do with nuclear weapons but whether to "invade [or] bomb and blockade" Japan.[5] At the June 18 White House meeting with the Joint Chiefs of Staff and service secretaries, the imminent existence of the atomic bomb only came up off the record at the tail end of the meeting—literally as an afterthought prompted by a question.

It was taken for granted by all involved—Stimson's Interim Committee, army leadership, Truman, and his closest advisors—that nuclear weapons would be employed as quickly as they became available. (See appendix L—acting chief of staff general Thomas T. Handy to command general, U.S. Army Strategic Air Forces, July 25, 1945, authorizing use of atomic bombs.) Ultimately, the closest thing to a written presidential authorization was Truman's scrawled approval on the July 30 draft of a press release on the bomb's use, which included a notation that it was not be released to the press until after he had left Potsdam.[6] (See appendix M—Atomic bomb press release authorization of President Harry S. Truman.)

The detonation of an atomic device in the New Mexico desert prompted not even the slightest thought of slowing up the world-wide movement of men and machines to the Pacific in anticipation of a prolonged invasion of mainland Japan that was expected to last for perhaps years into the future. After learning of the bomb, MacArthur ignored it, save for considering how to integrate the new weapon into plans for tactical operations at Kyushu and Hon-shu if its strategic use against cities failed to force a Japanese sur-render. Nimitz was of a similar mind. When briefed on the bomb he replied that "this is all very interesting," before adding, "in the meantime I have a war to fight."[7] Truman later summed up the matter at hand in the summer of 1945: "We did not know as yet what effect the new weapon might have, physically or psycholog-ically, when used against the enemy. For that reason the military advised that we go ahead with the existing military plans for the invasion for the Japanese home islands."[8]

As noted earlier, it was hoped that the sudden and unexpected use of the weapon might "shock" the Japanese military into sur-render before the invasion countdown ran out. A carefully consid-ered atomic bomb target set of Hiroshima, Niigata, Kokura, and Nagasaki had been developed by Secretary Stimson's Interim Com-mittee in conjunction with other agencies and would be approved by Stimson with Truman's concurrence at the Potsdam Confer-ence.[9] The bombs would be dropped as they became available, thus proving to the ruling Japanese militarists who maintained an iron grip on the government that the United States had more than one experimental bomb and that Japan would face "a rain of ruin from the air, the like of which has never been seen on this earth."[10] (See appendix N, "Potsdam Declaration, July 26, 1945.")

Even after two cities had been destroyed in a flash and the Soviet entry into the war dashed the last hopes of a negotiated end to hos-tilities, Emperor Hirohito's most senior military advisors counseled emphatically against surrender, maintaining that massive Amer-ican casualties during that nation's invasion of the Home Islands would decide the issue in Japan's favor. These same leaders, and, most importantly, War Minister Anami Korechika, subsequently acquiesced to the emperor's wishes upon receiving clear, heartfelt direction from Hirohito himself that Japan must surrender—and after it became apparent that continued use of the atom bomb would deny them the murderous "decisive battle" that held out at least some prospect of a negotiated settlement on their own terms. As Prime Minister Suzuki Kantarō observed after the news of the Nagasaki blast was announced during a meeting of Japan's Supreme War Council: "The United States, instead of staging the invasion, will keep on dropping atomic bombs."[11]

While all of this and more seems in hindsight to have advanced in a clear and obvious succession of events once atomic bombs began to explode, only one thing was crystal clear in the summer of 1945: when looking forward, the road to victory was going to be paved with untold thousands, indeed millions, of bodies, and far too many of them would be young Americans. While the reaction of the Japanese militarists who controlled the government could not be known, the benefits of direct Soviet military intervention could be predicted with a high degree of confidence if carried out in the all-out manner that Stalin promised. The end result would be twofold: vastly fewer U.S. casualties and a much shorter war. Said Truman: "The Chiefs of Staff were grim in their estimates of the cost in casualties we would have to pay to invade the Japanese mainland. As our forces in the Pacific were pushing ahead, paying a heavy toll in lives, the urgency of getting Russia into became more compelling. Russia's entry into the war would mean the saving of hundreds of thousands of American casualties."[12]

The quid pro quo arranged in Moscow the previous October called for the United States to provide a three-month supply of war stocks to support the Soviet armies involved in the war against Japan (see chapter 4). The immense and highly secret U.S. effort to accomplish this buildup was a complete success. It had been accomplished at great risk to the men sailing unescorted through Japanese waters on Liberty ships flying the Soviet hammer and sickle as well as to the Russians themselves, who risked the Japanese forces catching wind of what was up and severing the single, highly vulnerable rail line to the far eastern reaches of the Soviet Union.

The Soviets' rewards for entering the war against Japan were codified at the Yalta Conference (See appendix H, "Agreement regarding the Entry of the Soviet Union into the War against Japan") and the United States had painstakingly fulfilled its end of the bargain through Project Milepost, which had largely reached its impressive goals by mid-June, well before the Potsdam Conference. Now the time for the Soviets to pay up was rapidly approaching. On May 28 Stalin had personally informed Ambassador Averell Harriman and Truman's personal representative Harry Hopkins that "the Soviet Army will be properly employed on the Manchurian positions by August 8th." Subsequently, the Soviets gave every indication that they intended to keep their word.[13] But would they?

The Soviets had shown themselves to be tough negotiators. That was expected. Memories were still fresh and vivid, however, of the Soviets' recent calling for the Polish people to rise up against the Nazis then their refusing to come to the Poles' aid as the resistance, now fully exposed, was brutally destroyed piece by piece. Then there was Stalin's agreement to provide basing for American bombers, a principal aim of the U.S. military, only to find it almost immediately rescinded without explanation. There was also the arrest of Polish underground leaders, invited by the Soviets to begin negotiations on joining forces, who were instead arrested after entering Soviet-controlled territory. And these were only the major examples of duplicity. Now that the United States had made good on Milepost, and with Project Hula well underway, Truman wanted Stalin's personal assurance that the Soviets would carry out their end of the bargain.

Prior to the formal opening of the conference, Stalin paid a visit to Truman at his residence dubbed the "Little White House," and before the two had lunch, Stain agreed again, this time eye-to-eye with Truman, saying that Soviet forces would be "ready mid of August."[14] (See appendix O, "Truman-Stalin Meeting at Potsdam.")

Truman, in his contemporaneous writings, as noted earlier in this volume, was well pleased. He later wrote:

There were many reasons for my going to Potsdam, but the most urgent, to my mind, was to get from Stalin a personal reaffirmation of Russia's entry into the war against Japan, a matter which our military chiefs were most anxious to clinch. This I was able to get from Stalin in the very first days of the conference. We were at war, and all military arrangements had to be kept secret, and for this reason it was omitted from the official communique at the end of the conference. This was the only secret agreement made at Potsdam.[15]

But while the critical agreement with Stalin could not even be hinted at, other matters of importance were accomplished and could be reported, including other issues that concerned the United States—and Secretary of State Byrnes in particular—such as the nature of the postwar peace in Europe.[16] Indeed, during the press euphoria over Potsdam, ratification of the United Nations Charter had sailed through the U.S. Senate on July 28 by a vote of eighty-nine "yes" and two "no," a magnificent victory that Roosevelt had not lived to see. In an even deeper sense, however, "The personal meeting with Stalin and the Russians had more significance for me," wrote Truman, "because it enabled me to see at first hand what we and the West had to face in the future."[17]

As for upcoming military operations, there has been little—really, no—understanding among scholars today of what the United States was getting out of the Potsdam Conference beyond the seemingly vague understanding that now the wrap-up of the war with Japan would be both shorter and less costly. In fact, before the sessions even began Truman and Stalin had opened the door on July 17 to a level of cooperation and coordination that many during World War II and the long, dangerous Cold War that followed would find astounding. "On the first day of the conference," wrote Sergei Shtemenko of the Soviet General Staff, "the Soviet delegation confirmed our readiness to fulfill our obligations with regard to the war against Japan [and] General Antonov gave a detailed report on Soviet plans in the Far East."[18] (See appendix P for the second Tripartite Military Meeting, Thursday, July 26, 1945; and appen-

"I've Gotten What I Came For"

dix Q, "Planned U.S. Naval and Air Operations in Support of the Soviet Invasion of Manchuria.")

The simple fact is that both the United States and the Soviet Union were in a race not against each other but to get the Red Army *into* combat with Imperial Japan.

What drove all of this was American leaders' desire of to lessen the terrible cost of the coming tragedy on Japanese soil and the surrounding waters. Yet even today, with the explosion of documentation to the contrary, critics of the use of the atom bombs in Japan contend that the grotesquely high casualty estimates made for the planned invasion of Japan were a lie concocted after the fact in order to justify the use of atomic bombs. Instead, U.S. forced deployed the bombs for the exact reason Truman claimed: to prevent a far greater and prolonged bloodbath.

Truman's multiple references to Okinawa in his meeting with the Joint Chiefs of Staff and service secretaries—specifically his twice-used comment about the invasion operations representing "an Okinawa from one end of Japan to the other"—indicate clearly what he believed would be the magnitude of the fighting.[19] The Japanese Navy was essentially destroyed, but Japanese air power and aviation fuel were being carefully preserved for massed Kamikaze flights during the invasions.[20] More importantly, intelligence estimates demonstrated that Japan's field armies in the Home Islands were swelling rapidly, and there was ample time for them to train and arm recruits not only for the defense of the Tokyo area in 1946 but for the defense of Kyushu in the coming winter.

Future wars along the Asian littoral would demonstrate the limitations of America's industrial dominance when applied against enemies fighting an infantry-intensive war on rugged home ground. The situation facing the armed forces was painfully evident to the secretary of war. Stimson summed up his view of the meeting and the casualties question in his July 2, 1945, memo to the president:

> There is reason to believe that the operation for the occupation of Japan following the landing may be a very long, costly and arduous struggle on our part. The terrain, much of which I have

visited several times, has left the impression on my memory of being one which would be susceptible to a last ditch defense such as has been made on Iwo Jima and Okinawa and which of course is very much larger than either of those two areas. According to my recollection it will be much more unfavorable with regard to tank maneuvering than either the Philippines or Germany [because of the extensive network of dikes, canals, and rice paddies].

If we once land on one of the main islands and begin a forceful occupation of Japan, we shall probably have cast the die of last-ditch resistance. The Japanese are highly patriotic and certainly susceptible to calls for fanatical resistance to repel an invasion. Once started in actual invasion, we shall in my opinion have to go through with an even more bitter finish fight than in Germany. We shall incur the losses incident to such a war and we shall have to leave the Japanese islands even more thoroughly destroyed than was the case with Germany. This would be due both to the difference in the Japanese and German personal character and the differences in the size and character of the terrain through which the operations will take place.[21]

Stimson had been a colonel of artillery during the brutal fighting of World War I, and Truman would not take lightly his appraisal of the targeted Japanese terrain gained from direct examination on multiple occasions between the wars. On the subject of casualties, the President did not need to have it explained to him what Stimson meant by "an even more bitter finish fight than Germany," since he and everyone else who had taken part in the June 18 meeting knew that it had cost roughly a million "all-causes" American casualties to defeat the Nazis, and that U.S. casualties were actually small when compared to those of the major allies. Moreover, Marshall told the president the same thing at the meeting when he stated that, because of Japan's mountainous terrain, "the problem would be much more difficult than it had been in Germany."

Stimson's warning in his July 2, 1945, memo to Truman that U.S. forces "shall incur the losses incident to such a war" was equally clear. For anyone not understanding the reference, Stimson spelled it out in his high-profile *Harper's* article after the defeat of Japan: "We estimated that if we should be forced to carry this plan to its conclusion, the major fighting would not end until the latter part of 1946, at the earliest. I was informed that such operations might be expected to cost over a million casualties."[22]

The belief that total casualties "might" exceed a million men—roughly the same number that had been experienced by America in the war against Germany—was far below the two to five million implied by Hoover's memoranda yet was double the figure of five hundred thousand being briefed to Pacific-bound servicemen and being used by Stimson himself at least through May 1945. Were the escalating estimates of Japan's manpower potential and its widely trumpeted mobilization responsible for Stimson's change, or was he simply restating the army planning staff's "Saipan ratio," which guided its manpower decisions for 1945?

Stimson's fears aside, the casualty estimates coming from "always conservative" planners were grim enough.[23] "There were all kinds of estimates as to the cost of it in manpower," remarked Lieutenant General John Hull, chief of the Operations Division, "and had the Japanese continued fighting and fought as hard for their homeland as you would expect them to . . . it would have been a bloody operation. . . . The casualty estimates ran everything from a few hundred thousand to a million men to do the thing."[24]

Truman's widely quoted postwar statement in the official Air Force history of its operations during World War II has also been called into question. The president wrote Air Force historian James Lea Cate: "When the message came to Potsdam that a successful atomic explosion had taken place in New Mexico, there was much excitement and conversation about the effects on the war. . . . I asked General Marshall what it would cost in lives to land on the Tokyo Plain and other places in Japan. It was his opinion that such an invasion would cost at a minimum one-quarter million casualties, and might cost as much as a million, on the American side alone."[25]

To some, the president's statement of what was said in an oral presentation by General Marshall seemed insufficient, and an examination of the historiography and a very small selection of some of the more readily accessible documents led author Kai Bird to conclude his *New York Times* article "The Curators Cave In" by claiming, "No scholar of the war has ever found archival evidence to substantiate claims that Truman expected anything close to a million casualties, or even that such large numbers were conceivable."[26]

When it later turned out that there was, in fact, a considerable amount of documentation available, the question was recast by Professor Barton Bernstein as (emphasis in original) "fundamentally about what *top* U.S. officials—not lower and middle-level people—believed." Wrote Bernstein: "No scholar has been able to find any *high-level* supporting archival documents from the *Truman months* before Hiroshima that, in unalloyed form, provides even an explicit estimate of 500,000 casualties, let alone a million or more."[27]

The relevance of this narrow focus on the period after Truman became president appears questionable, however, since this frequently cited contention ignores the fact that the government's manpower policy for 1945 was formulated in the winter of 1944–1945 and that the huge hikes in Selective Service inductions were publicly announced and implemented months before Truman took the oath of office.[28] Nevertheless, the Hoover memorandum of May 30, 1945, and the subsequent memos between President Truman and his most senior civilian advisers—the Truman-Grew-Hull-Stimson-Vinson exchange—unquestionably meet the evolving criteria of critics.

Truman's statement in the Air Force history was found wanting on other grounds as well. A lack of references to a "formal" meeting on the atom bomb in the diaries of several participants at the Potsdam Conference led Bernstein to discount it as (emphasis in original) "Truman's postwar, dubious claim of Marshall's *alleged* pre-Hiroshima casualty estimates." Bernstein maintains not only that "no such meeting took place at Potsdam" but that "there is no record of such a discussion or such an estimate."[29]

The atomic bomb, however, was still a closely guarded secret when the "Log of the President's Trip to the Berlin Conference" was created, yet multiple Truman diary entries imply—and British diplomatic papers specifically indicate—that such a meeting

"I've Gotten What I Came For"

did indeed take place on July 18, 1945.[30] It was referenced, however, simply as "The president conferred with the Secretary of State and a number of his advisors in the forenoon," in the "Log of the President's Trip," and it was immediately on the heels of this meeting that Truman brought Winston Churchill the telegrams detailing the successful atom bomb test in the New Mexico desert.[31] Nevertheless, discussions of the atomic bomb at these meetings are not even hinted at. Similarly, even the momentous event of Truman being notified on the evening of July 16 that the atomic bomb had just been successfully tested in the New Mexico desert also escapes mention.

Following their working lunch, the prime minister wrote in a memorandum that the president was weighted down by the "terrible responsibilities that rested upon him in regard to the *unlimited* effusion of American blood" expected during the invasion (emphasis in original).[32] Churchill later spoke for both his outgoing coalition government and the new Labour government when he said: "We were resolved to share the agony. . . . [of] the final and perhaps protracted slaughter."[33] Ironically, these back-to-back meetings at Potsdam were one month to the day after Truman's White House conference with the Joint Chiefs, Stimson, and Forrestal. (See appendix R, "Extract from the Log of the President's Trip to the Berlin Conference, July 18, 1945.")

Truman has also been taken to task for the wide variety of figures he later gave for possible American casualties resulting from an invasion of Japan. As a result, the charge that Truman's "postwar claims oscillated so widely that no responsible analyst should trust any particular recollection on this subject" is often parroted.[34] To this, one must point out the obvious: there can be no single "right" number since the invasion never took place. Truman was entitled to his personal opinions, and, as Robert Maddox has wryly noted, virtually all of the figures he used over a span of some twenty years originally appeared in wartime documents.[35]

This particular criticism also begs a question: Why should one expect Truman to be any more skilled at counterfactual analysis than the scholars criticizing him many decades after the fact?[36] There is far more utility in examining the projected, or *pro*factuals—

the many variables and unknowables that leaders and planners during World War II had to consider when planning ahead in time for the effects of weather, opposition, logistics, and so on. This must not be confused with counterfactual analysis and is exactly what both American and Japanese military staffs were, and still are, paid to do.

Some scholars have for years—indeed, decades— picked over the bones of every decision relating to the use of nuclear weapons against Imperial Japan. Every nuance of Truman's most casual asides has been examined, parsed, and psychoanalyzed as critics of the decision have tried to prove that the president lied when he stated that the atom bombs were dropped in the hope that they would induce a defeated Japan to surrender before U.S. forces— being gathered in the Pacific from as far away as the battlefields of Germany—were forced into a prolonged, bloody ground invasion.

In 1945, however, Truman and his senior military and civilian advisors had no such luxury. The clock was ticking on the invasion countdown, and George M. Elsey, who handled the atomic bomb message traffic at Potsdam and worked closely with Truman throughout his presidency, later remarked: "You don't sit down and take time to think through and debate ad nauseam all the points. You don't have time. Later somebody can sit around for days and weeks and figure out how things might have been done differently. This is all very well and very interesting and quite irrelevant."[37]

The largely unknown exchange between Truman and his most senior civilian advisers in the wake of the Hoover memorandum, and his subsequent meeting with Marshall and the other Joint Chiefs, should make Truman's priorities clear. Yet the answer to what Truman actually believed will never find universal concurrence. The primary participants in these events were long gone even before the Enola Gay controversy of the 1990s, but key people from their personal staffs remembered well the context in which decisions affecting the lives of millions had to be made.

Elsey, who would later serve for many years as the president of the American Red Cross, was then a "watch officer" for the White House Map Room, where the progress of the war was graphically charted and updated daily for presidents Roosevelt and Truman.

"I've Gotten What I Came For"

He was also the only member of the select Map Room staff that knew that an atomic bomb was being developed. Elsey noted the close attention Truman paid to growing Japanese troop strength and remembered "Admiral Leahy discussing the invasion plans with the President in the Map Room prior to our departure for Potsdam." He also emphasized "the concern they both had as to the size of the Japanese forces available to oppose us." Elsey stated that during the course of "many conversations" with the President that fateful summer, Truman made it very clear that he "was deeply worried about the casualties that would inevitably be incurred in an invasion."[38]

And the beliefs of the country's most senior military man, General Marshall, have also been called into question by Truman crit-ics who have only a thin understanding of the documents that they were using as the basis of their contentions. While they maintain, without citing any evidence, that Marshall didn't actually believe casualties would be as bad as was feared and even suppressed large casualty estimates, it is important to note that Marshall certainly never refuted, even obliquely, Truman's statements that he was the source of the casualty estimates that the president used in both his memoirs and the Air Force history. What Marshall told his biographer, Forrest Pogue, was that conquering Japan by invasion would have been "terribly bitter and frightfully expensive in lives and treasure." He argued that claims the war would have ended soon, even without the use of atomic weapons, "were rather silly" and maintained that "it was quite necessary to drop the bomb."[39]

Did this reflect the true beliefs of Roosevelt and Truman's most trusted military advisor, or was it simply an effort by Marshall to provide cover for his commander in chief? One of his key assistants in the immediate postwar period, George F. Kennan, was unequivocal: "I have no doubt that our leaders, General Marshall among them, had good reason to anticipate a casualty rate of dreadful and sickening proportions in any invasion of Japan."[40]

Air-Raid Casualties and Property Damage in Japan

IX. EXHIBITS

EXHIBIT A-1

Air-raid casualties and property damage in Japan, by prefectures

	Type of bomb		Casualties				Building damages		
	*Explo.	*Incend.	Dead	*Serious injured	*Sligh. injured	*Tota. burned	Par. burned	*Tota. *Demo.
Hokkaido	428	----------	1,276	518	324	4,802	19	831
Aomori	2,157	52,307	1,494	240	367	15,577	17	192
Iwate	6,700	3,380	728	452	232	4,346	71	556
Miyagi	1,119	1,951	1,173	1,900	9	12,328	319	63
Akita	1,353	----------	123	49	77	38	----------	56
Yamagata	180	----------	78	25	41	84	15	4
Fukushima	1,926	7,027	499	257	301	1,268	67	241
Ibaragi	3,012	220,089	1,789	1,130	1,257	26,878	255	965
Tochigi	432	9,727	668	358	996	10,943	118	401
Gumma	2,884	301,234	974	484	971	14,338	179	288
Saitama	2,241	40,524	528	180	888	5,432	97	163
Chiba	6,047	95,453	1,438	774	995	20,876	285	265
Tokyo	11,436	419,380	88,204	19,597	51,469	765,815	3,050	4,021
Kanagawa	6,970	568,377	6,204	2,926	12,021	143,934	460	990
Niigata	30	----------	809	412	1,694	11,325	78	11
Toyama	8	----------	2,232	456	3,390	22,766	25	42
Ishikawa	27	8	4	60	----------	----------	----------	----------
Fukui	30	----------	74	43	77	1	----------	6
Yamanashi	121	48,409	930	363	1,037	18,489	191	29
Nagano	26	798	37	35	19	78	----------	28
Gifu	696	402,393	1,233	524	981	26,133	357	385
Shizuoka	7,327	459,856	5,679	2,111	9,178	70,551	1,811	4,060
Aichi	10,766	993,626	11,279	5,706	8,745	159,334	4,948	9,046
Mie	3,005	111,181	3,067	2,581	1,637	35,662	966	1,788
Shiga	327	2,554	59	57	184	34	6	16
Kyoto	277	3,516	227	205	367	77	20	120
Osaka	767	67,660	13,236	179	18,626	352,713	4,992	8,218
Hyogo	8,011	347,106	12,235	6,317	16,588	180,345	2,478	6,787
Nara	----------	3,033	73	86	156	89	33	11
Wakayama	1,285	4,113	1,932	1,903	3,633	28,369	71	1,220
Tottori	42	5	80	61	31	29	----------	2
Shimane	90	----------	52	32	58	----------	----------	----------
Okayama	1,262	50,670	1,709	351	524	25,752	504	14
Hiroshima	885	170,114	70,631	19,942	45,079	88,196	2,460	7,337
Yamaguchi	11,889	136,073	3,797	923	2,739	18,683	891	765
Tokushima	195	6,100	1,144	373	568	18,026	81	223
Kagawa	1	1	1,352	424	630	15,982	292	48
Ehime	452	10	217	520	1,183	27,825	194	394
Kochi	500	4,036	584	161	735	11,573	167	231
Fukuoka	2,676	77,166	4,625	2,389	2,622	49,534	3,744	767
Saga	----------	317	221	18	132	703	18	156
Nagasaki	3,550	20,376	20,766	25,053	932	24,695	160	1,834
Kumamoto	1,992	57,272	1,031	753	1,122	13,738	139	381
Oita	3,344	4,403	564	363	547	2,854	304	437
Miyazaki	6,386	10,996	685	249	544	8,109	82	384
Kagoshima	4,404	60,174	2,417	1,315	1,677	36,320	238	1,160
Okinawa	----------	----------	----------	----------	----------	----------	----------	----------
Karafuto	----------	----------	----------	----------	----------	----------	----------	----------
Total	117,256	4,761,415	268,157	109,854	195,983	2,265,644	30,202	54,936

Figures are for September 30, 1945 with the exception of Tokushima (figures for June 30, 1945) and Kagoshima (figures for July 31, 1945) *Explo. = Explosive *Incend. = Incendiary *Serious = Seriously *Sligh. = Slightly *Tota. = Totally *Par. = Partially

197

DOC. 1. Japanese Casualties during the U.S. bombing campaign. *Final Report Covering Air-Raid Protection and Allied Subjects in Japan*, United States Strategic Bombing Survey, Pacific, no. 62 (Tokyo: United States Strategic Bombing Survey, Civilian Defense Division, 1947), 197. The data in this chart is compiled from Japanese records. It does not include totals by prefecture for partially damaged buildings and forest fires, which were contained in the original chart.

APPENDIX B

Memorandum on Ending the Japanese War

MEMORANDUM

ON

ENDING THE JAPANESE WAR

From Herbert Hoover

I believe there is just a bare chance of ending the
Japanese war if an adequate declaration of Far Eastern
policy be made by the United States and Britain jointly,
and if possible with China. The President has already
taken an admirable step in this direction which might
now be further advanced.

The following is my own view of American objectives
and the interpretation of them into such a declaration:

1. As this war arose fundamentally over
Japanese invasion of Manchuria, the first point in such
declaration is the restoration of Manchuria to China.
It is an essential step to the establishment of the
sanctity of international agreements.

2. For reparations to China, it should be
declared that all Japanese Government property in China
must be handed to the Chinese.

3. As the militarist party in Japan has proved
a menace to the whole world, a third point in such a
declaration should be to insist upon the unconditional
surrender of the whole Japanese Army and Navy and their
equipment.

4. In view of the military caste by inheritance
among the Japanese people which even assassinates Japanese
opposition, they cannot be trusted with a military establishment. Therefore, the third point is continued disarmament
for a long enough period (probably a generation) to dissolve

DOC. 2. The first two pages of "Memorandum on Ending the Japanese War,"
with "From Herbert Hoover" blue-penciled across the top in President Truman's
handwriting. The second page contains the first of two warnings of a potential cost of
between "500,000 to 1,000,000 American lives." Found in State Dept., WWII, White
House Confidential Files, box 43, Harry S. Truman Papers, Harry S. Truman Library
and Museum (HSTLM).

the whole military caste and its know-how.

5. As certain Japanese officers are charged with violation of the rules of war and human conduct, they should be surrendered for fair trial by the Allies.

6. As certain islands held by Japan are necessary protection against the future and to enforce disarmament, the next point of declaration could be the ceding of these islands to the Allies.

Beyond this point there can be no American objectives that are worth the expenditure of 500,000 to 1,000,000 American lives.

7. Encouragement to Japan to accept such points and a part saving of face could be had by further necessary points in the declaration.

(a) That the Allies have no des re to destroy either the Japanese people or their government, or to interference in the Japanese way of life; that it is our desire that the Japanese build up their prosperity and their contributions to the civilized world.

(b) That the Japanese retain Korea and Formosa as trustees under the world trustee system. The Koreans and Formosans are today incapable of self-government, they are not Chinese, and the Japanese have proved that under the liberal elements of their country that they are capable administrators. Those countries have been Japanese possessions for over fifty years and their annexation has been admitted by treaties of America, Britain and China.

THE WHITE HOUSE   WAR DEPARTMENT
WASHINGTON SECRETARY'S OFFICE

June 9, 1945

MEMORANDUM FOR THE SECRETARY OF WAR

FROM: Harry S. Truman

      The attached paper was submitted to
me by Mr. Hoover and I should like for you to
submit to me your analysis of it. After you
have done so, we can discuss it.

      In view of your long experience in
far eastern affairs, I should especially value
your judgment.

DOC. 3. Typed memo from President Truman to Secretary of War Henry L. Stimson, dated June 9, 1945. This memo indicates that Truman had seen the Hoover memorandum and took it seriously enough to request both a written and oral analysis from his key advisors. Truman's bold signature is in the same medium-blue pencil as his note on the original Hoover memorandum (see document 2). Stimson answered: "We shall in my opinion have to go through with an even more bitter finish fight than in Germany. We shall incur the losses incident to such a war and we shall have to leave the Japanese islands even more thoroughly destroyed than was the case with Germany." Found in Stimson "Safe File" Japan (After 7/41), box 8, Records of the Secretary of War, RG 107, National Archives (NA), College Park MD.

APPENDIX C

The Historiography of Hiroshima
The Rise and Fall of Revisionism

MICHAEL KORT

Michael Kort is professor of social science at Boston University's College of General Studies. He received his BA in history from Johns Hopkins University and his MA and PhD in Russian history from New York University. He is the author of numerous books on the history of the Soviet Union and the Cold War, including *The Soviet Colossus: History and Aftermath* (sixth edition, 2006); *The Columbia Guide to the Cold War* (1998); *The Columbia Guide to Hiroshima and the Bomb* (2007); *A Brief History of Russia* (2008); and *The Vietnam War Reexamined* (Cambridge University Press, 2017).

In preparing "The History of Hiroshima: The Rise and Fall of Revisionism" for this volume, the author has taken the opportunity to correct several minor errors that found their way into the original as it was published in the *New England Journal of History*. Portions of this appendix have been adapted from Kort's *The Columbia Guide to Hiroshima and the Bomb*.

"Every now and then a notion or idea arises that is radically wrong."[1] In making this statement in *Harry S. Truman and the Cold War Revisionists* (2006), distinguished Truman scholar Robert H. Ferrell was taking to task a large cadre of academic historians who during the past half century judged the foreign policy of Harry S. Truman as being primarily responsible for causing the Cold War. As the title of Ferrell's book indicates, these historians are known as "revisionists," in juxtaposition to the so-called "orthodox" historians who generally have defended Truman's foreign policy, and no aspect of the orthodox/revisionist debate has generated more controversy than Truman's decision to use the atomic bomb against Japan at the end of World War II.

The "radically wrong" idea in this case is the revisionist contention that the use of the bomb was militarily unjustified. That judgment in turn has several component parts, although individual revisionist historians generally have not adhered to them all. The most important are that the atomic bomb was not necessary to force a Japanese surrender in August 1945; that Truman knew it; that he did not use the bomb for military reasons against Japan but rather as a diplomatic tool against the Soviet Union, which in turn played a major role in causing the Cold War; and that after the war he inflated the casualty estimates—from tens of thousands to several hundreds of thousands—for the projected American invasion of Japan to justify the use of the bomb.

Notwithstanding piles of books and reams of journal articles that have made all or part of this case in one way or another, there is no compelling evidence to support any of it and overwhelming documentary evidence demonstrating the opposite. Yet that judgment gained wide acceptance in academia between the mid-1960s and early 1970s and remained the conventional wisdom there—dogma is not too strong a word—well into the 1990s, when a series of path-breaking books and articles, several by historians working outside academia's cloistered ivory towers and ivied walls, demonstrated beyond a reasonable doubt just how false it was. Still, it is probably the case that the discrediting of the revisionist critique of Truman's decision to use the atomic bomb against Japan comes as a surprise to many, if not most, of the readers of *Truman and the Bomb* and this appendix.

The Early Debate

The debate over the use of the atomic bomb against Japan dates from August 1945. Truman's first critics spoke out after the attacks on Hiroshima and Nagasaki, even before Japan formally surrendered on September 2, arguing mainly on the basis of pacifist or religious principles.[2] A different type of argument emerged in mid-1946 in the *Saturday Review of Literature*, where Norman Cousins and Thomas K. Finletter accused the United States of using atomic weapons against Japan as a diplomatic tool to limit Soviet influence in East Asia, not as a military weapon to end the war.

Thus, in a chronological sense, Hiroshima "revisionism" actually debuted before "orthodoxy."[3]

In 1948 the British physicist and Nobel laureate P. M. S. Blackett, a pro-Soviet Marxist, gave the revisionist case a more comprehensive presentation in *Military and Political Consequences of Atomic Energy*, a volume published in the United States with some revisions as *Fear, War, and the Bomb: Military and Political Consequences of Atomic Energy*. Blackett argued that Japan would have surrendered before the end of 1945 without the atomic bombs or the Soviet entry into the war (which took place on August 8, two days after Hiroshima and one before Nagasaki). He relied on the conclusion of the United States Strategic Bombing Survey's (USSBS) *Summary Report (Pacific War)*, published in July 1946, that in the face of continued American conventional bombing Japan would have surrendered "certainly" before December 31, 1945, and "in all probability" before November 1, "even if Russia had not entered the war, and even if no invasion had been planned or contemplated."

This categorical statement was destined to achieve talismanic status in the revisionist arsenal in the 1960s and retain it for three decades. As will be discussed here, when in the mid-1990s several historians finally took a close look at evidence the USSBS had collected, in particular its interrogations of Japanese officials, they found that the survey's conclusion contradicted its own evidence. In any event, Blackett gave Hiroshima revisionism another talismanic slogan when he proclaimed that "the dropping of the atomic bombs was not so much the last military act of the second World War, as the first major operation of the cold diplomatic war with the Russians now in progress."[4]

Blackett's argument found little favor in the United States. During the late 1950s and early 1960s aspects of these early revisionist arguments were incorporated by prominent leftist historians William Appleman Williams and D. F. Fleming in their respective volumes on American foreign policy, *The Tragedy of American Diplomacy* (1959) and *The Cold War and Its Origins* (1961). However, the revisionist case, still lacking a documentary foundation, did not make a significant impact on American public or scholarly opinion. Instead, the so-called orthodox position held sway.

Oddly enough, Hiroshima "orthodoxy" emerged as a reaction to the early revisionist criticism of Truman's decision.

The orthodox argument first appeared in print in a December 1946 *Atlantic Monthly* article by Massachusetts Institute of Technology president Karl T. Compton and then in February 1947, more comprehensively and persuasively, in a *Harper's Magazine* article by Henry L. Stimson, secretary of war from 1940 until late 1945. Stimson laid out the basic orthodox position that the atomic bomb had been the best way to bring about a Japanese surrender and end the war as quickly as possible with a minimum loss of American lives and was used for those reasons alone. In 1948 he reinforced his original argument in his autobiography, *On Active Service in War and Peace.*[5]

Between the mid-1950s and early 1960s several prominent scholars backed up the orthodox position, notably military historian Louis Morton and retired Harvard University professor Samuel Eliot Morison. Then Pulitzer Prize–winning historian Herbert Feis endorsed Stimson's case in *Japan Subdued: The Atomic Bomb and the End of the War in the Pacific* (1961). To be sure, Feis accepted the 1946 conclusion of the USSBS that a combination of a blockade and conventional bombing could have ended the war during late 1945. More fundamentally, however, he stressed that the decision to use the bomb was "governed by one reason which was deemed imperative: that by using the bomb, the agony of the war might be ended most quickly and many lives be saved." Meanwhile, Robert J. C. Butow's *Japan's Decision to Surrender* (1954), the early postwar era's landmark study of Japanese decision making during the last year of the war and an invaluable and highly authoritative resource to this day, stressed the crucial importance of Hiroshima and Nagasaki, along with the Soviet entry into the Pacific War, in breaking the political logjam in Tokyo and bringing about a surrender.[6]

The Rise of Revisionism and "Atomic Diplomacy"

The orthodox consensus came under assault in the mid-1960s against the backdrop of the Vietnam War. The book that did the most to shift the nature of the discussion and, at least in academic circles, tilt the scales against Truman was *Atomic Diplo-macy: Hiroshima and Potsdam* by Gar Alperovitz, who mounted a direct assault on America's use of the atomic bomb by insisting that it was used not for military but rather diplomatic reasons and that its real target was not Japan, the country that was attacked, but the Soviet Union, presumably an American ally at the time. Specifically, Alperovitz argued that in the summer of 1945 the Japanese were prepared to surrender if granted terms permitting them to keep their emperor, that Truman and his top advisors knew it, and that Washington deliberately withheld those terms, instead demanding unconditional surrender and ignoring Japanese efforts to end the war. Washington's "two overriding considerations" for bombing Hiroshima and Nagasaki were to keep the Soviet Union out of the war in the Far East, thereby limiting its postwar gains in that region, and to pressure Moscow to moderate its demands and accommodate American concerns regarding postwar Eastern Europe. This "atomic diplomacy" in turn precipitated the Cold War.[7]

Atomic Diplomacy was not an easy read. In formulating what may be called the hard-line revisionist position on the bombing of Hiroshima, Alperovitz laced his 275-page narrative with more than 1,400 endnotes. In many paragraphs almost every sentence has a citation; many sentences have two. After a while the clutter of notes seems like a swarm of gnats that must be swatted away so one can get at the text itself. Still, by their sheer number and density, the notes gave *Atomic Diplomacy* a scholarly veneer that impressed many readers, and, although it debuted to mixed reviews, the book was enthusiastically welcomed by enough historians on the political left to set in motion a process that eventually put the Hiroshima decision on the defensive. In some vocal circles *Atomic Diplomacy* quickly achieved iconic status.

The enthusiasm was misplaced. Some commentators, including several prominent Cold War revisionists, pointed out that Alperovitz either lacked any evidence to back up his claims or had stretched the meager evidence he cited beyond its breaking point. Eventually a few historians dug deeper—most notably and comprehensively Robert James Maddox, whose critique of *Atomic Diplo-*

macy appeared in 1973. Maddox found that Alperovitz's footnotes could not be trusted. For example, Maddox pointed out that Alperovitz misled his readers about the context of important statements. Thus, while Alperovitz tells his readers that in April 1945 Truman said the Soviets could "go to hell" if they did not make concessions regarding the composition of the Polish government, an accurate reading of the relevant primary sources shows Truman was referring to a possible Soviet boycott of the founding conference of the United Nations if Stalin did not get his way on Poland, in which case the United States would proceed with the conference while the Soviets could "go" elsewhere.

Maddox also convincingly demonstrated how Alperovitz used ellipses to change the meaning of statements, such as when he deleted key words from a Truman reference to a statement by Secretary of State James Byrnes regarding the atomic bomb. Alperovitz implies that Byrnes was discussing the bomb's use as a diplomatic weapon against the Soviet Union; however, both the words omitted via ellipses and Truman's next sentence make it clear that Byrnes was referring to the bomb's use to dictate terms to Japan "at the end of the war." Maddox added that there were similar examples throughout *Atomic Diplomacy*, which is why he understandably found it "disconcerting" that such a work could "be considered a contribution to the historical literature."[8]

Its fatal flaws notwithstanding, *Atomic Diplomacy* had a major impact. While even many revisionist historians shied away from Alperovitz's essentially conspiratorial thesis about the bombing of Japan, they borrowed some of his ideas to construct their own critiques of American policy during World War II and the early postwar period. Martin Sherwin provided a notable example of that approach in *A World Destroyed: The Atomic Bomb and the Grand Alliance* (1975). Sherwin disagreed with Alperovitz in grudgingly granting that the primary motive for dropping the bomb was to end the war quickly with a minimum loss of lives, but he also found anti-Soviet diplomatic motives deeply entwined in the decision. He added that determining with precision the extent to which these "secondary considerations" influenced the Hiroshima decision "defies an unequivocal answer."[9]

By the mid-1970s the revisionist enterprise, albeit a more moderate version than that presented by Alperovitz, was flourishing. The specific idea of atomic diplomacy had lost some battles, but it appeared to be winning the war. Many academics, while rejecting the Alperovitz thesis as a whole, wove bits and pieces of it into their own critiques of the bombing of Hiroshima or of Truman's and Stimson's subsequent defense of it. The revisionist case became an expansive tapestry embroidered with a myriad of shapes and forms. Some of the better-received books that modified or extended the revisionist case in one direction or another included Gregg Herken's *The Winning Weapon: The Atomic Bomb and the Cold War, 1945–1950* (1981), Robert L. Messer's *The End of an Alliance: James F. Byrnes, Roosevelt, Truman, and the Origins of the Cold War* (1982), and Leon Sigal's *Fighting to a Finish: The Politics of War Termination in the United States and Japan* (1988). Meanwhile, in 1985 Alperovitz published an expanded and updated version of *Atomic Diplomacy*, the main change being a sixty-page introduction.

Whatever their differences, by the 1980s the revisionists agreed that the atomic bomb had not been necessary to force a Japanese surrender in August 1945 and that there was no evidence to support Truman's claims for wartime casualty estimates in the hundreds of thousands had the United States been forced to invade Japan. Beyond that, their scenarios varied. In *Dubious Victory: The United States and the End of World War II* (1973), Lisle A. Rose vigorously rejected the atomic diplomacy thesis but maintained that Japan would have surrendered without an invasion.

Barton J. Bernstein argued in a series of journal articles that Truman had used the bomb primarily to force a Japanese surrender, thereby accepting a key point of the orthodox analysis. He agreed with the revisionists, however, that Japan could have been compelled to surrender during 1945 without an invasion or the bomb and that after the war Truman and Stimson exaggerated the number of casualties they had expected from an invasion of Japan in order to justify the bomb's use. Over the next two decades, Bernstein established himself as the most prominent proponent of the moderate revisionist position in general and what may be called the low casualty estimates argument in particular.[10]

The Revival of Orthodoxy

Revisionism's heyday lasted through the 1980s and into the early 1990s. Then the historiographical ground began to shift. During the 1990s a new body of scholarly work emerged, often based on hitherto unavailable documents, that countered many of the revisionist arguments, among them the characterization of the atomic bomb as a diplomatic weapon in 1945, the claim that Japan would have surrendered before the planned U.S. invasion had the bomb not been used, and allegations that projected casualty figures for the expected invasion and ultimate defeat of Japan were lower than those cited by supporters of the decision to use the bomb. The historians who produced these new books and journal articles provided powerful validation for America's use of atomic bombs against Japan. In the process, they destroyed the pillars that had supported the various versions of the revisionist case.

The first of these works was *MacArthur's ULTRA: Codebreaking and the War Against Japan, 1942–1945* (1992) by military historian Edward J. Drea, a scholar fluent in Japanese. Drea's focus was not on the Hiroshima decision per se but on the U.S. Army's codebreaking operation in the Pacific, called ULTRA, that beginning in 1944 provided General Douglas MacArthur invaluable information in his campaign against Japanese forces in the southwest Pacific theater. ULTRA reports—which were not declassified until the mid-1970s—were forwarded on a daily basis to top U.S. policymakers in Washington, including White House officials, along with diplomatic, or MAGIC, intercepts.

What ULTRA showed during late June and throughout July was a massive Japanese buildup of unanticipated scale on the southernmost home island of Kyushu, precisely where the first stage of the two-stage invasion of Japan, called Olympic, was scheduled to take place on November 1. (The second stage, Coronet, was aimed at the Tokyo plain and scheduled for March 1946. The overall plan to invade Japan was designated Downfall.) Not only did the buildup testify to Japan's determination to fight to the bitter end, but it invalidated any previous military estimates of the casualties such an invasion would cost. ULTRA showed that by early August the number of Japanese defenders on Kyushu was almost double what the U.S. had expected (ULTRA actually underestimated the number of Japanese troops by a third) and that Olympic would be "very costly indeed."[11] Drea's evidence thus undermined two key parts of the revisionist case: that Japan was seriously considering surrender in the summer of 1945 and that the lower casualty estimates cited by revisionists, all of which dated from before American military planners learned of the Japanese buildup on Kyushu, were the ones accepted by the top American decision makers in Washington.

In 1993 the Hiroshima debate took an unusual turn when it became a heated public issue in which academics and scholars had to share the podium with a wide range of interested non-specialists. The cause of the furor was a proposed exhibit by the Smithsonian Institution's National Air and Space Museum (NASM) in Washington DC on the bombing of Hiroshima, planned to mark the fiftieth anniversary of that event. The NASM curators drew heavily on revisionist scholarship, but to their apparent surprise their narrative of the event did not go unchallenged. When the exhibit's script became public knowledge, NASM was accused of presenting both the decision to use the atomic bomb and its consequences in an unfair light. The core of the dispute was the context in which the bombing took place.

Two points in particular were lightning rods for critics. First, the original NASM script called the American fight against Japan a "war of vengeance" while opining that the Japanese were fighting a "war to defend their unique culture against Western imperialism." Second, critics complained, the exhibit stressed Japanese suffering from the atomic bombs without adequately highlighting the brutality and destruction of Japan's war of aggression in East Asia. The Air Force Association, a veterans group, played a prominent role in criticizing the NASM script, but it was only one of many critics.

Academic historians plunged into the fray on both sides. Revisionist scholars defending the exhibit insisted that the issue was scholarly research (their own) based on primary source documents versus the emotional reactions of their detractors, many of whom were elderly veterans. They complained that critics of NASM wanted to censor legitimate scholarship, a charge that ignored the existence of scholarship that contradicted what was in the NASM's script. One academic who had served on NASM's advisory group of scholars suggested the disagreement was between "memory and history," the former flawed and faded as it emerged from the hearts and minds of aging, emotional veterans, and the latter reliable and reputable as it emerged from the research of unbiased, up-to-date scholars. Whatever its self-serving pretentiousness, the phrase caught on in revisionist circles. But the exhibit was mortally wounded. The Senate unanimously adopted a resolution critical of the exhibit and in January 1995 it was cancelled.[12] Then, as if on cue, came a series of books and scholarly articles that demonstrated convincingly that those who had relied on "memory" during the NASM debate had not shown faulty recall after all.

The books included biographies of Truman by two leading scholars in the field, Robert H. Ferrell, whose *Harry S. Truman: A Life* appeared in 1994, and Alonzo L. Hamby, whose *Man of the People: A Life of Harry S. Truman* was published in 1995. Each included a detailed chapter on the Hiroshima decision that refuted the revisionist claims, from Japan's presumed readiness to surrender prior to August 6 to Truman's alleged use of the atomic bomb as a diplomatic weapon against the Soviet Union. Stanley Weintraub's *The Last Great Victory: The End of World War II, July/August 1945* (1995), a day-by-day chronicle of the last month of the Pacific War, provided the grim context that ultimately dictated the use of the bomb.[13]

These wide-ranging works were accompanied by works that focused exclusively on the Hiroshima decision, or more narrowly on certain aspects of it, which collectively shattered the revisionist case. In *Weapons for Victory: The Hiroshima Decision Fifty Years Later* (1995), Robert James Maddox convincingly dismantled the atomic diplomacy thesis, demonstrating how it rested not on the documentary record but on unsupported allegations and distortions of the historical record. Maddox documented how Truman, far from using the atomic bomb as a diplomatic weapon against the Soviet Union, attempted to maintain good relations with the

Soviet Union before and during the Potsdam Conference. Maddox further showed how MAGIC intercepts—in particular the cables between Japan's foreign minister in Tokyo and its ambassador in Moscow—and the ULTRA intercepts made it clear to American leaders that Japan was unwilling to surrender on terms remotely consistent with minimum Allied war aims and was instead preparing vigorously for the expected American invasion. Maddox also cited solid documentary evidence that Truman and his advisors saw casualty estimates for the anticipated American invasion of Japan of five hundred thousand or more and that the president feared staggering losses should the invasion take place.

Robert P. Newman's *Truman and the Hiroshima Cult* approached the Hiroshima decision topic by topic, with individual chapters defending policies such as demanding unconditional surrender and not providing Japan with a demonstration of a nuclear explosion. Most devastating to the revisionist case was Newman's demolition of the USSBS assertion that Japan would have surrendered "certainly prior to December 31, 1945, and in all probability prior to November 1, 1945" absent the atomic attacks on Hiroshima and Nagasaki and the Soviet entry into the war. By reviewing the testimony of the Japanese officials the USSBS had interrogated in 1945, he demonstrated that it is impossible to read that testimony objectively and not deduce that the USSBS reached its conclusion of a Japanese surrender during 1945 by ignoring its own evidence.[14]

Alperovitz meanwhile returned to the fray with *The Decision to Use the Atomic Bomb and the Architecture of an American Myth.* This massive tome—two "books" totaling more than eight hundred pages and written with the aid of seven collaborators—debuted to decidedly mixed and often critical reviews. Even a relatively sympathetic reviewer like moderate revisionist J. Samuel Walker wrote: "The fact that the book is thoughtful, original, and engaging does not, in my estimation, make it convincing."[15] Indeed, the book's flaws constitute one of the few subjects related to Hiroshima on which Robert James Maddox and Barton J. Bernstein some years later found a small patch of common ground—the former commenting that Alperovitz's handling of his sources in *The Decision to Use the Atomic Bomb* "is, if anything, even more outlandish than that found in *Atomic Diplomacy*," and the latter noting Alp-erovitz's "selective use" of the MAGIC cables and that the volume "had vulnerabilities very similar to those of his 1985 revision."[16]

Casualty Projections, "Unconditional Surrender" and Japan's Surrender, and Operation Downfall

The claim that after the war Truman and some of his advisors exaggerated casualty projections of an invasion and final defeat of Japan—specifically that those projections reached five hundred thousand or more—for decades was one of the main pillars of the revisionist case.[17] That pillar collapsed with the first thorough examination of the issue, "Casualty Projections for the U.S. Invasions of Japan, 1945–1946: Planning and Policy Implications" by military historian D. M. Giangreco. Writing in the *Journal of Military History*, Giangreco explained that in military hands these projections took three forms: medical estimates, manpower estimates, and strategic estimates. He then demonstrated that there was substantial documentation for high-end casualty projections—which, to be sure, varied widely—from both military and civilian sources that reached upward of five hundred thousand. Equally important, one estimate that reached Truman—from former president Herbert Hoover, who had high-level government contacts—led the president to convene an important meeting with the Joint Chiefs of Staff and top civilian advisors on June 18, 1945, to discuss the projected invasion of Japan. In short, as Giangreco stressed in a later article in the *Pacific Historical Review*, Truman both saw and was concerned about high-end casualty estimates prior to the scheduled invasion. His claims to that effect were not postwar concoctions.[18]

Nor did the thesis that unconditional surrender was responsible for extending the war fare well in the light of new scholarship. In "Japan's Delayed Surrender" (1995), Herbert Bix concluded that "it was not so much the Allied policy of unconditional surrender that prolonged the Pacific war, as it was the unrealistic and incompetent actions of Japan's leaders."[19] The intransigence of Japan's leaders prior to Hiroshima was further documented by Lawrence Freedman and Saki Dockrill in "Hiroshima: A Strategy of Shock"

(1994) and, most thoroughly and convincingly, by Japanese historian Sadao Asada in "The Shock of the Atomic Bomb and Japan's Decision to Surrender—A Reconsideration" (1998). Asada's extensive use of Japanese-language sources convinced him the United States did not miss an opportunity to end the war before Hiroshima when it refused to modify its demand for unconditional surrender. Rather, if "any opportunity were missed, it may have been Japan's failure to accept the Potsdam Declaration on July 26."[20]

Of course, revisionists were not silent during the 1990s. For example, Barton J. Bernstein published several journal articles reaffirming various aspects of the moderate revisionist case. J. Samuel Walker provided a concise summary of that point of view in *Prompt and Utter Destruction: Truman and the Use of Atomic Bombs Against Japan* (1997). In *The Invasion of Japan: Alternative to the Bomb* (1994), John Ray Skates argued for low-end casualty estimates in the projected invasion of Japan and added that the unconditional surrender policy prolonged the war. John D. Chappell, who chronicled growing American war weariness and concern about rising casualties during 1945 in *Before the Bomb: How American Approached the End of the Pacific War* (1997), agreed that the unconditional surrender prolonged the war. Still, the weight of the evidence overwhelmingly and increasingly favored orthodox arguments.[21]

The 1990s wave of new orthodox scholarship culminated in Richard B. Frank's *Downfall: The End of the Imperial Japanese Empire* (1999), a meticulous and cogently argued volume that soon gained widespread recognition as the definitive work on the end of the Pacific War. Frank brought together evidence from other scholars and added a great deal of his own to produce a book that left virtually every aspect of the revisionist case in tatters. His comprehensive overview of casualty estimates prior to the planned invasion of Japan supported historians who had argued for high-end figures. He pointedly rejected the thesis that modifying the demand for unconditional surrender to include the preservation of the imperial institution would have shortened the war. As J. Samuel Walker put it in a review of *Downfall*, Frank's analysis of the diplomatic and military evidence "drives a stake into the heart of the most cherished revisionist contention—that Japan was seeking peace and the United States prolonged the war by refusing to soften its demand for unconditional surrender." Frank himself concluded that "alternatives to the atomic bombs carried no guarantee that they would end the war" and added that the "hard choices" American leaders made in 1945 "had been vindicated."[22]

The Debate Since the Year 2000

As the new century began, Gian P. Gentile expanded his critique of the USSBS and its conclusions in *How Effective is Strategic Bombing? Lessons Learned from World War II to Kosovo* (2001). Robert P. Newman, while focusing on the ill-fated NASM exhibit, updated his critique of revisionist accounts of Hiroshima in *Enola Gay and the Court of History* (2004). The book that received the most attention was Tsuyoshi Hasegawa's *Racing the Enemy: Stalin, Truman, and the Surrender of Japan* (2005), which supported parts of the revisionist narrative while discarding others. Hasegawa wrote that Japan was not prepared to surrender before the events of August 6–9. At the same time, he backed Alperovitz by arguing that the United States was "racing" to deploy the bomb before Soviet military preparations in the Far East were complete in order to force an early Japanese surrender and keep the Soviet Union out of the Pacific War. Hasegawa added that during the Potsdam Conference, having realized the United States had the atomic bomb, Stalin began "racing" to get the Soviet Union into the war before the bomb forced Tokyo to surrender. He also maintained that Tokyo surrendered not because of the atomic attacks on Hiroshima and Nagasaki but because of the Soviet declaration of war.[23]

Although *Racing the Enemy* received several enthusiastic reviews, critics soon pointed out that key parts of Hasegawa's case were not sustained by his sources. For example, the documentary evidence is overwhelming that Truman wanted the Soviets to enter the war and that on August 8 he was very pleased to learn that they had done so. David Holloway, a leading authority on Soviet military and nuclear policy, has argued convincingly that Soviet documents contradict Hasegawa's contention that at Potsdam Stalin began his own "race" to enter the war. And, as Sadao Asada has stressed, Japanese documents clearly support the primacy of the atomic bombs in finally compelling Japan's surrender.[24]

Like Hasegawa's work, *American Prometheus: The Triumph and Tragedy of J. Robert Oppenheimer* (2005) by Kai Bird and Martin J. Sherwin was also well received, winning the Pulitzer Prize and other awards. In the critical section dealing with the use of atomic bombs and Japanese surrender the authors rehash the standard critique of Truman's decision found in Hiroshima revisionism. Unsupported allegations abound unbuttressed by any evidence. Bird and Sherwin, long-time proponents of "atomic diplomacy," ignore the new and extensive body of distinguished scholarship on this subject and at times resort to distortions of American intelligence information. One clear example of this the implication that an intercepted Japanese cable that reached Truman's desk said that "unconditional surrender is the only obstacle to peace," a phrase that does not appear in any of the intercepted cables.

If "atomic diplomacy" needed a *coup de grâce*, it was delivered in 2007 by Wilson D. Miscamble's *From Roosevelt to Truman: Potsdam, Hiroshima, and the Cold War*. After a meticulous examination of what Truman and Secretary of State James F. Byrnes actually did, as opposed to what Byrnes in a few instances may have said, Miscamble justifiably concluded, "Fanciful notions of 'atomic diplomacy' must be consigned to the historical dustbin."[25]

The year 2007 also saw the publication of three volumes that provide overviews of the Hiroshima debate. Two are anthologies. *The End of the Pacific War: Reappraisals*, edited by Tsuyoshi Hasegawa, contains original entries with diverging positions on the orthodox/revisionist divide. *Hiroshima in History: The Myths of Revisionism*, edited by Robert James Maddox, as its title implies, contains entries evaluating the competing claims surrounding the Hiroshima decision. The author is confidently critical of revisionism; all are reprints of previously published articles with the exception of Maddox's update on the scholarship of Alperovitz. Finally, this reviewer published *The Columbia Guide to Hiroshima and the Bomb*.[26] Aside from an overview of the Hiroshima debate, it contains almost two hundred documents that enable the reader to see that a careful examination of those documents will convince objective investigators that the revisionist critique of the atomic bomb decision truly was "radically wrong."

Since 2007 the pace of publication of Hiroshima volumes has slowed, with only eight books of any significance, three moderate revisionist and five orthodox (one of which was subsequently republished in an updated and greatly expanded edition), appearing. The revisionist works are very different in terms of structure and focus but two share common features, as they are authored by former students of Barton Bernstein and, pretentions aside, none of the three does anything to resuscitate the revisionist case. Instead, they are very much part of the trend by revisionists to ignore inconvenient documentation, a trend that both surprised and disturbed scholars such as Robert Ferrell and Arthur Schlesinger Jr. (see chapter 1).

Atomic Tragedy: Henry L. Stimson and the Decision to Use the Bomb Against Japan (2008), by Sean Malloy, is a short monograph which argues that Secretary of War Henry Stimson betrayed his core values and his belief in moral statesmanship by acquiescing to the use of the atomic bomb against Japan. Malloy also snipes at Truman for using the bomb but offers nothing substantial or new to suggest practical alternatives to the bomb's use. *Hiroshima: The World's Bomb* (2008), by Andrew J. Rotter, is based almost exclusively on secondary sources and does little more than repeat, without any additional supporting evidence, arguments already made more competently by Bernstein and J. Samuel Walker. The last quarter of the book is a superficial survey of post–World War II nuclear weapons proliferation. It concludes with a cliché-ridden "epilogue" about the wrongs of attacking civilians that, along with other disturbing juxtapositions, comes perilously close to equating Nazi genocide with the British and American military measures, in particular the bombing of German cities, that were vital to winning the war and destroying the Nazi regime.[27]

Meanwhile, orthodox defense of the Hiroshima decision has been significantly reinforced. *Hell to Pay: Operation Downfall and the Invasion of Japan, 1945–1947* (2009), by D. M. Giangreco, is a groundbreaking study of how the United States and Japan were preparing for the American invasion of the home islands scheduled to begin in the fall of 1945. Giangreco demonstrates, once again, that Japan was not prepared to surrender prior to bombing of Hiroshima and that American casualty estimates for the upcoming invasion were in the many hundreds of thousands. He then makes use of heretofore unexamined American and Japanese operational and planning documents to demolish the notion that Japan's military lacked the means to mount an effective resistance to the upcoming invasion. That invasion, had it taken place, would have resulted in a "disastrous confrontation" involving weapons of mass destruction and an enormous loss of life on both sides.[28]

Wilson Miscamble's *The Most Controversial Decision: Truman, the Atomic Bombs, and the Defeat of Japan* (2011) is a superb scholarly overview of the events that culminated in the bombing of Hiroshima and the best short (150 pages) introduction to the subject in print. It is ideal for college and university classroom use and is available in paperback. In addition, along with clearly outlining how and why the United States arrived at its decision to use atomic weapons against Japan and refuting the main revisionist claims in the process, Miscamble—in his chapter "Necessary, But Was it Right?"—offers the best discussion of the morality of the Hiroshima decision this reviewer has encountered.[29]

In his new revisionist work HIROSHIMA NAGASAKI: *The Real Story of the Atomic Bombings and Their Aftermath* (2011), Paul Ham repeats revisionist claims that the use of atomic weapons was horrific, unnecessary, and a moral disaster. Reviewing the book, Richard Frank, the author of *Downfall: The End of the Imperial Japanese Empire*, found it marred by "sensationalism" and added that Ham's use of crucial Japanese sources resembled "a process more like alchemy than historical inquiry." One important example that Frank cites is Ham's effort to prove intercepted Japanese cables demonstrate that Japan was prepared to surrender had the United States been prepared to permit the retention of the emperor. The reality is that the Japanese were demanding not only retention of the emperor but that the old order remain largely in place with much of its power, a situation that would have left the emperor with what amounted to power over the Allied occupation commander and the authority to block any reform programs.[30] This, of course, was totally unacceptable to the United States and its allies, who were determined, as they were with their effort to denazify Germany, to uproot the dictatorial, expansionist, and militarist forces in Japan that had caused World War II.

As with virtually all of the revisionist works published in recent decades, Ham maintains, despite contemporaneous evidence to the contrary, that it was not the atomic bomb that forced Japan's surrender but the entry of the Soviet Union into the war. D. M. Giangreco takes this notion on directly in a greatly expanded 2017 edition of *Hell to Pay*, which includes two new "Soviet chapters" among its many additions and updates. Giangreco details the massive and direct American support to the Soviet invasion of Manchuria through the top-secret projects Milepost and Hula agreed to at the Yalta Conference and states: "If there was a 'race' involving the United States and Soviet Union in the Far East, it was a race by both allies to get Red armies *into* the war against Japan as quickly as possible."[31]

Another response to the new revisionism is David Dean Barrett's *140 Days to Hiroshima*, a volume that offers a comprehensive and definitive account of the events and decision making that culminated in the American use of atomic weapons against Japan in August 1945. Barrett's meticulous and balanced review of the evidence makes it clear that the circumstances at the time justify Truman's decision to use atomic weapons. He convincingly demonstrates that the Japanese government was not prepared to surrender on terms acceptable to the United States and its allies prior to the attacks on Hiroshima and Nagasaki, that President Truman and his top advisors understood this, and that Truman's sole objective in resorting to atomic weapons was to end the war as soon as possible and thereby save American lives. Barrett further demonstrates that there were estimates for American casualties in the projected invasion of Japan that exceeded five hundred thousand and that the use of atomic bombs against Hiroshima and Nagasaki was the key factor in bringing about Japan's surrender.[32]

Most recently, Waldo Heinrichs, a World War II veteran, and Marc Gallicchio published *Implacable Foes: War in the Pacific, 1944–1945* (2017), a massive, meticulously researched volume that, as the title indicates, covers the last year of the war in the entire Pacific theater. Going over areas covered by other historians but unearthing yet more evidence from personal accounts, U.S. government records, and military correspondence, Heinrichs and Gallicchio reveal more fully than ever the war of bloody attrition Japan was waging as U.S. forces closed in on the home islands and Tokyo's determination to fight to the bitter end to avoid surrender terms acceptable to the Allies, regardless of the military and civilian casualties involved. Their book powerfully reinforces the case that the atomic bombs were essential to breaking the morale of the military officers who controlled the Japanese government and thereby enabling Emperor Hirohito, finally, to intervene and get Japan to accept the Allied terms that finally ended World War II. As the authors write in concluding their book, given the circumstances they faced, "Truman and Marshall understood that the atomic bomb had been indispensable and that it alone had brought the kind of victory they sought."[33]

After his collaboration with Heinrichs, Gallicchio examined the closely related issue of unconditional surrender in *Unconditional: The Japanese Surrender in World War II*. That issue is beyond the scope of this essay. However, in crafting his defense of unconditional surrender as being crucial to the American policy, strongly supported by its allies, of uprooting Japanese militarism and reforming Japanese society, a policy that ultimately was successful, Gallicchio also provides compelling evidence that the atomic bombings of Hiroshima and Nagasaki were essential to bringing about that unconditional surrender.

Gallicchio meticulously reviews the commitment of Japan's military leaders to break America's will by fighting a protracted battle on their home islands and the information garnered by MAGIC and ULTRA that made Truman and is advisors aware of this fact. He then concludes, "There is no evidence that the Japanese would have agreed to subordinate the emperor and the entire government to the Supreme Allied Commander of the Allied powers before the atomic bombs and the Soviet entry into the war." While Gallicchio does not try to evaluate whether the atomic bombs or the Soviet entry into the war were more decisive, he leaves no doubt that the atomic bombs were essential to ending the war within days rather than after a drawn-out battle on terms that "began a process that transformed Japan from a military dictatorship into a more democratic and peaceful nation." Gallicchio adds that to have compromised on those terms would have meant a "sacrifice of the war's objectives."[34]

APPENDIX D

The Manhattan Project

A Chronology of Its Expansion and Subsequent Congressional Investigations

1942

June 28, 1942—President Franklin D Roosevelt signs Executive Order 8807 establishing the Office of Scientific Research and Development (OSRD) to mobilize American science for the war effort. This included engaging in nuclear fission research for the purpose of weaponization, and its director, Vannevar Bush, reported solely to President Roosevelt.

August 13, 1942—Manhattan Engineering District is established under Major General Leslie Groves of the U.S. Army's Corps of Engineers for the purpose of creating an atomic bomb. This would later be called the "Manhattan Project."

September 26, 1942—The top secret Manhattan Project is granted authority to use the highest wartime priority rating by the War Production Board.

September 29, 1942—Under Secretary of War Robert P. Patterson authorizes the Corps of Engineers to acquire fifty-six thousand acres in Tennessee for Manhattan Project's Site X, which will become the Oak Ridge laboratory and production site for uranium production at Clinton Engineer Works.

November 16, 1942—General Groves and physicist Robert Oppenheimer visit Los Alamos, New Mexico, and designate it as the location for Site Y, the Manhattan Project's principal research and design laboratory. Oppenheimer becomes the director of the Los Alamos facility.

December 2, 1942—Chicago Pile-1, the first nuclear reactor, goes critical at the University of Chicago under the leadership and design of physicist Enrico Fermi. It achieved its self-sustaining reaction just one month after construction was started.

1943

January 16, 1943—General Groves visited the proposed site of a plutonium production complex near Pasco, Washington, code-named Site W. The federal government quickly acquired the land under its war powers authority and established the Hanford Engineer Works.

February 1, 1943—Congressman John Jennings of Tennessee submits a resolution in the House of Representatives requesting creation of a select committee to investigate a pattern of inadequate compensation to landowners at and near the Clinton Engineer Works.

March–April 1943—Representative Hal Holmes, in whose district the Hanford plant was located, requests information from the War Department about the resultant land acquisitions. He receives "data sufficient to answer questions from his constituents" and agrees to cooperate with the Manhattan Project.

April 7, 1943—Senator Harry Byrd of Virginia introduces a bill drafted by a Justice Department official in charge of its Lands Division of property condemnations for the Hanford Plant and expresses "skepticism that the War Department [can] keep the project secret in view of the public character of the condemnation proceedings."

June 17, 1943—Secretary Stimson's failure to answer an inquiry regarding extensive and unexplained land acquisitions in the Hanford area prompts the chairman of the Senate Special Committee to Investigate the National Defense Program, Harry S. Truman, to call for an explanation. Stimson convincers Truman to not pursue the matter but Truman quickly learns more through other War Department sources.

July 9, 1943—Chairman of the House Military Affairs Committee Andrew J. May opens an inquiry into the charges made by Representative Jennings (see February 1, 1943), which would include public hearings.

July 1943—President Roosevelt declares Los Alamos, as well as the massive Oak Ridge and Hanford sites, to be military districts not subject to state control.

July 17, 1943—In answer to a question about the huge federal land accusation in Washington by Judge Lewis B. Schwellenbach of the U.S. District Court for the Eastern District of Washington, who was also a former U.S. senator from that state, Senator Truman improperly reveals that it was "for the construction of a plant to make a terrific explosi[ve] for a secret weapon that will be a wonder." (See chapter 2.)

November 1943—Michigan congressman Albert J. Engel of the House Subcommittee on War Department Appropriations presses for information on the construction at Oak Ridge and states his intention to go to the site. He is dissuaded by Under Secretary of War Robert P. Patterson.

December 7, 1943—Persistent inquiries by chairman of the Subcommittee on Military Appropriations, Senator Elmer Thomas of Oklahoma, and others prompt Investigating Committee chairman Truman to send one of the committee's investigators to the now-massive Hanford Engineer Works. The man was denied entry.

1944

February 18, 1944—With pressure building in the House of Representatives for more information and perceiving Congressman Engel's persistent efforts as a harbinger of things to come, a carefully limited system for informing Congress is instituted. Secretary Stimson, Army Chief of Staff George C. Marshall, and OSRD director Vannevar Bush hold a secret meeting of House leaders from both parties in the hope that a background briefing on the project might serve to better safeguard its secrecy and financial support. The leaders included Speaker Sam Rayburn, Majority Leader John W. McCormack, and Minority Leader Joseph W. Martin.

March 13, 1944—Secretary Stimson refuses requests by Senator Truman that the military liaisons officers assigned to his

```
                                    Washington, D. C.
                                    July 15, 1943


Honorable Lewis B. Schwellenbach
United States District Judge
Spokane, Washington

Dear Low:

You don't know how very much I appreciated your letter of
the First. I have been covered up with work just as you have been
and have put off from day to day writing to you.

I know something about that tremendous real estate deal, and I
have been informed that it is for the construction of a plant
to make a terrific explosion for a secret weapon that will be
a wonder. I hope it works.

I am sending you a copy of the report which the Committee made
on the Jeffries-Patterson quarrel. You could change the names
around and it would fit exactly for the Wallace-Jones fuss. I
didn t see any reason for making two reports on the same subject,
and I didn't think it would be exactly ethical for a special
Committee authorized by the Senate and appointed by the Vice
President to make an investigation of the appointing authority.
These scraps between key men in the Administration should be
fought out in the back room of the White House and not in the news-
papers.

I sure hope you have a pleasant visit in Wisconsin, and that I
will have an opportunity to make an investigation of this real
estate deal some time in the near future.

                                    Sincerely yours,


HST:MLD                             Harry S. Truman,U.S.S.
encl.
```

DOC. 4. Senator Harry S. Truman to Judge Lewis B. Schwellenbach: July 15, 1943, "for the construction of a plant to make a terrific explosi[ve] for a secret weapon that will be a wonder." Correspondence File, 1934–45, Schwellenbach, Lewis B. folder, box 193, Senate-Vice Presidential Papers, Truman Papers, HSTLM.

Investigating Committee by the War Department be allowed to inspect construction in the area of the Hanford facility. Under considerable pressure by fellow senators—including Washington state's Monrad Wallgren—once word of the secret meeting between House and Manhattan Project leaders had leaked out, Senator Truman had made requests immediately after the meeting and again on 10 March.

June 10, 1944—Although the House of Representatives remained the principal source of pressure for more information on the Manhattan Project, a meeting similar to that with House leaders in February was held with key members of the Senate to forestall trouble from that quarter. Participants included Secretary of War Stimson; Major General George J. Richards, representing the War Department budget officer; OSDR director Vannevar Bush; Senate Majority Leader Alben W. Barkley; Minority Leader Wallace H. White; Senior Minority Member Styles Bridges; and Appropriations Chairman Elmer Thomas.

December 1944—The Senate Special Committee to Investigate the National Defense Program, under James M. Meade after vice president elect Harry S. Truman's departure, is persuaded by the War Department to not become involved in Justice Department infighting over land acquisitions in the Hanford, Washington, area that might have led to the Manhattan Project being dangerously exposed to widespread publicity.

1945

Late February 1945—Congressman Engel of the House Subcommittee on War Department Appropriations again presses Under Secretary of War Patterson for information on the "extravagance and waste" at the Oak Ridge facility and threatens to withhold funding if he is barred from examining the site. Secretary of War Stimson prevails upon Congressman John Tabor on Engle's committee and House Speaker Rayburn to convince Engel to delay any inspection of Oak Ridge and not hold up funding on the floor of the House.

The U.S. Army Special Study, *Manhattan: The Army and the Atomic Bomb*, describes the results of Congressman Engle's relentless pressure:

This experience convinced the Secretary of War and the Manhattan commander, as well as other project leaders, that more and more members of Congress would be demanding current information about Manhattan's activities. Consequently, they arranged to have a selected delegation from each House visit

Clinton and, if they wished, also Hanford. With the President's approval for this plan, Groves and Stimson, accompanied by the Secretary's aide, Col. William H. Kyle, visited Clinton on 10 April to prepare "for future trouble with Congressmen." Upon the unexpected death of Roosevelt on the twelfth, the inspection trip to Clinton was delayed, but only temporarily. In May, after President Truman had given his assent, Speaker Rayburn helped select five members from the House Appropriations Committee—Clarence Cannon, the chairman, George H. Mahon, J. Buell Snyder, Engel, and Taber. Under the careful guidance of the Manhattan commander and the district engineer, the five congressmen spent two days inspecting the Clinton Engineer Works. The legislators returned to Washington convinced that public funds had been well spent and prepared to support the project's budgetary requests for FY 1946.[1]

APPENDIX E

"Between You, the Boss [Truman], and Me"

Assigned by the War Department as the military liaisons to then-senator Harry S. Truman's Investigative Committee during World War II, Major General Frank Lowe and Brigadier General Harry Vaughn both later worked directly for "The Boss" in 1950. Vaughn served as his longtime military aide and Lowe operated independently under presidential orders as Truman's eyes and ears in Korea during the Korean War. This letter from Lowe to Truman and Vaughn after the Communist Chinese entered the war inadvertently reveals that this closed trio of former and current artillery officers had been discussing "the fissuring of the atom many times . . . in '42 and '43." And shared none of this knowledge with the civilian members of the committee. (See chapter 2.)

~~TOP SECRET~~ (?) (Only as between you, The Boss + me)

Tokio,
2 Dec '50

Dear Harry:-

Subject: Atom Bomb.

This is a subject that, in so far as the armed forces are concerned, I know little about & have no desire to know more.

The Boss will recall our talks in '42 & '43 anent the Manhattan Project—when we discussed the fissuring of the atom many times. I told him of my intimate association with Dr. Robert H. Goddard, the rocket expert & now dead, who was my classmate in prep & at Tech. Bob had discussed this objective with me many times. Also in my report on my mission to England in 1941—I touched upon this subject & The Boss has a copy of the report.

Now I am informed via press release of The President's Declaration + his subsequent release also the British reaction, so I shall have the temerity to say my bit.

(a.) Of course it is a decision for The

DOC. 5. Major General Frank Lowe to Brigadier General Harry Vaughn, December 2, 1950, restricted to "between you, The Boss [Truman], and me." Box 245, President's Secretary's File, HSTLM.

Appendix E

nor interference, inside or outside the USA. This is a USA weapon — not a UN, nor a British nor any other country. The British have their own aims & objectives — mostly selfish à la the Balkans (Churchill) in W.W. #2. I can tell you, very confidentially, that all is not beer & skittles out here, between the English & the British, especially the colonials from Australia & even Canada, many of whom prefer very much indeed to be associated with us (the USA)

(b) When, as & if it be decided to use the atom bomb, naturally, Gen MacArthur will be charged with the responsibility of its use in the theatre of operations but I doubt if he knows much more than I do of its best applications & I feel very strongly, that informed Air-force (specialists) officers should have voice, & strong voice, in determining the time, place & target. There is, at least, one high ranking Air Force officer out here who should, in my opinion, have highest level participation in all atom bomb use decisions out here.

Maj. Gen. Harry H. Vaughan, USA
The White House,
Washington, D.C.

Faithfully
Frank.

APPENDIX F

Secretary of War Henry Stimson to Truman on Atom Bomb Development

SECRET

WAR DEPARTMENT
WASHINGTON

April 24, 1945.

Dear Mr. President:

I think it is very important that I should have a talk with you as soon as possible on a highly secret matter.

I mentioned it to you shortly after you took office but have not urged it since on account of the pressue you have been under. It, however, has such a bearing on our present foreign relations and has such an important effect upon all my thinking in this field that I think you ought to know about it without much further delay.

Faithfully yours,

Henry L. Stimson

Secretary of War.

The President,
The White House.

DECLASSIFIED
E. O. 11652. Sec. 3(E) and 5(D) or (E)
OSD letter, April 12, 1974
By NLT-___, NARS Date 2-2-76.

DOC. 6. The April 24, 1945, request for a meeting on the development of the atomic bomb contains Truman's written notation to his appointment secretary to set up an appointment for the next day. "Folder no. 1, War Dept.—1945," box 35, White House confidential file, White House central files, HSTML.

U.S. Navy Combatant Ships under Project Hula

Appendix

U.S. Navy Combatant Ships Transferred to the USSR Under Project HULA, May–September 1945

U.S. Designations	Soviet	Transfer Date	Disposition
Charlottesville (PF 25)	EK-1	12 Jul.	1949-returned
Long Beach (PF 34)	EK-2	"	"
Belfast (PF 35)	EK-3	"	1960-scrapped
Glendale (PF 36)	EK-6	"	1949-returned
San Pedro (PF 37)	EK-5	"	"
Coronado (PF 38)	EK-8	"	"
Ogden (PF 39)	EK-10	"	"
Allentown (PF 52)	EK-9	"	"
Machias (PF 53)	EK-4	"	"
Sandusky (PF 54)	EK-7	"	"
Tacoma (PF 3)	EK-11	16 Aug.	"
Sausalito (PF 4)	EK-16	"	"
Hoquiam (PF 5)	EK-13	"	"
Pasco (PF 6)	EK-12	"	"
Albuquerque (PF 7)	EK-14	"	"
Everett (PF 8)	EK-15	"	"
Bisbee (PF 46)	EK-17	26 Aug.	"
Gallup (PF 47)	EK-22	"	"
Rockford (PF 48)	EK-18	"	"
Muskogee (PF 49)	EK-19	"	"
Carson City (PF 50)	EK-20	"	"
Burlington (PF 51)	EK-21	"	"
Bayonne (PF 21)	EK-25	2 Sep.	"
Poughkeepsie (PF 26)	EK-27	"	"
Gloucester (PF 22)	EK-26	9 Sep.	"
Newport (PF 27)	EK-28	"	"
Bath (PF 55)	EK-29	"	"
Evansville (PF 70)	EK-30	"	"
Fancy (AM 234)	T-272	21 May	1960-scrapped
Marvel (AM 262)	T-274	"	"
Measure (AM 263)	T-275	"	"
Method (AM 264)	T-276	"	"
Mirth (AM 265)	T-277	"	"
Nucleus (AM 268)	T-278	"	"
Rampart (AM 282)	T-282	"	"
Disdain (AM 222)	T-271	22 May	"
Indicative (AM 250)	T-273	"	"
Palisade (AM 270)	T-279	"	1957-stricken

U.S. Designations	Soviet	Transfer Date	Disposition
Penetrate (AM 271)	T-280	"	1960-scrapped
Peril (AM 272)	T-281	"	1960-scrapped
Admirable (AM 136)	T-331	19 Jul.	1958-stricken
Adopt (AM 137)	T-332	"	1960-stricken
Astute (AM 148)	T-333	"	1960-scrapped
Augury (AM 149)	T-334	"	1960-scrapped
Barrier (AM 150)	T-335	"	1956-scrapped
Bombard (AM 151)	T-336	"	1963-stricken
Bond (AM 152)	T-285	17 Aug.	1960-scrapped
Candid (AM 154)	T-283	"	1958-stricken
Capable (AM 155)	T-339	"	1960-scrapped
Captivate (AM 156)	T-338	"	"
Caravan (AM 157)	T-337	"	"
Caution (AM 158)	T-284	"	"
LCI(L) 584	DS-38	10 June	1956-stricken
LCI(L) 585	DS-45	"	1955-returned
LCI(L) 590	DS-34	"	"
LCI(L) 591	DS-35	"	1956-stricken
LCI(L) 592	DS-39	"	"
LCI(L) 593	DS-31	"	"
LCI(L) 665	DS-36	"	1955-returned
LCI(L) 667	DS-40	"	"
LCI(L) 668	DS-41	"	1956-stricken
LCI(L) 675	DS-42	"	"
LCI(L) 943	DS-43	"	1945-combat loss
LCI(L) 949	DS-44	"	1955-returned
LCI(L) 950	DS-32	"	1956-stricken
LCI(L) 586	DS-37	14 June	1956-scrapped
LCI(L) 587	DS-33	"	1956-stricken
LCI(L) 521	DS-8	29 Jul.	1955-returned
LCI(L) 522	DS-2	"	"
LCI(L) 523	DS-3	"	"
LCI(L) 524	DS-4	"	"
LCI(L) 525	DS-5	"	1945-combat loss
LCI(L) 526	DS-46	"	1955-returned
LCI(L) 527	DS-7(?)	"	"
LCI(L) 551	DS-48	"	"
LCI(L) 554	DS-9	"	1945-combat loss

DOC. 7. "U.S. Navy Combatant Ships Transferred to the USSR under Project Hula, May–September 1945," by Richard A. Russell, *Project Hula: Secret Soviet-American Cooperation in the War Against Japan* (Washington DC: Naval Historical Center, Department of the Navy, 1997), 39–40.

U.S. Designations	Soviet	Transfer Date	Disposition	U.S. Designations	Soviet	Transfer Date	Disposition
LCI(L) 557	DS-10	"	1955-returned	YMS 285	T-610	27 Aug.	1945-sunk
LCI(L) 666	DS-50	"	1956-scrapped	YMS 287	T-611	3 Sep.	1955-stricken*
LCI(L) 671	DS-47	"	1945-combat loss				
LCI(L) 672	DS-1	"	1945-combat loss	SC 537	BO-304	26 May	1954-mothballed
LCI(L) 945	DS-6	"	1955-returned	SC 646	BO-310(?)	"	1956-destroyed
LCI(L) 946	DS-49	"	"	SC 647	BO-308	"	1956-stricken
				SC 661	BO-303	"	1954-mothballed
YMS 143	T-522	17 May	1956-stricken	SC 674	BO-306	"	1956-scrapped
YMS 144	T-523	"	1946-scrapped	SC 687	BO-301	"	"
YMS 428	T-525	"	1956-stricken	SC 657	BO-307	5 June	1954-stricken
YMS 435	T-526	"	"	SC 660	BO-311	"	1956-stricken
YMS 145	T-524	22 May	1956-destroyed	SC 663	BO-318	"	1955-stricken
YMS 59	T-521	6 June	1956-stricken	SC 673	BO-316	"	"
YMS 38	T-593	19 Jul.	1955-scrapped	SC 713	BO-313	"	"
YMS 42	T-592	"	1955-stricken	SC 986	BO-305	"	1954-stricken
YMS 75	T-590	"	1956-destroyed	SC 1021	BO-312	"	1955-stricken
YMS 139	T-594	"	1955-scrapped	SC 1060	BO-317	"	"
YMS 178	T-588	"	1956-destroyed	SC 500	BO-319	10 June	1956-destroyed
YMS 184	T-595	"	1955-stricken	SC 634	BO-309	"	1955-stricken
YMS 216	T-596	"	"	SC 675	BO-314	"	1956-stricken
YMS 237	T-589	"	1956-stricken	SC 1295	BO-320	"	1960-destroyed
YMS 241	T-591	"	1956-destroyed	SC 1324	BO-315	"	1956-stricken
YMS 272	T-597	"	"	SC 685	BO-302	19 Jul.	1948-stricken
YMS 273	T-598	"	1956-stricken	SC 538	BO-321	17 Aug.	1956-stricken
YMS 295	T-599	"	1956-destroyed	SC 643	BO-322	"	"
YMS 260	T-527	2 Aug.	1956-stricken	SC 752	BO-325	"	1955-stricken
YMS 33	T-603	17 Aug.	1956-destroyed	SC 754	BO-324	"	"
YMS 85	T-604	"	"	SC 774	BO-323	"	1956-stricken
YMS 100	T-602	"	"	SC 997	BO-326	"	1956-scrapped
YMS 266	T-601	"	1956-stricken	SC 1007	BO-332	"	1960-destroyed
YMS 288	T-600	"	1956-destroyed	SC 1011	BO-327	"	1955-stricken
YMS 301	T-605	"	1955-stricken*	SC 1031	BO-328	"	1960-destroyed
YMS 88	T-608	27 Aug.	"	SC 1364	BO-331	"	1956-scrapped
YMS 180	T-609	"	"	SC 1365	BO-329	"	1955-stricken
YMS 135	T-606	"	"	SC 756	BO-335	2 Sep.	1956-destroyed
YMS 332	T-607	"	"				

* subsequently transferred to the Peoples Republic of China

Soviet Designations
EK (storozhevoi korabl)–escort vessel
T (tralshik)–minesweeper
DS (desantiye suda)–landing ship
BO (bolshiye okhotniki za povodnimi lodkami)–large hunters
   for submarines

U.S. Designations
PF–frigate
AM–minesweeper
LCI(L)–large infantry landing craft
YMS–motor minesweeper
SC–subchaser

Sources: Department of the Navy, *Ships Data: U.S. Naval Vessels*, vol. II, 1 January 1949 (NAVSHIPS 250-012) (Washington: Bureau of Ships, 1949); S. S. Berezhnoi, *Flot SSSR: Korabli i suda lendliza: Spravochnik* [The Soviet Navy: Lend Lease Ships and Vessels: A Reference] (St. Petersburg: "Belen," 1994).

Appendix G

APPENDIX H

Agreement regarding the Entry of the Soviet Union
into the War against Japan

U.S. Department of State, *Foreign Relations of the United States, Diplomatic Papers, Conversations at Malta and Yalta, 1945* (Washington DC: United States Department of State, Government Printing Office, 1955), 984.

L/T Files
Top Secret[1]

Agreement

The leaders of the three Great Powers—the Soviet Union, the United States of America and Great Britain—have agreed that in two or three months after Germany has surrendered and the war in Europe has terminated the Soviet Union shall enter into the war against Japan on the side of the Allies on condition that:

1. The status quo in Outer-Mongolia (The Mongolian People's Republic) shall be preserved;

2. The former rights of Russia violated by the treacherous attack of Japan in 1904 shall be restored, viz:

(*a*) the southern part of Sakhalin as well as all the islands adjacent to it shall be returned to the Soviet Union,

(*b*) the commercial port of Dairen shall be internationalized, the preeminent interests of the Soviet Union in this port being safeguarded and the lease of Port Arthur as a naval base of the USSR restored,

(*c*) the Chinese-Eastern Railroad and the South-Manchurian Railroad which provides an outlet to Dairen shall be jointly operated by the establishment of a joint Soviet-Chinese Company it being understood that the preeminent interests of the Soviet Union shall be safeguarded and that China shall retain full sovereignty in Manchuria;

3. The Kuril islands shall be handed over to the Soviet Union.

It is understood, that the agreement concerning Outer-Mongolia and the ports and railroads referred to above will require concurrence of Generalissimo Chiang Kai-Shek. The President will take measures in order to obtain this concurrence on advice from Marshal Stalin.

The Heads of the three Great Powers have agreed that these claims of the Soviet Union shall be unquestionably fulfilled after Japan has been defeated.

For its part the Soviet Union expresses its readiness to conclude with the National Government of China a pact of friendship and alliance between the USSR and China in order to render assistance to China with its armed forces for the purpose of liberating China from the Japanese yoke.

И. Стајин[2]

Franklin D Roosevelt

Winston S. Churchill

February 11, 1945.

APPENDIX I

Secretary Stimson's Proposed Program for Japan

Copy HLS

NNO 730069

DECLASSIFIED
E.O. 116___
Authority ___
By ERC ___ NARS, Date 4/12/74

MEMORANDUM FOR THE PRESIDENT.

Proposed Program for Japan

1. The plans of operation up to and including the first landing have been authorized and the preparations for the operation are now actually going on. This situation was accepted by all members of your conference on Monday, June 18th.

2. There is reason to believe that the operation for the occupation of Japan following the landing may be a very long, costly, and arduous struggle on our part. The terrain, much of which I have visited several times, has left the impression on my memory of being one which would be susceptible to a last ditch defense such as has been made on Iwo Jima and Okinawa and which of course is very much larger than either of those two areas. According to my recollection it will be much more unfavorable with regard to tank maneuvering than either the Philippines or Germany.

3. If we once land on one of the main islands and begin a forceful occupation of Japan, we shall probably have cast the die of last ditch resistance. The Japanese are highly patriotic and certainly susceptible to calls for fanatical resistance to repel an invasion. Once started in actual invasion, we shall in my opinion

DOC. 8. Secretary of State Stimson's "Proposed Program for Japan" and cover letter handed to President Truman on July 2, 1945. Stimson "Safe File" Japan (After 7/41), box 8, Records of the Secretary of War, RG 107, NA. The full text, minus the cover letter was later published in Henry L. Stimson, "The Decision to Use the Atomic Bomb," *Harper's Magazine*, February 1947, 97–107. First, second, and final drafts in Stimson "Safe File."

have to go through with an even more bitter finish fight than in
Germany. We shall incur the losses incident to such a war and we shall
have to leave the Japanese islands even more thoroughly destroyed
than was the case with Germany. This would be due both to the
difference in the Japanese and German personal character and the
differences in the size and character of the terrain through which
the operations will take place.

4. A question then comes: Is there any alternative to such
a forceful occupation of Japan which will secure for us the
equivalent of an unconditional surrender of her forces and a
permanent destruction of her power again to strike an aggressive
blow at the "peace of the Pacific"? I am inclined to think that
there is enough such chance to make it well worthwhile our giving
them a warning of what is to come and a definite opportunity to
capitulate. As above suggested, it should be tried before the
actual forceful occupation of the homeland islands is begun and
furthermore the warning should be given in ample time to permit a
national reaction to set in.

We have the following enormously favorable factors on our
side - factors much weightier than those we had against Germany:

Japan has no allies.

Her navy is nearly destroyed and she is vulnerable to
a surface and underwater blockade which can deprive her of sufficient food and supplies for her population.

On the other hand, I think that the attempt to
exterminate her armies and her population by gunfire or other
means will tend to produce a fusion of race solidity and antipathy
which had no analogy in the case of Germany. We have a national
interest in creating, if possible, a condition wherein the Japanese
nation may live as a peaceful and useful member of the future
Pacific community.

5. It is therefore my conclusion that a carefully timed
warning be given to Japan by the chief representatives of the
United States, Great Britain and, if then a belligerent, Russia,
calling upon Japan to surrender and permit the occupation of her
country in order to insure its complete demilitarization for the
sake of the future peace.

This warning should contain the following elements:

The varied and overwhelming character of the
force we are about to bring to bear on the islands.

The inevitability and completeness of the
destruction which the full application of this force
will entail.

The determination of the allies to destroy
permanently all authority and influence of those who
have deceived and misled the country into embarking
on world conquest.

that if in saying this we should add that we do not
exclude a constitutional monarchy under her present
dynasty, it would substantially add to the chances
of acceptance.

6.   Success of course will depend on the potency of the
warning which we give her. She has an extremely sensitive national
pride and, as we are now seeing every day, when actually locked with
the enemy will fight to the very death. For that reason the
warning must be tendered before the actual invasion has occurred
and while the impending destruction, though clear beyond per-
adventure, has not yet reduced her to fanatical despair. If Russia
is a part of the threat, the Russian attack, if actual, must not
have progressed too far. Our own bombing should be confined to
military objectives as far as possible.

Sgd Henry L Stimson

APPENDIX J

Proposal for Increasing the Scope of Casualty Studies

SECRET

21 July 1945

MEMORANDUM FOR: Dr. Edward L. Bowles.

Subject: Proposals for Increasing the Scope of
Casualty Studies.

Recently, as you know, I have been trying to gather and organize information bearing on the problem of casualties in the Pacific War. It seems to me most important that the facts relating to this question be surveyed thoroughly and coordinated into a single well integrated picture. Such a study should be available for consideration in connection with the total casualties to be expected in the Japanese war, the rate at which land invasion should be pushed ahead in Japan or held back while attrition by air and blockade proceeds, and the relative apportionment of effort between the Army Air Forces and the Army Ground Forces and within each Force. The reason why a study of casualties would have such diverse applications is that the big cost to the nation in this war will be dead and disabled Americans. Consequently, in evaluating one plan or another, the expected casualties should be estimated as accurately as possible. It appears to me that at present adequate studies of the casualty problem are not being made.

The most basic problem in the Japanese war is the establishment of what is necessary to cause Japan to capitulate. There is a very important historical study which can be made in this connection but apparently has never been made either in the War Department or outside. The object of the study is to determine to what extent the behavior of a nation in a war can be predicted from the behavior of her troops in individual battles. If the study shows that the behavior of nations in all historical cases comparable to Japan's has in fact been invariably consistent with the behavior of the troops in battle, then it means that the Japanese dead and ineffectives at the time of defeat will exceed the corresponding number for the Germans. In other words, we shall probably have to kill at least 5 to 10 million Japanese.

DECLASSIFIED

SECRET

DOC. 9. William B. Shockley to Edward L. Bowles, expert assistant to the secretary of war, "Proposal for Increasing the Scope of Casualty Studies," with attached paper "Historical Study of Casualties," by Quincy Wright, July 21, 1945. Studies conducted at the direction of Secretary of War Henry L. Stimson. Box 34, War Department study in Edward L. Bowles Papers, Library of Congress, Washington DC

This might cost us between 1.7 and 4 million casualties including 400,000 to 800,000 killed.

However, as I mentioned, the historical study referred to above has not been made. I have discussed it with Colonel MacCormack of MIS and also with Professor Quincy Wright of the University of Chicago. Professor Wright has directed a large number of studies on the history of war during the past 20 years and in 1942 published "A Study of War" in two volumes. I discussed this problem with Professor Wright about two weeks ago and he is unacquainted with any such study. He feels, however, that such a study has considerable promise of enabling better predictions to be made as to the course of the war and the reactions of Japan. I do not want to give the impression that such a study would furnish a complete guide to the future of the war, but merely that it would illuminate the situation from a new and unexplored angle and might well affect our conclusions in an important way.

In addition to the study mentioned above concerning the breaking point of the nation, studies are needed on the casualty ratios between Japanese and U.S. troops in battle. Some studies along these lines have already been carried out in G-2 and more are in progress. At present the studies break a number of campaigns down into casualties by day of the campaign. One interesting finding of these studies is that the ratio between the Jap killed and U.S. killed is much more consistent between the one campaign and another when the landing phase and mopping up phases are eliminated. This consistency applies only to the Pacific campaigns studied, these being quite different from the Southwest Pacific campaigns. The following Table summarizes these findings:

Campaign	Ratio of Jap Killed to U.S. Killed	
	Entire Campaign	Middle Third (a)
Saipan	8 (b)	11
Guam	9 (b)	10
Iwo Jima	4 (b)	8
Okinawa	14.5 (c)	11
Leyte	22 (b)	39
Luzon	22 (b)	25

- 2 -

(a) This corresponds to the interval between the time when one-third the Japs are killed and the time when two-thirds are killed. Values are based on data collected by G-2.

(b) Values from "Health", pg. 15, 31 May 1945.

(c) Based on data collected by G-2.

These values suggest that in areas where the tactical situation resembles that met in the first four campaigns listed, the major part of the campaign will be fought with a ratio of about 10 Japs killed for every U.S. killed.

It would be worthwhile, in my opinion, to extend these casualty studies of the various campaigns so as to correlate them with information regarding the cause of our casualties (i.e. whether by rifle, machine gun, mortar, etc.) and with our ammunition expenditures. In particular, every effort should be made to establish definitely the reason for the marked difference between the values for the Southwest Pacific and the others.

So far as I can make out, there are severe organizational difficulties in the War Department to making integrated studies. In exploring the possibilities, I have found some data and studies in each of the following: Surgeon General's Office, Army Ground Forces, G-1 and G-2. It is, for example, the function of G-2 to study Japanese casualties but except in the case of a special request such as I made for information on casualty ratios, they do not deal with U. S. casualties. Similarly it is not the function of any of the groups mentioned to correlate the casualties with ammunition expenditures. What is needed apparently is some sort of an organization set up at a suitably high level with informal contacts with all parts of the War Department which can contribute to the problem. This organization, which might, in fact, merely be a committee from the interested sections, could then assign projects in such a way as to end with an integrated picture where now there are uncorrelated studies.

To summarize, it appears to me that two specific recommendations may be in order:

1. A historical study of defeated nations should be undertaken and an attempt made to relate the behavior of the nation to the behavior of her troops. Professor Wright has indicated a willingness to guide such a study and has suggested certain former students whom

- 3 -

Appendix J   161

he believes capable of carrying out the details. At my request,
Professor Wright plans to prepare an outline which we could use
as a basis for setting up such a project.

2. A suitable agency for carrying out integrated
casualty studies should be formed so as to combine and supplement
the studies presently being made.

W. B. Shockley,
Expert Consultant,
Office of the Secretary of War.

- 4 -

*Discussion of American Casualties at President Truman's
Meeting with the Joint Chiefs of Staff and
Service Secretaries, June 18, 1945*

President Truman, had only recently retired as a highly respected colonel in the Reserve Officer Corps. After serving with distinction as a battery commander during the Meuse-Argonne Offensive in the First World War, the former Missouri "dirt farmer" had retained his commission and rose through the ranks to become the commander of the 381st Artillery Regiment from 1932 to 1935 and was then offered command of the 379th Artillery Regiment in 1935. During this period, the 379th's sister regiments, the 380th and 381st were commanded by artillery officers who would later serve in Truman's administration: Harry Vaughan as Military Aide and John Snyder as Treasury Secretary.[1] The president's cousin was Major General Ralph Truman.

Truman took his commission seriously and immersed himself in soldiering in spite of his increasing duties in a series of political positions. He was a familiar figure at the artillery range at Fort Riley, Kansas.[2] After arriving in Washington as a newly elected U.S. senator, he admitted in a letter to his wife that he "played hooky" from a meeting of the Senate Appropriations Committee to attend a lecture by Douglas Southall Freeman on General Robert E. Lee at the Army War College.[3] On another occasion, when Colonel Snyder paid a visit to him in Washington, the two artillerymen drove over to the Gettysburg battlefield to perform what the army today calls a "terrain walk" in order to examine the military aspects of the ground that Union and Confederate forces fought over in 1863.[4] The Transportation Act of 1940 (or Wheeler-Truman Act) was formulated by Truman and greatly increased America's preparedness for war. He was also an active member of three key armed services committees—the Military Affairs Committee, the Military Subcommittee of the Appropriations Committee, and Chairman of the Senate Special Committee to Investigate the National Defense Program—so when he went to General Marshall and offered to rejoin the Regular Army he was politely rebuffed by the chief of staff, who said: "Senator, you've got a big job to do right up there at the Capitol with your Investigating Committee. Besides, this is a young man's war. We don't need old stiffs like you."[5]

In some ways, Truman's working knowledge of the nuances of military planning and analysis has worked to the detriment of historians, and this can be no more clearly seen than in the well-worn misperceptions of what was actually said by the participants of that Monday afternoon meeting in the White House Cabinet Room. A less knowledgeable—or astute—president would have needed the Joint Chiefs' opinions expressed in more basic terms, which would have not only been helpful to the president, but also to later researchers poring over the meeting's transcript. Truman, however, used the same form of verbal shorthand, based on a common understanding of both the methodologies and assumptions used to formulate military analyses, as his peers around the table. Marshall's steady guidance was evident throughout the sixty-minute discussion, and President Truman himself made it a point to look beyond the numbers to the impact in human terms. The principal participants in this meeting with President Truman were Marshall, King, Leahy, Stimson, General Ira C. Eaker (substituting for Arnold), Navy Secretary James Forrestal, and Assistant Secretary of War John J. McCloy. Extended portions of the meeting's minutes are presented below, with additional commentary on the institutional context in which the participants were operating, and the various methodologies used in making casualty projections:

Details of the Campaign against Japan

Extracted from minutes of meeting held at the White House 18 June 1945 at 1530.[6]

> THE PRESIDENT stated that he had called the meeting for the purpose of informing himself with respect to the details of the campaign against Japan set out in Admiral Leahy's memoran-

dum to the Joint Chiefs of Staff of 14 June. He asked General Marshall if he would express his opinion.

GENERAL MARSHALL pointed out that the present situation with respect to operations against Japan was practically identical with the situation which had existed in connection with the operations proposed against Normandy. He then read, as an expression of his views, the following digest of a memorandum prepared by the Joint Chiefs of Staff for presentation to the President, J.C.S. (1388):

Our air and sea power has already greatly reduced movement of Jap shipping south of Korea and should in the next few months cut it to a trickle if not choke it off entirely. Hence, there is no need for seizing further positions in order to block Japanese communications south of Korea. General MacArthur and Admiral Nimitz are in agreement with the Chiefs of Staff in selecting 1 November as the target date to go into Kyushu because by that time:

a. If we press preparations, we can be ready.

b. Our estimates are that our air action will have smashed practically every industrial target worth hitting in Japan as well as destroying huge areas in the Jap cities.

c. The Japanese Navy, if any still exists, will be completely powerless.

d. Our sea action and air power will have cut Jap reinforcement capabilities from the mainland to negligible proportions.

Important considerations bearing on the 1 November date rather than a later one are the weather and cutting to a minimum Jap time for preparation of defenses. If we delay much after the beginning of November the weather situation in the succeeding months may be such that the invasion of Japan, and hence the end of the war, will be delayed up to 6 months.

An outstanding military point about attacking Korea is the difficult terrain and beach conditions which appear to make the only acceptable assault areas Fusan in the southeast corner and Keijo, well up the western side.[7] To get to Fusan, which is a strongly fortified area, we must move large and vulnerable assault forces past heavily fortified Japanese areas. The operation appears more difficult and costly than an assault on Kyushu. Keijo appears an equally difficult and costly operation. After we have undertaken either one of them we still will not be as far forward as going into Kyushu.

The Kyushu operation is essential to a strategy of strangulation and appears to be the least costly worthwhile operation following Okinawa. The basic point is that a lodgment in Kyushu is essential, both to tightening our strangle hold of blockade and bombardment on Japan, and to forcing capitulation by invasion of the Tokyo Plain.

We are bringing to bear against the Japanese every weapon and all the force we can employ, and there is no reduction in our maximum possible application of bombardment and blockade, while at the same time we are pressing invasion preparations. It seems that if the Japanese are ever willing to capitulate short of complete military defeat in the field, they will do it when faced by the completely hopeless prospect occasioned by (1) destruction already wrought by air bombardment and sea blockade, coupled with (2) a landing on Japan indicating the firmness of our resolution, and also perhaps coupled with (3) the entry or threat of entry of Russia into the war.

With references to clean up of the Asiatic mainland, our objective should be to get the Russians to deal with the Japs in Manchuria (and Korea if necessary) and to vitalize the Chinese to a point where, with assistance of American air power and some supplies, they can mop out their own country.

CASUALTIES. Our experience in the Pacific war is so diverse as to casualties that it is considered wrong to give any estimate in numbers. Using various combinations of Pacific experience, the War Department staff reaches the conclusion that the cost of securing a worthwhile position in Korea would almost certainly be greater than the cost of the Kyushu operation. Points on the optimistic side of the Kyushu operation are that: General MacArthur has not yet accepted responsibility for going ashore where there would be disproportionate casualties. The nature of the objective area gives room for maneuver, both on

the land and by sea. As to any discussion of specific operations,
the following data are pertinent: [See table 1.]

Table 1: General MacArthur's Operations 1 March 1944–1 May 1945

Campaign	U.S. Casualties Killed, Wounded, Missing	Jap Casualties Killed and Prisoners (not inc. wounded)	Ratio U.S. to Jap
Leyte	17,000	78,000	1:4.6
Luzon	31,000	156,000	1:5
Iwo Jima	20.000	25,000	1:1.25
Okinawa	34,000 (Ground) 7,700 (Navy)	81,000 (incomplete count)	1:2
Normandy (1st 30 days)	42,000	[—]	[—]

Notes: The record of General MacArthur's operations from 1 March 1944 through 1 May 1945 [northwestern New Guinea and the Philippines] shows 13,742 U.S. soldiers killed compared to 310,165 Japanese soldiers killed, or a ratio of 1 to 22.[8]

It is at this point in the discussion, that historians—military
and civilian alike—invariably lose track of exactly what the participants are saying. The numbers above were used solely as a base
to establish ratios of U.S. to Japanese casualties during the most
recent campaigns. A ratio which stripped U.S. wounded from
the equation and measured only killed to killed (which the Japanese casualties almost invariably were) is presented for comparative purposes, as well as a U.S. casualty total for the first third
of the fighting in the Normandy Campaign with no ratios given.
After the presentation of casualty ratios, casualty numbers are
not used. Instead, there are references to operations or portions
of operations. These references do not refer to the baseline figures, which are frequently quoted by authors and historians, but
to the ratios they spawned and which only *suggest* how casualties
from the much larger Japanese and American forces involved in
the first of the two invasion operations might play out. [POST-
PUBLICATION ADDITION: This was explicitly stated by Lincoln
in a memo to his chief, Lieutenant General John E. Hull, during
the formulation of the JWPC paper: "about 30,000 for the first 30

days (which are the casualties we have experienced in Luzon to date [160 days]) is about a balanced estimate."][9]

> There is reason to believe that the first 30 days in Kyushu should not exceed the price we have paid for Luzon. It is a grim fact that there is not an easy, bloodless way to victory in war and it is the thankless task of the leaders to maintain their firm outward front which holds the resolution of their subordinates. Any irresolution in the leaders may result in costly weakening and indecision in the subordinates. . . .

The "price" Marshall refers to is one American battle casualty for every five Japanese, and not the specific number of casualties from the smaller operation on Luzon. The limitation of the estimate to the "first 30 days" was made because the ratio could very easily change as U.S. soldiers and Marines started to fight their way into the mountains against additional Japanese divisions moving down from northern Kyushu. Detailed speculation beyond thirty days could come back to haunt the chief of staff, and even the first thirty-day projection is hedged by the qualifier "there is reason to believe."

> GENERAL MARSHALL said that he had asked General MacArthur's opinion on the proposed operation and had received from him the following telegram, which General Marshall then read:

> "I believe the operation presents less hazards of excessive loss than any other that has been suggested and that its decisive effect will eventually save lives by eliminating wasteful operations of nondecisive character. I regard the operation as the most economical one in effort and lives that is possible. In this respect it must be remembered that the several preceding months will involve practically no loss in ground troops and that sooner or later a decisive ground attack must be made. The hazard and loss will be greatly lessened if an attack is launched from Siberia sufficiently ahead of our target date to commit the enemy to major combat. I most earnestly recommend no change in OLYMPIC. Additional subsidiary attacks will simply build up our final total casualties."

As noted earlier, the opening portion of MacArthur's statement and the numbers supplied by his staff could not be used.

> GENERAL MARSHALL said that it was his personal view that the operation against Kyushu was the only course to pursue. He felt that air power alone was not sufficient to put the Japanese out of the war. It was unable alone to put the Germans out. General Eaker and General Eisenhower both agreed to this. Against the Japanese, scattered throughout mountainous country, the problem would be much more difficult than it had been in Germany. He felt that this plan offered the only way the Japanese could be forced into a feeling of utter helplessness. The operation would be difficult but no more so than the assault in Normandy. He was convinced that every individual moving to the Pacific should be indoctrinated with a firm determination to see it though.

The statement that "the problem would be much more difficult than it had been in Germany" is telling, and it is not contradicted by the follow-up statement that "the operation would be difficult but not more so than the assault in Normandy." Use of the words "in Normandy" instead of "on Normandy" indicates that Marshall was not limiting his comment to the initial "D-Day" landings, which suffered extremely low casualties on four of the five beachheads, but to the total campaign, which saw incremental advances through the tangled hedgerow country as American forces positioned themselves for a breakout from the Normandy Peninsula. There were 133,316 American and 91,223 British battle casualties during the Normandy Campaign, which took place from June 6 through August 31, 1944.[10]

> ADMIRAL KING agreed with General Marshall's views and said that the more he studied the matter, the more he was impressed with the strategic location of Kyushu, which he considered the key to the success of any siege operations. He pointed out that within three months the effects of air power based on Okinawa will begin to be felt strongly in Japan. It seemed to him that Kyushu followed logically after Okinawa. It was a natural

setup. It was his opinion that we should do Kyushu now, after which there would be time to judge the effect of possible operations by the Russians and the Chinese. The weather constituted quite a factor.[11] So far as preparation was concerned, we must aim for Tokyo Plain; otherwise we will never be able to accomplish it. If preparations do not go forward now, they cannot be arranged for later. Once started, however, they can always be stopped if desired.

GENERAL MARSHALL agreed that Kyushu was a necessity and pointed out that it constituted a landing in the Japanese homeland. Kyushu having been arranged for, the decision as to further action could be made later.

THE PRESIDENT inquired if a later decision would not depend on what the Russians agreed to do. It was agreed that this would have considerable influence.

THE PRESIDENT then asked Admiral Leahy for his views of the situation.

ADMIRAL LEAHY recalled that the President had been interested in knowing what the price in casualties for Kyushu would be and whether or not that price could be paid. He pointed out that the troops on Okinawa had lost 35 percent in casualties. If this percentage were applied to the number of troops to be employed in Kyushu, he thought from the similarity of the fighting to be expected, that this would give a good estimate of the casualties to be expected. He was interested therefore in finding out how many troops are to be used in Kyushu.

Leahy apparently did not believe that the presented figure of thirty-four thousand for ground force battle casualties offered a true picture of losses on Okinawa and used the total number of casualties to formulate the 35 percent figure. Since Leahy, as well as the other JCS members and Truman, also already knew approximately how many men were to be committed to the Kyushu fight, he was obviously making an effort—commonly done in such meetings—to focus the participants' attention on the statistical consequences of the disparity.

ADMIRAL KING called attention to what he considered an important difference in Okinawa and Kyushu. There had been only one way to go on Okinawa. This meant a straight frontal attack against a highly fortified position. On Kyushu, however, landings would be made on three fronts simultaneously and there would be much more room for maneuver. It was his opinion that a realistic casualty figure for Kyushu would lie somewhere between the number experienced by General MacArthur in the operations on Luzon and the Okinawa casualties.

As intelligence-gathering operations were currently discovering, however, and postwar prisoner interrogations and direct ground observations after the war would confirm, the Japanese had, through a process of elimination, correctly deduced the exact invasion beaches on Kyushu as well as the probable time that the invasion would be launched. The effort to fortify the beach areas and inland positions would begin in earnest in July and was to continue throughout the months leading up to the invasion. Unknown to Admiral King at the time of the June 18 meeting, the three-pronged landings on Kyushu "with much more room to maneuver" were effectively going to become three frontal attacks.

GENERAL MARSHALL pointed out that the total assault troops for the Kyushu campaign were shown in the memorandum prepared for the President as 766,700. He said, in answer to the President's question as to what opposition could be expected on Kyushu, that it was estimated at eight Japanese divisions or about 350,000 troops. He said that divisions were still being raised in Japan and that reinforcement from other areas was possible but it was becoming increasingly difficult and painful.

Marshall's figure of 766,700 differs only slightly from that of MacArthur's headquarters which gives 766,986 as the number of men to be landed within a month and a half of the invasion.[12] The U.S. portion of all ratios presented did not just represent the casualties from the units in contact with the enemy but the total force versus total force numbers. Participants at the meeting were familiar with ongoing total casualty figures, which determined the number of troops that could be fielded on a given day, and thus knew that the actual casualty figures were considerably higher. For discussion purposes, however, inclusion of nonbattle injuries, including psychiatric breakdowns and disease, is uncommon in such meetings because: (1) they are not directly inflicted by the enemy, and (2) a portion of the affected will eventually return to duty. Noncombat casualties tend to only be added to discussions if the manpower pool for replacements is so low, or the ability to get replacements to units needing reconstitution is so difficult, that the ability to accomplish a mission is directly affected. In the case of Okinawa, the intensity and prolonged nature of the fighting resulted in an extraordinarily large number of nonbattle casualties that were so severe that, excluding the killed in action, 61,471 battle and nonbattle casualties were missing from the ground units present for duty strength at the end of June, weeks after the heaviest fighting had ended.[13]

THE PRESIDENT asked about the possibility of reinforcements for Kyushu moving south from the other Japanese islands.

GENERAL MARSHALL said that it was expected that all communications with Kyushu would be destroyed.

ADMIRAL KING described in some detail the land communications between the other Japanese islands and Kyushu and stated that as a result of operations already planned, the Japanese would have to depend on sea shipping for any reinforcement.

ADMIRAL LEAHY stressed the fact that Kyushu was an island. It was crossed by a mountain range, which would be difficult for either the Japanese or the Americans to cross. The Kyushu operation, in effect, contemplated the taking of another island from which to bring increased air power against Japan.

The assurances of the Joint Chiefs were all true enough as stated, but they skirted the fact that the "island" was bigger in size and population than some American states, and that Kyushu was largely self-sufficient militarily. Moreover, it was questionable if the mountains would be a greater barrier for the foot-mobile Japanese or the invading American forces, who would have to fight through the southern portion of them and then form a noncontiguous defensive line of comparatively isolated hilltop positions for the duration of the war. Truman, who had been monitoring the rising casualty figures from Okinawa on a daily basis, was very well aware of this and cut to the bottom line.[14]

THE PRESIDENT expressed the view that it was practically creating another Okinawa closer to Japan, to which the Chiefs of Staff agreed.

THE PRESIDENT then asked General Eaker for his opinion of the operation as an airman.

GENERAL EAKER said that he agreed completely with the statements made by General Marshall in his digest of the memorandum prepared for the President. He had just received a cable in which General Arnold also expressed complete agreement. He stated that any blockade of Honshu was completely dependent upon airdromes on Kyushu; that the air plan contemplated employment of 40 groups of heavy bombers against Japan and that these could not be deployed without the use of airfields on Kyushu. He said that those who advocated the use against Japan of air power alone overlooked the very impressive fact that air casualties are always much heavier when the air faces the enemy alone and that these casualties never fail to drop as soon as the ground forces come in. Present air casualties are averaging 2 percent per mission, about 30 percent per month. He wished to point out and to emphasize that delay favored only the enemy and he urged that there be no delay.

THE PRESIDENT said that, as he understood it, the Joint Chiefs of Staff after weighing all the possibilities of the situation and considering all possible alternative plans were still of the unanimous opinion that the Kyushu operation was the best solution under the circumstances.

The Chiefs of Staff agreed that this was so.

THE PRESIDENT then asked the Secretary of War for his opinion.

MR. STIMSON agreed with the Chiefs of Staff that there was no other choice. He felt that he was personally responsible to the President more for his political than for military considerations. It was his opinion that there was a large submerged class in Japan who do not favor the present war and whose full opinion and influence had never yet been felt. He felt sure that this submerged class would fight and fight tenaciously if attacked on their own ground. He was concerned that something should be done to arouse them and to develop any possible influence they might have before it became necessary to come to grips with them.

THE PRESIDENT stated that this possibility was being worked on all the time. He asked if the invasion of Japan by white men would not have the effect of more closely uniting the Japanese.

MR. STIMSON thought there was every prospect of this. He agreed with the plan proposed by the Joint Chiefs of Staff as being the best thing to do, but he still hoped for some fruitful accomplishment through other means.

The other means included a range of measures, from increased political pressure brought to bear through a display of Allied unanimity at the upcoming conference in Potsdam to the untested atomic weapons then in production that many hoped would "shock" the Japanese into surrender.

THE PRESIDENT then asked for the views of the Secretary of the Navy.

MR. FORRESTAL pointed out that even if we wished to besiege Japan for a year or a year-and-a-half, the capture of Kyushu would still be essential. Therefore, the sound decision is to proceed with the operation against Kyushu. There will still be time thereafter to consider the main decision in the light of subsequent events. . . .

The question of how long it would take an air-sea blockade to force a Japanese surrender had been a hotly debated topic among mid- and senior-level military planners for over two years. Approximately a year and a half from the full establishment of airpower on Okinawa, where some bases for medium-range bombers were already in operation, was believed to be the outer limit of how long it would take such a course to work. It was the consensus of the military leadership that such a blockade could not be made fully effective without additional bases established farther north on Kyushu. The merits of unconditional surrender were briefly touched on at this point.

> THE PRESIDENT said he considered the Kyushu plan all right from the military standpoint, and so far as he was concerned, the Joint Chiefs of Staff could go ahead with it; that we can do this operation and then decide as to the final action later.

A short discussion of the British, Chinese, and Portuguese roles in ending the war ensued, and the president moved to wrap up the meeting.

> THE PRESIDENT reiterated that his main reason for this conference with the Chiefs of Staff was his desire to know definitely how far we could afford to go in the Japanese campaign. He had hoped that there was a possibility of preventing an Okinawa from one end of Japan to the other. He was clear on the situation now and was quite sure that the Joint Chiefs of Staff should proceed with the Kyushu operation. . . .

President Truman's comment about the invasion operations representing "an Okinawa from one end of Japan to the other"— now made twice—is an unequivocal indication of what he believed would be the magnitude of the fighting. The Japanese Navy was essentially destroyed, but Japanese air power was being preserved for the invasions. Japan's field armies in the Home Islands were swelling rapidly, and there was ample time to train recruits not only for the defense of the Tokyo area in 1946 but for the defense of Kyushu in the coming winter.

> ADMIRAL KING said he wished to emphasize the point that, regardless of the desirability of the Russians entering the war, they were not indispensable and he did not think we should go so far as to beg them to come in. While the cost of defeating Japan would be greater, there was no question in his mind but that we could handle it alone. He thought that the realiza-

tion of this fact should greatly strengthen the President's hand in the forthcoming conference.

THE PRESIDENT and the Chiefs of Staff then discussed certain other matters.

The "certain other matters," according to McCloy, was the atomic bomb.[15]

APPENDIX L

General Thomas Handy's Atomic Bomb Authorization

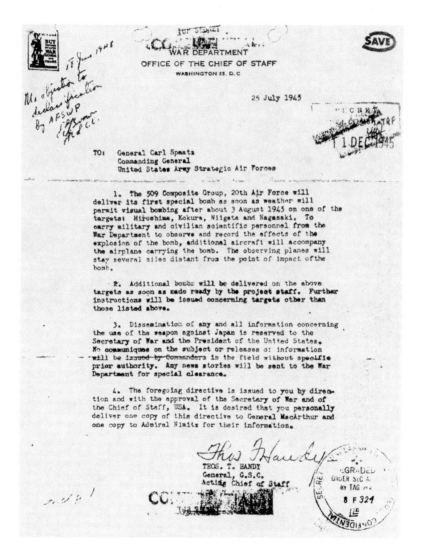

DOC. 10. Acting chief of staff general Thomas T. Handy to command general,
U.S. Army Strategic Air Forces, July 25, 1945, authorizing use of atomic bombs.
From Robert J. Maddox, "The Biggest Decision: Why We Had to Drop the
Atomic Bomb," *American Heritage* 46, no. 3 (May–June 1995): 70.

APPENDIX M

Atomic Bomb Press Release

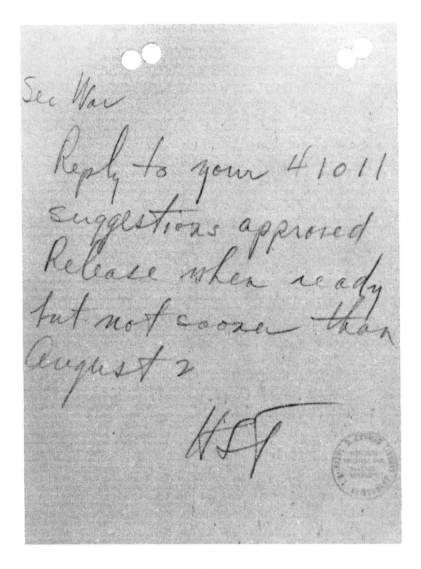

DOC. 11. Atomic bomb press release authorization—"Release when ready but
not sooner than August 2"—of President Harry S. Truman, July 30, 1945.
"Folder no. 1—War Dept.—1945," box 35, White House confidential file,
Whiter House central files, HSTML.

Potsdam Declaration, July 26, 1945

1. We—the President of the United States, the President of the National Government of the Republic of China, and the Prime Minister of Great Britain, representing the hundreds of millions of our countrymen, have conferred and agree that Japan shall be given an opportunity to end this war.

2. The prodigious land, sea and air forces of the United States, the British Empire and of China, many times reinforced by their armies and air fleets from the west, are poised to strike the final blows upon Japan. This military power is sustained and inspired by the determination of all the Allied Nations to prosecute the war against Japan until she ceases to resist.

3. The result of the futile and senseless German resistance to the might of the aroused free peoples of the world stands forth in awful clarity as an example to the people of Japan. The might that now converges on Japan is immeasurably greater than that which, when applied to the resisting Nazis, necessarily laid waste to the lands, the industry and the method of life of the whole German people. The full application of our military power, backed by our resolve, will mean the inevitable and complete destruction of the Japanese armed forces and just as inevitably the utter devastation of the Japanese homeland.

4. The time has come for Japan to decide whether she will continue to be controlled by those self-willed militaristic advisers whose unintelligent calculations have brought the Empire of Japan to the threshold of annihilation, or whether she will follow the path of reason.

5. Following are our terms. We will not deviate from them. There are no alternatives. We shall brook no delay.

6. There must be eliminated for all time the authority and influence of those who have deceived and misled the people of Japan into embarking on world conquest, for we insist that a new order of peace, security and justice will be impossible until irresponsible militarism is driven from the world.

7. Until such a new order is established and until there is convincing proof that Japan's war-making power is destroyed, points in Japanese territory to be designated by the Allies shall be occupied to secure the achievement of the basic objectives we are here setting forth.

8. The terms of the Cairo Declaration shall be carried out and Japanese sovereignty shall be limited to the islands of Honshu, Hokkaido, Kyushu, Shikoku and such minor islands as we determine.

9. The Japanese military forces, after being completely disarmed, shall be permitted to return to their homes with the opportunity to lead peaceful and productive lives.

10. We do not intend that the Japanese shall be enslaved as a race or destroyed as a nation, but stern justice shall be meted out to all war criminals, including those who have visited cruelties upon our prisoners. The Japanese Government shall remove all obstacles to the revival and strengthening of democratic tendencies among the Japanese people. Freedom of speech, of religion, and of thought, as well as respect for the fundamental human rights shall be established.

11. Japan shall be permitted to maintain such industries as will sustain her economy and permit the exaction of just reparations in kind, but not those which would enable her to re-arm for war. To this end, access to, as distinguished from control of, raw materials shall be permitted. Eventual Japanese participation in world trade relations shall be permitted.

12. The occupying forces of the Allies shall be withdrawn from Japan as soon as these objectives have been accomplished and

there has been established in accordance with the freely expressed will of the Japanese people a peacefully inclined and responsible government.

13. We call upon the government of Japan to proclaim now the unconditional surrender of all Japanese armed forces, and to provide proper and adequate assurances of their good faith in such action. The alternative for Japan is prompt and utter destruction.

U.S. Department of State, *Foreign Relations of the United States: The Conference in Berlin* (Washington DC: Government Printing Office, 1960), 2:1474–76.

APPENDIX O

Truman-Stalin Meeting at Potsdam

"Truman-Stalin Meeting, Tuesday, July 17, 1945, Noon" from notes by Charles E. Bohlen, chief of the U.S. State Department's East European Division and interpreter for President Harry S. Truman. U.S. Department of State, *Foreign Relations of the United States: The Conference in Berlin* (Washington DC: Government Printing Office, 1960), 2:43–47.

JULY 17, 1945, POTSDAM, GERMANY

PRESENT[1]

UNITED STATES

President Truman

Secretary Byrnes

Mr. Bohlen

Fleet Admiral Leahy[2]

SOVIET UNION

Generalissimo Stalin

Foreign Commissar Molotov

Mr. Pavlov

Mr. Vyshinsky

740.00119 Potsdam/7–1745

12. July 17.[3]

M. S.[4] late.
Truman—[blank]
S—Chinese—delayed   fly—no doctors
Tr—glad to—   looking forw—
S—Personal relationship
Truman—no difficulty in agreeing—
S—added—questions
T—no.
M[5]—reads—some already on agenda—i e 1 division on German fleet. 2 Reparations. 3 Polish Question—continued of continued—Art[6]—London Govt—western frontiers of Poland—(on list)

S—Yalta—did not decide frontiers of[7]
M—trusteeships for USSR.

S—no question of changing regime of trusteeship—settled S. F.[8]—but maybe stupid—division of Italian colonies—other nationals—roughly [one word illegible]

M—relations with Axis satellite—
T—on ours
M—Spain Franco regime
T—ready—
B[9]—trusteeship—other than Italian
M—yes—
S—Italian & other colonies.
T—what time
S—5 proposed—M & Eden
B—I know habits of rise late—getting—opportunity
T—5 today—4—after that
S—I have changed my habits since
B—[blank]

T—Gen Marshall like your Chiefs—they ready to discuss—Antonov—Air Marshal.[10]

T—Chiefs of staff—no.

S—ours in Berlin could not attend.   Re Franco—I should like to explain—F. regime not result of internal conditions

of Spain—imposed on Spain—by Ger—Italian—thus a danger to
Uni. Nations   This regime harmful—by giving shelter to
different fascist remnants—we thought it proper to break off with
present regime & give change

T—I hold no brief for Franco   study

S—right.

T—I would like—certain matters—first to US—take into
consider—orderly—way—but—reasons

T—pleasure to meet for am[11]—your present—welfare Soviet
          repsv& U J I   am here to—be yr friend—deal
directly yes—or no—no diplomat

S—good—help—work—USSR—always go along with US.

T—Byrnes.

B—[blank]

T—friends—all subject differences settle—frankly

S—good   of course difference—but.

T—Churchill—called—

S—[one word illegible]

B—[blank]

S—I think so—Labor—surprise

T—expressed same 2 to 1   80 majority

S—yes—people won't throw out W Ch[12]—self Preservation

T—yes—1944 R[13]

S—clever—Eng less clear Jap war—for—Russians & Amer—do
their duty   Eng think war mainly

T—P. M[14] offerd—

S—peculiar—mentality—bombed by Ger—not Japan
war over for them—these feelings may work vs[15] P. M.
US people—give power to finish task—can Brit ask that—they
believe war over—little interest in war vs Japan—may be

T—we are—not in dire straits as Eng was in re Germany—

S—we ready mid of Aug   needs agreement with China
[one word illegible]

T—I think that

S—O M[16] agreed—long negations[17]—R. R. Dairen. P. A[18]—
differences.   Soong—not hopeful by cable—I noticed S
understood us than Chungking[19]

T—yes—I had long talk[20]   He understands

S—he prepared to return to Chungking—& persuade return end of July—He asked a statement assurance[21]   re M[22]—part of China—sovereignty—gave that assurance

S—asked assurances deal only with central govt & not with any nucleus. one Army—he had in mind Com army   we shall give full assurances

T—very happy to hear that—settle matter

S—National 1 govt 1 army Treaty agreed—not.   Ch 30 in place of 20 as Czech.[23] agree—non-interference Ch internal affairs Soong—Sinkiang—Conflict—Ch author. & local pop—no assistance to rebels—[one word illegible]—special provisions—vs. interference could not help—suggested concession—Ch [one word and figure illegible] %—rest non Chinese local native schools set up. Soong agreed—won't be able to calm by stick—improvements—Soong agreed.

T—Soong—reasonable.

B—pts of differenc—failure on—misunderstanding.

S—in Yalta agreement[24]   said—re RR.   joint preeminent interests. be safeguard—same in Dairen & P. A. The Chinese don't recognize preeminent int & get around it—what is our preeminent interests—no profits—equally divided—altho built by Russian money—no guards as Japs had—Chinese protect RR themselves—old treaty[25] 80 yrs—back to China   we suggest 30 yrs—agreed   satisfaction—but what preem int lie—like to 1 maj[26] vote on board of RR—Russian director   they want Chinese director—& no maj—Dairen Chinese administration

B—jt administration

S—yes—but 1 Chinese maj—we propose—City Council—jt—board. Russian part

T—effect on our right—

S—free port—open—[one word illegible].

T—open door

S—not all smooth with Chinese—that is why he went home

S—mid August—as agreed at Yalta—we keep word

M   }   keep words [see appendix H]

T

B—in accordance—with Yalta—OK—in excess difficult

S—our wishes—more liberal than Yalta—restoration of Russian rights—entitled to station troops—80 yrs exclusively Russian—we have formal right—not done so we do not wish to add or deceive Chungking   don't understand horse trading—slow. try to wangle every thing—big pictures—very

T—big—Chin

B—   }   main interest free port [see appendix H]

T—

B—when here from Soong

S—end July—to finish negotiation—Chinese 22 years no ties—no repre—can't lose what one does not have.

APPENDIX P

Tripartite Military Meeting of the U.S., Soviet,
and British Chiefs of Staff, July 26, 1945

From U.S. Department of State, *Foreign Relations of the United States: The Conference in Berlin* (Washington DC: Government Printing Office, 1960), 2:408–17.

POTSDAM, JULY 26, 1945, 3 P.M.

PRESENT

UNITED STATES

General of the Army Marshall

Fleet Admiral King

General of the Army Arnold

Lieutenant General Hull

Vice Admiral Cooke

Major General Norstad

Major General Deane

Rear Admiral Gardner

Rear Admiral Maples

Captain McDill

SOVIET UNION

Army General Antonov

Admiral of the Fleet Kuznetsov

Marshal of Aviation Falaleyev

Lieutenant General Slavin

Admiral Kucherov

Secretariat

Brigadier General McFarland

Captain Moore

Interpreters

Lieutenant Chase

Major Evsekov

J. C. S. Files

Joint Chiefs of Staff Minutes

TOP SECRET[1]

GENERAL ANTONOV asked GENERAL MARSHALL if he would preside at the meeting.

GENERAL MARSHALL said that he appreciated the honor but under the circumstances he suggested General Antonov preside and he hoped that he would accept.

GENERAL ANTONOV asked if General Marshall had had an opportunity to become acquainted with the answers to the five questions General Marshall had given him at the meeting on 24 July[2] (See Annex to these minutes).[3] He said that Generalissimo Stalin had handed the written answers to President Truman yesterday at eleven o'clock a.m.

GENERAL MARSHALL said that he was sorry that he had not seen the answers which had been prepared by General Antonov.

GENERAL ANTONOV then read the answer to the first question as follows:—

The Soviet Command agrees to establish in Petropavlovsk and Khabarovsk radio stations for transmitting weather data in accordance with the request made in a letter from President Truman delivered on 23 July 1945.[4] The Soviet Command is ready to accept and use the radio stations and equipment proposed in that letter for the above purpose.

As regards the personnel for maintaining and operating the stations, we consider it wiser to use Soviet personnel which already has a great deal of experience in working with American radio stations.

In addition to these two stations we shall increase the network of local stations in order to give better information on weather.

When the reading of the answer to the first question was completed, GENERAL ANTONOV asked if he should proceed to read the answers to the remaining questions. GENERAL MARSHALL replied that the United States Chiefs of Staff would prefer to discuss the answer to each question as it was read.

ADMIRAL KING said that the United States Chiefs of Staff were disappointed that American personnel was not acceptable for liaison purposes at the central weather stations, since they felt that it would increase the efficiency of the Russian effort as well as our own. He thought, therefore, that we should request reconsideration of this point. If American personnel were used, he said that it was the intention to have 18 officers and 42 enlisted men at Khabarovsk and 9 officers and 24 enlisted men at Petropavlovsk. He had a memorandum relating to the details of equipment and personnel[5] which he thought the Russian High Command should have for use in connection with the reconsideration requested.

GENERAL ANTONOV said that Russian personnel had had experience in the use of the equipment and in the communication procedure in the vicinity of Sevastopol and Odessa as well as near Murmansk. The proposal to use Russian personnel had been made because it had been considered that the operation of these stations would then be more simple. However, if the United States Chiefs of Staff insisted on American personnel at these stations, there would be no objection to employing them.

ADMIRAL KING then gave General Antonov the memorandum he had previously mentioned.

GENERAL ANTONOV pointed out that he had not received an answer as to whether the United States Chiefs of Staff insisted on the use of American personnel.

GENERAL MARSHALL said that the United States Chiefs of Staff would prefer to use American personnel and pointed out that the major service rendered by this personnel would be to U.S. naval forces and to the strategic air forces. For this reason he thought that American personnel would be more satisfactory.

GENERAL ANTONOV said that the first question could then be considered solved and American liaison personnel would be employed at the stations under discussion.

GENERAL ANTONOV then read the answer to the second question as follows:—

Separate zones of naval and air operations are to be set up for the United States and the U.S.S.R. in the Sea of Japan. The boundary between these zones will be along the lines connecting Cape Boltina on the coast of Korea to point 40° north 135° east to point 45° 45' north 140° east thence along the parallel 45° 45' north to the line connecting Cape Crillon (Kondo) (on the southern tip of southern Sakhalin) with Cape Soya Missaki (Soyasaki) (on the northern tip of Hokkaido).

The U.S.S.R. naval and air forces will operate north of this line. United States naval and air forces will operate to the south of this line. This line shall be the limiting line of operations for surface and submarine craft and for aviation.

Depending upon circumstances in the future, this boundary line may be subject to change.

United States naval and air operations north of this boundary line and Soviet naval and air operations south of this boundary line will be subject to coordination.

In the Sea of Okhotsk there shall be a zone of mutual operations for the naval and air forces of the United States and the Soviet Union. Operations in the Okhotsk Sea will take place in accordance with mutual agreements.

In the Bering Sea there shall be a zone of mutual operations of our Pacific Fleet and aviation and the United States Fleet and aviation bounded on the north, east and south by a line going from Cape Dezhnev to Diomede Island and thence along the boundary of the territorial waters of the U.S.S.R. and the United States to parallel 51° 30' north and thence through 50° 35' north

157° east; thence to 49° 50' north 156° 20' east and thence along the parallel 49° 50' north to the Fourth Kurile Strait.

The remainder of the Bering Sea as well as bordering regions of the Pacific Ocean shall be the zone of operations of the United States Fleet.

GENERAL MARSHALL said that the line of demarcation for sea and air operations in the Sea of Japan was acceptable.

ADMIRAL KING said that he desired to confirm the proposed conditions in the Sea of Okhotsk. He said he understood that this sea would be free for operations of both the United States Navy and the Navy of the Soviet Union and that coordination would be arranged through mutual understanding and cooperation. He asked also if the area to the north of the red line shown on the chart[6] prepared by the Russian Chiefs of Staff, and described in the answer to the second question, was subject to joint control by the United States and the Soviet Navies, in the same manner as in the Sea of Okhotsk.

ADMIRAL KING's understanding was confirmed by ADMIRAL KUZNETSOV.

GENERAL MARSHALL said that with this understanding, the proposals by the Russian Chiefs of Staff were acceptable.

GENERAL ANTONOV repeated that the areas as set forth in answer to the second question were for both sea and air operations, and there was agreement on this answer.

GENERAL ANTONOV then read the answer to the third question as follows:—

The boundary line between operational zones of the United States and Soviet air forces in Korea and Manchuria shall be as follows: Cape Boltina, Changchun, Liaoyuan, Kailu, Chihfeng, Peking, Tatung and thence along the southern boundary of Inner Mongolia.

United States aviation will operate south of this line including all the above-named points. U.S.S.R. aviation will operate north of this line. Depending upon future conditions this line is subject to change. United States air operations north of this line and Soviet air operations south of this line must be coordinated.

GENERAL ARNOLD said he would like to call attention to the fact that the boundary line as proposed by the Russian Chiefs of Staff would deprive the United States air forces of certain railroad centers and lines of communication north of the line as targets unless each individual mission were arranged for separately. He asked if the United States air forces could send missions north of the boundary line within 24 hours after application had been made to the local Russian authorities. He thought that if his understanding as to local coordination was correct, the desired operations of the United States air forces could be worked out satisfactorily. He called the attention of the Russian Chiefs of Staff to the range of the heavy bombers, medium bombers, and light bombers, as indicated on a map which he presented,[7] and pointed out where the United States bombing effort could be made effective to the north of the boundary line.

AIR MARSHAL FALLALEV said that the boundary line suggested by the Russian Chiefs of Staff was to the northward of the principal railroad junctions. These junctions would therefore be available to attack by the United States air forces. If it became necessary to attack targets to the north of the line, reliable communications would permit arrangements to be made within 24 hours. Since, however, the communication might not always be reliable, this question might involve some difficulties.

GENERAL MARSHALL said that with the understanding that if the means of communication for coordinating attacks north of the boundary line were too slow, the question of its position would be discussed again, the proposals made by the Russian Chiefs of Staff were acceptable. However, he said, there was an additional matter he would like to raise in regard to both the second and third questions previously discussed. This concerned the flight of individual reconnaissance aircraft, and he asked that the Russian Chiefs of Staff comment on this point.

AIR MARSHAL FALLALEV said that it was considered that as a general rule, the boundary proposed should apply to reconnaissance aircraft as well as to bombing flights. When necessary to fly reconnaissance aircraft beyond the boundary line, the flight should be coordinated through the liaison officers.

GENERAL ANTONOV then read the answer to the fourth question as follows:—

The Soviet Command agrees that beginning with military operations of the Soviet Union against Japan, to establish liaison groups between the American and Soviet commanders in the Far East. To accomplish this liaison it is suggested that there be Soviet liaison groups with General MacArthur, with Admiral Nimitz, and in addition, in Washington, to have a Soviet Military Mission.

American liaison groups will be located with the Soviet High Commander in the Far East, Marshal Vassilievski, in Khabarovsk; and with the commander of the Soviet Pacific Fleet, Admiral Yemashev, in Vladivostok.

The Soviet Command is ready to accept the radio-teletype equipment for installation at the indicated points.

GENERAL MARSHALL said that the proposal of the Russian Chiefs of Staff appeared entirely acceptable, but he wished to ask if it was the intention that the liaison groups to be provided should make it possible for immediate coordination of operations. He asked if operations in the Sea of Okhotsk, for example, or in any other special area, would normally be referred to Washington and Moscow, or whether the necessary decisions would be made in the field with the minimum delay.

GENERAL ANTONOV replied that Marshal Vassilievski is the commander in chief of all forces of the Soviet Union in the Far East. Marshal Vassilievski had authority to solve all questions of local coordination which were included in the tasks assigned him by the High Command of the Soviet Union. He said that similarly Admiral Yemashev is the commander in chief of all Russian naval forces in the Pacific. He said that these two officers would be able to solve the questions of coordination of action within the limits of the questions and answers which were being discussed here.

GENERAL MARSHALL said that the statement of General Antonov made the answer to the fourth question entirely acceptable.

GENERAL ANTONOV then referred back to the third answer and asked if the question of liaison was now clear.

GENERAL MARSHALL replied that his question had concerned the employment of reconnaissance aircraft and that he considered the question of liaison as provided for in the fourth answer entirely satisfactory. He said, moreover, that as the operations proceeded he hoped that there would develop such an intimacy in liaison that we would find later that the commanders in the field would develop an even greater intimacy. This would of course depend on them.

GENERAL ANTONOV read the answer to the fifth question as follows:—

The Soviet Command agrees to select ports and airfields for ships and planes in need of repairs and to make available, as far as possible, repair facilities and medical assistance to the personnel of the above-mentioned ships and planes.

For this purpose we can designate:—

a. Naval ports: In the Japanese Sea, Port Nakhodka (America Strait); in the Okhotsk and Bering Sea regions—Nikolaevsk, on the Amur, and Petropavlovsk, on Kamchatka.

b. Airfields: In the region of Vladivostok, in the region of Alexandrovsk on Sakhalin Island and in the region of Petropavlovsk on Kamchatka.

GENERAL MARSHALL said that the proposals of the Russian Chiefs of Staff were entirely acceptable.

GENERAL ARNOLD asked if the matter of identification of aircraft at the Russian airbases which would be available to United States aircraft would be handled as a local matter. He said that sometimes a plane was so disabled that it was necessary to come into a landing field from any direction, identifying itself by radio signal only.

AIR MARSHAL FALLALEV said that the names of airfields, methods of approach, corridors and other details would be furnished and that the requirements of the aircraft and personnel upon landing would be provided. He said that a disabled aircraft, after making a certain signal, could land from any direction without other formality. Aircraft crews should be instructed, however, not to fly over such ports as Vladivostok, because of the danger of being fired upon by anti-aircraft batteries.

GENERAL ARNOLD pointed out that his inquiry was in regard to whether arrangements of this nature would be made locally, to which AIR MARSHAL FALLALEV replied that the principle was being established here, and that the details would be determined on the spot by the commanders in the field.

GENERAL ANTONOV said that he now considered that the five questions given him by General Marshall on 24 July had been answered. He wished, however, to make an additional statement in regard to them. He said that he considered that all of the arrangements provided for under the five questions would come into being on the entry of Russia into the war against Japan.

GENERAL MARSHALL asked if it would be possible to get the communication equipment discussed in the first question into Siberia before that date, or if it would be necessary to wait until after Russia had entered the war.

GENERAL ANTONOV said that preliminary arrangements for the liaison wireless stations could be made beforehand, and that agreements could be reached with reference to each particular question raised.

GENERAL ANTONOV said that at the meeting on 24 July, ADMIRAL KING had pointed out that after the seizure of Kyushu communications might be opened from Kyushu to Vladivostok.[8] This line of communications was very important, since the Straits of Tsushima could be used throughout the year, whereas the route through the Kuriles and through La Perousse Strait was closed during part of the year by ice. He asked General Marshall when the invasion of Kyushu would take place and when the opening of the sea route from the south could be expected.

GENERAL MARSHALL said that the occupation of Kyushu depended on three factors. The first was the movement of troops from Europe. This was being done as rapidly as possible, and engineering troops were being moved first in order to prepare the way for the full application of air power. The movement involved two oceans and one continent, and although we could not be certain of carrying out the entire movement on schedule, and were now somewhat behind on both personnel and cargo, he hoped that all difficulties would be overcome. The second factor was the movement of large amounts of supplies from the Solomons, New Guinea, and Halmahera, north to the Philippines and Okinawa, to be loaded on assault ships for the tremendous amphibious effort against Kyushu. The third factor was the recent withdrawal of our divisions engaged in the Philippines and Okinawa from heavy fighting, and the problem of rehabilitation and training for the next operation.

Finally, he said, the weather conditions in the area made landings in September and early October too hazardous to undertake, although this was not a controlling factor as to date. At the present time he expected the landing on Kyushu to take place the last part of October.

GENERAL MARSHALL said further that the assault on Japan by naval and air forces which would extend also to Korea and the Liaotung Peninsula would be continued and increased. By these means he anticipated that by the time of the landing on Kyushu we will have destroyed Japanese oil, other material production, and communications, and will have virtually destroyed the Japanese air force. He said that ADMIRAL KING has added that the Japanese Navy would be destroyed as well. He said that all plans for the operation against Kyushu were complete, shipping was being assembled, the construction of bases was proceeding at top speed, and the operations of the United States Fleet and all air forces would proceed with increased vigor from now on. He thought, however, that the Tsushima Strait could not be opened before the end of October. The difficulties of opening Tsushima Strait would involve the sweeping of the passage for mines. The most serious threat to these operations would be from Japanese suicide planes which had caused us so much difficulty in previous operations.

GENERAL ANTONOV said that he would be much pleased if the route to Vladivostok via Tsushima Strait could be opened in October since by that time communications through the Kuriles and La Perousse Strait would be closed by ice.

GENERAL MARSHALL said he understood and appreciated the urgent necessity to the Russian Chiefs of Staff of opening the southern route and said that we would do all in our power to clear the straits as early as possible. General Marshall said that ADMI-

RAL KING had pointed out that the operations to open Tsushima Strait could not take place until after the landing in Kyushu and until after our air forces were established in northwestern Kyushu. It would be necessary, of course, for our minesweepers to have adequate air cover during their operations in clearing the straits of mines. The time required to establish the necessary airfields would depend to a large degree on Japanese resistance in Kyushu and the straits might not be opened until the middle of December or about six weeks after the first landing on Kyushu. He pointed out that we would make every effort to expedite the operation for the benefit of our forces as well as for the benefit to the Russians. He wanted to make this point clear since he desired to avoid any misunderstanding as to our capabilities in clearing Tsushima Strait for traffic to Vladivostok.

GENERAL MARSHALL then read a memorandum[9] which he said related to this discussion and which gave the progress, from partial reports, covering the last ten days of naval and air action against Japan.

GENERAL ANTONOV expressed his appreciation for the information contained in the memorandum read by GENERAL MARSHALL.

GENERAL MARSHALL said that the United States Chiefs of Staff were prepared to furnish to the Russian Chiefs of Staff, until operations against Japan were commenced by the Soviet Union, a weekly report of operations similar to that contained in the memorandum, through General Deane or his naval associate. Thereafter, reports of such operations would be furnished through the commanders in the field.

GENERAL ANTONOV said that he would be glad to receive this information and asked if there were any other questions to be considered at this meeting.

GENERAL MARSHALL said that directions had been given to furnish the Russian Chiefs of Staff with copies of the minutes of this meeting in order to provide a means of determining if there was a mutual understanding of the conversations which had taken place. In the absence of comment by the Russian Chiefs of Staff, it would be assumed that the record was a correct basis for understanding and guidance.

GENERAL ANTONOV said that he would examine the minutes and if he had any comment he would inform the United States Chiefs of Staff thereof.[10]

GENERAL MARSHALL said that it was planned that he, Admiral King and General Arnold would leave for the United States tomorrow. Admiral Leahy would remain until the conference was completed. He said that the principal assistants of the Chiefs of Staff, Admiral Cooke, General Hull and General Norstad would remain at the conference to handle any matters that might arise. He said that if he, Admiral King and General Arnold leave tomorrow as planned, he desired to take this occasion to express for the United States Chiefs of Staff their appreciation for the opportunity afforded to discuss these important matters with the Russian Chiefs of Staff. He was gratified that they had been able to reach decisions so satisfactory to all.

GENERAL ANTONOV also expressed his pleasure and satisfaction over the results of the conference and said that he hoped that his close contact with General Marshall would be continued in the future so that all questions that might arise might be settled promptly. He then gave General Marshall a map showing the areas which had been considered in the discussion.[11]

GENERAL MARSHALL said that he regretted that through a misunderstanding the United States Chiefs of Staff had not received the answers to the five questions and were, therefore, not well prepared for the afternoon's discussion. He thanked General Antonov for his patience in reading the answers which he had presented.

Planned U.S. Naval and Air Operations in Support of the Soviet Invasion of Manchuria

---

For the benefit of our forces as well as for the benefit to the Russians.

—GENERAL GEORGE C. MARSHALL AT THE POTSDAM CONFERENCE

As early as the spring of 1943, the Combined Chiefs of Staff reported to the president of the United States and British prime minister that the U.S. military's "present strategic concept does not contemplate further amphibious operations west of the ALEUTIANS. Our forces there will assume a defensive role until conditions are favorable to operations in support of RUSSIA in the KAMCHATKA PENINSULA–Siberian area."[1]

As the Pacific war progressed, U.S. contingency planning—codenamed Keelblocks—was conducted in the event that the Soviet Union was attacked by Japan and entered the Pacific war. Though generally defensive in character, such as protecting Siberia's Kamchatka Peninsula and the Komandorskie Islands, located between Kamchatka and Alaska's Aleutian Islands, U.S. forces also considered offensive operations. For example, in order to ensure that the sea lanes to Russian ports remained open, Keelblocks 2 would see U.S. forces help secure Kamchatka from Japanese attack and build airfields there. Once this was done, a major amphibious assault would be launched against the nearby Japanese air and naval base complex at Paramushiro Island as a prelude to seizing or neutralizing the northern half of the 800-mile-long Kurile chain.

Army chief of staff General George C. Marshall as well as Admirals Ernest J. King and Chester W. Nimitz, respectively the chief of naval operations and Pacific Fleet commander, believed that the available manpower and resources were far too limited to sustain a major assault far to the north in 1944 and would severely undercut the critical drives across the central and southwest Pacific. Thus, after the ejection of Japanese forces from the Aleutian Islands, operations against Japanese forces in the Kuriles were kept just persistent enough to leave them guessing as to U.S. intentions but nothing more. Nimitz did, however, inform Vice Admiral Frank J. Fletcher, the aggressive North Pacific Force commander, that the military's "strategic concept still includes the possibility of a northern assault in 1945."

During the U.S.-Soviet negotiations of October 14–17, 1944, as part of the Moscow Conference, Soviet premier Joseph Stalin pledged that the Soviet Union would enter the war with Imperial Japan within three months of the defeat of Germany. To launch a massive offensive thousands of miles from Europe against the Japanese, Russian forces required that the United States supply much of the food, fuel, war supplies, and even the trucks to haul them both before and during the offensive.[2] The United States moved immediately to prepare the Soviet Union for the coming war through a massive expansion of the Lend-Lease program— codenamed "Milepost"—that was administered not through Congressionally established Lend-Lease channels but secretly by the War Department (see chapter 3).

Immediately before the U.S.-Soviet agreement in October 1944 that led to the establishment of Milepost, the part the Soviets would likely play in an expanded war was examined in a comprehensive, weeklong series of war games held at the American embassy in Moscow. Their objective, according to the chief of the U.S. Military Mission there, Major General John R. Deane, was to "point up the problems that would arise in connection with Soviet and Soviet-American operations in Siberia."[3]

The games operated from the premise that if the Japanese struck first they would be able to quickly cut the vital Trans-Siberian rail line at numerous vulnerable points as well as interdict Lend-Lease shipping through the Sea of Okhotsk between the Kuril Islands and Sakhalin, a long West Virginia–sized island shared by the Soviet Union and Japan. This was reaffirmed in other studies before and after the Yalta Conference.[4] In such an event, according to war game results, American forces already stretched to the max by our own offensives far to the south and with limited assistance from the Soviets, would have to overcome Japanese naval and air elements in the Kurils, southern Sakhalin (Japanese Karafuto), and the northernmost Japanese home island Hokkaido that were attacking and closing the various ocean straits between Soviet Kamchatka and their major far eastern port of Vladivostok. The key element in securing this objective, war gamers and General Deane believed, would be a major campaign to seize the dangerous Japanese bases on the adjoining islands of Paramushiro and Shumshu across the Pervyy Kurilskiy Strait from Soviet forces in the Kamchatka Peninsula.[5] Such an operation, however, was simply not in the cards, and Deane concluded that "objectives in the northern Kuriles or Kamchatka are not suitable as positions from which to provide contributory support, commensurate with costs, to our over-all objectives in the war against Japan. Furthermore, examination so far has indicated that there will be deficiencies in forces and resources, particularly in service support units, required for a major operation in the North Pacific on the scale of a Paramushiro-Shimushu [sic] operation."[6]

The Pentagon's Joint Planning Staff agenda prepared for the Yalta Conference stated that when discussing the matter with their Soviet counterparts Marshall and King should "emphasize" that this would entail a "difficult campaign" along the heavily defended straits long-controlled by the Japanese and "indicate to the Russians that any operations by us to open sea routes to Sea of Okhotsk–Amir River ports will be extremely costly and at the expense of our own efforts toward Japan from the south; that because of limitation of means, the probability of amphibious operations in the North Pacific in 1945 is remote."[7]

The Soviets were given no encouragement to believe that amphibious operations would be launched in the Kurils. On the third day of deliberations, Admiral King recited almost verbatim from the briefing paper and when the Soviet Navy's Commander in Chief, Admiral Nikolay Gerasimovich Kuznetsov, then asked directly "if the capture of an island in the Kurils was planned for 1945," King reiterated that the "means were not available to undertake it as well as the other operations which had been planned." But King left the door at least partially ajar in case the Japanese inflicted some catastrophe on the Soviet supply lines when he added, "however, as always, it [is] a question of the relative importance of the various operations under consideration."[8]

Several days later, General Marshall and the Red Army's chief of staff, General Alexei E. Antonov, briefly discussed the virtual certainty that Imperial forces in the region would attack first "if the Japanese obtained any intimation of the Russian concentration and intention." With Soviet honor on the line, Antonov stated that the Soviets would take responsibility for keeping open the La Perouse Strait along the northern Japanese island of Hokkaido.[9] Admiral Kuznetsov, however, was not fully confident that his forces were up to the task of keeping this strait open and maintained some hope that American warships would defend the shipping. During conversations with his American counterpart, "Kuznetsov asked about U.S. escorts for the convoys to the Soviet Far East after the Soviet Union entered the war, but King said that the Navy would be concentrated in the south in the Sea of Japan and that the Soviets could expect no escorts."[10]

The U.S. alternative to a direct commitment in the Kurils was to ramp up the naval side of the Lend-Lease expansion by helping the Soviets establish a modest amphibious capability before they entered the war.[11] Discussions were already in the works to set up a training regime for the Soviet sailors who would man the vessels supplied under Milepost. This was to be done by setting up a secret base at an existing facility, Fort Randall at Cold Bay, Alaska, where their sailors could quickly learn to operate the hundreds of combat ships coming to them under Milepost. The first wave of 2,300 "Project Hula" sailors arrived from Vladivostok before the end of March. Ultimately, some 15,000 Soviet naval personnel were trained at Fort Randall and manned the 149 Made-in-USA minesweepers, subchasers, frigates, LCI assault craft, and LSM-sized floating workshops turned over by the end of August 1945.[12] (See appendix G—U.S. Navy combatant ships transferred to the USSR under Project Hula, May–September 1945.)

The distance between the La Perouse Strait splitting Hokkaido from Sakahlin and the inner zone of the American lake that the Philippine Sea had become is roughly equivalent to the expanse from New Orleans to Halifax, with the distance to the Japanese base on Paramushiro a further seven hundred miles along the Kurile chain. American military leaders had consistently been crystal clear that only the direst circumstances would prompt American fleet elements to be carved from the southern drives aimed directly at the Japanese Home Islands.

Project Hula substantially lessened the danger that these drives might be weakened by the need to defend the critical supply line to Russia. The Soviets maintained at the Yalta Conference that their forces "will occupy southern Sakhalin as quickly after the beginning of hostilities as possible and will do this without American help." In addition, "The Soviet Navy will deny La Perouse Strait to the Japanese but it will be difficult to permit friendly surface movements through the La Perouse Strait until a Soviet Navy base and shore artillery are established."[13]

The need for the Soviets to establish a naval base adjacent to the La Perouse after seizing the Japanese portion of Sakhalin would be greatly lessened by the mass of "blue water" (oceangoing) warships and amphibious craft coming through Hula. Nevertheless, prudence dictated that the U.S. Navy be ready to open the sea lanes themselves if the Japanese succeeded in foiling Soviet efforts. Admiral Chester W. Nimitz, commander in chief of Pacific Ocean areas, had been kept abreast of developments at the Yalta Conference, and though neither he nor Admiral King had to actually seize islands in the Kurils to keep the Milepost supplies flowing, Nimitz wanted to know if they now might have to "modify our present concept for a KURILES Operation."[14]

Admiral King replied on February 20 that "in view of the Russian requirement" that supplies continue to flow, "this is being examined here [Washington] and your planner should examine it likewise." King, as noted earlier, was confident that Project Hula would decisively tilt control of the Okhotsk Sea in the Soviet's favor and he closed by stating that "the Russians will in fact be able to control the LA PEROUSE STRAIT subsequent to seizure and occupation of lower SAKHALIN."[15] A month later King instructed Nimitz to also "explore question of establishing line of communications to Sea of JAPAN thru TSUSHIMA STRAIT." Located far to the south off Korea, it remained ice-free year around unlike the La Perouse, which begins to freeze over in October.[16]

But while keeping the supplies flowing through the Okhotsk Sea could be economically accomplished by a modest force even without Russian assistance as long as no amphibious operations were involved, clearing the constricted Tsushima Strait was another matter entirely. Tsushima island lies squarely in the middle of the passage formally named Korea Strait north of the island and Tsushima Strait on the south. Easily mined, it was lined with shore batteries and ringed by airfields.

Nimitz warned that even though Japan's "fleet has been greatly reduced [and] air force has suffered severe losses," such an operation could only be launched after certain islands near Shanghai China were first seized for airbase development. Further, this could only be done after Japanese air power became "so weak as to permit the occupation of such bases." He added that the Chinese islands in question were "not well adapted to development."[17]

Nimitz promised to further evaluate the possibilities once his reconnaissance capabilities on soon-to-be-invaded Okinawa were effective and stated that such an operation would "contribute directly to accomplishment of the overall objective of U.S. forces as well as the preparation of RUSSIA to assist."[18] On April 5, Nimitz reported to King that Admiral William F. Halsey, commander Third Fleet, "is now engaged in planning operations . . . to establish line of communications into SEA OF JAPAN via either LA PEROUSE or KOREA [-Tsushima] STRAIT." Subsequent communications from King reemphasized that any plans needed to focus on "maintaining a convoy route without securing positions in KAMCHITKA or the KURILES."

On May 21 Nimitz informed King that Keelblocks 3 and 4 planning was nearing completion with option four, calling for Admiral Fletcher's North Pacific Force being augmented by three fleet and seven escort carriers, as well as more than two dozen destroyers plus a heavy bomber group and reconnaissance elements for use against "HOKKAIDO and the southern KURILES as necessary to support Russian operations in SAKHALIN or cover convoy movements."[19]

Coordination with Soviet forces in the Far East was still in its infancy, and Halsey judged that if called upon to support the Red Army's invasion of Japanese Karafuto, the Third Fleet's strikes against Hokkaido would be far enough removed from Sakhalin itself that there would be no risk at all of Russian casualties in a friendly fire incident. Those strikes would still be able to isolate the Japanese defenders from support. Both the Soviet and U.S. commands were, however, concerned about the largescale northward expansion of American submarine operations into the Sea of Japan above the Tsushima-Korea Straits because of the possibility of accidental clashes and the risks to American subs from the U.S. Navy's own aircraft.[20]

An effective blockade of the East China Sea by U.S. naval and air elements prevented nearly all movement of Japanese ships between China and Japan, but "minefields in KOREA STRAITS have prevented access by submarines to profitable shipping traffic lanes in the JAPAN SEA" from Manchuria and Korea. Though a small number of subs were periodically sent through the straits in order to literally "test the waters," this situation did not change until the very carefully planned and executed Operation Barney was launched in early June 1945 with American submarines entering through the south and exiting through the La Perouse more than a thousand miles to the north.[21]

Due to the great distances involved, Admiral Nimitz requested guidance on whether to have severely damaged submarines put in at Vladivostok or Sovetskaya Gavan and if the still-neutral Russians could supply pilotage through the shallow Tartary Strait to the latter port, which was presumably more secure from Japanese intelligence and observation than Vladivostok. King replied that "pending receipt of guidance from MOSCOW," Sovetskaya Gavan would indeed be the "preferred" port for refuge and repairs.[22]

During the Potsdam Conference's July 24 Tripartite Military Meeting—and as he had done at the Yalta Conference and despite Project Hula—Soviet chief of staff Antonov asked if the United States would operate against the Kuriles in order to open the line of communications to Siberia once hostilities commenced with Japan. But cognizant of the U.S. chiefs' earlier refusal to commit themselves to launching amphibious operations in the islands, Antonov this time added that the Soviets had "some strength in Kamchatka and would like to assist with some forces."

As before, the United States did not have the resources to engage in such an operation without weaking its efforts far to the south. Admiral King reiterated that "it would not be possible to operate against the Kuriles." King did, however, have Keelblocks in his back pocket and—likely much to the relief of the Soviet chiefs—added what they'd long wanted to hear, "that he saw no reason why a line of communications could not be maintained through the Kuriles."[23]

Throughout the Potsdam Conference the Joint Chiefs insured that Admiral Nimitz as well as the U.S. Army and Strategic Air Forces commanders in the Pacific, Generals Douglas MacArthur and Carl A. Spaatz, were kept fully informed in all decisions that Admiral King and General George C. Marshall reached with their Soviet counterparts: Soviet chief of staff General Alexei E. Antonov, navy commander in chief Admiral Nikolay G. Kuznetsov, and Air Marshal Fedor Y. Falaleyev. After the July 24 Tripartite Military Meeting—early in the morning on the other side of the globe from Potsdam—the green light was now given to burst open the door that the Japanese would hurriedly slam shut once the Soviet Union declared war.

Nimitz, in accordance with earlier Keelblocks plans, ordered that Cruiser Division 5's three cruisers immediately ready themselves for assignment to Admiral Fletcher's North Pacific Force. In a separate message to Vice Admiral John H. Towers, Commander, Air Force, Pacific Fleet, Nimitz also called for "six escort carriers with two Flag Officers to concentrate in MARSHALLS in near future for use in KEELBLOCKS 4 if required" and instructed Towers to "warn COMSERVPAC to be continually prepared on short notice" to supply support elements to the carriers. With the Soviet Union still a "neutral" nation hampered by highly vulnerable rail and sea supply lines, Nimitz added: "Utmost secrecy directed."[24]

In addition to Cruiser Division 5, there were destroyers and long-range reconnaissance aircraft ordered north to bolster Fletcher's Task Force 92, which would soon begin clearing the Kuriles of Japanese shipping. Subsequently, the six "baby flat tops" of Carrier Divisions 23 and 26, with yet more cruisers and destroyers, were ordered by Towers to gather at Eniwetok, where they would form Task Force 49 under Rear Admiral Harold G. Martin. From there they would be sent north to be folded into Fletcher's command.[25]

These actions were initiated the morning after the July 24 meeting of the U.S. and Soviet chiefs of staff, who held their second and final meeting two days later (see appendix P—Potsdam: the second Tripartite Military Meeting, Thursday, July 26, 1945). The following agreements were to "become effective upon Soviet entry into the war" and, with subsequent clarifications, included:

- The establishment of U.S. weather stations at Petropavlovsk on the Kamchatka Peninsula plus Khabarovsk just beyond the northeastern tip of Manchuria and an increase in the number of Russian station feeding them weather data.[26]

- That U.S. and Soviet surface forces will operate without restrictions in the Seas of Japan and Okhotsk and that air and submarine forces will operate on their own sides of demarcation lines running through the Sea of Japan and Bering Sea. Operations would be coordinated by mutual understanding and cooperation and it was agreed that, depending upon circumstances in the future, boundary lines may be subject to change and that these changes would be effected by local (theater) liaison without reference to Washington or Moscow.[27]

- The boundary line between operational zones of the U.S. and Soviet air forces in Korea and Manchuria will be Cape Boltina at the 41st parallel on Korea's northeast coast through to Peking (Beijing) and thence along the southern boundary of Inner Mongolia. For U.S. aircraft to attack targets or make reconnaissance flights north of the boundary line or the Soviets to its south, coordination would be effected by local (theater) liaison without reference to Washington of Moscow within 24 hours after application. It was further agreed that position of the line would be reconsidered if communications proved too slow to effect prompt coordination.[28]

- Agreement with the Soviet Command to the establishment liaison groups between the American and Soviet commanders in the Far East beginning with military operations of the Soviet Union against Japan. Soviet Joint Chiefs of Staff liaison groups would operate with General MacArthur and Admiral Nimitz in addition to a Soviet Military Mission in Washington. The American liaison groups will be located with the Soviet High Commander in the Far East, Marshal Aleksandr Vasilevsky in Khabarovsk, and with the Commander of the Soviet Pacific Fleet, Admiral Ivan Yemashev in Vladivostok. The Soviet Command was ready to accept the radio-teletype equipment for installation at the Soviet headquarters and that liaison would be effected by these commanders without reference to Washington or Moscow.[29]

- That "after D-Day"—the Soviet declaration of war and invasion of Manchuria—Russian and American air and naval craft in emergencies will have access to the nearest friendly facility "where they may obtain repairs, servicing, medical care, and otherwise be assisted in making a speedy return to combat. . . ." Though all Soviet bases would be available to U.S forces in an "Extreme emergency . . . certain [Soviet] ports, airfields or areas where maximum facilities would be available" were:

  (a) Naval ports: in the JAPANESE SEA, port NAHODKA (American Strait); in the OKHOTSK and BERING SEA REGIONS, NIKOLAEVSK, on the AMUR, and PETROPAVLOVSK, on KAMCHATKA.

  (b) Airfields: in the region of VLADIVOSTOK, in the region of ALEXANDROVSK on SAKHALIN ISLAND and in the region of PETROPAVLOVSK on KAMCHATKA.

- Action—Agreed with the understanding that the method of identification of damaged aircraft arriving at Soviet fields would be established by the Commanders in the Field.[30]

With these matters out of the way, Soviet chief of staff Antonov broached a "very important" matter: "The Straits of Tsushima could be used throughout the year, whereas the route through the Kuriles and through La Perousse Strait was closed during part of the year by ice. He asked General Marshall when the invasion of Kyushu would take place and when the opening of the sea route from the south could be expected."[31]

Despite the ships and men cycling through Project Hula and the U.S Pacific Fleet preparing to punch a big hole in the Japanese barrier stretching along the Kuriles from Hokkaido to Kanchatka plus assist in reopening the La Perousse Strait to the west, the Soviets were understandably nervous about a cutoff of shipping due to ice. They had by now received shipments totaling more than a million tons of supplies to support the coming war with Imperial Japan through the top-secret Milepost program (see chapter 3), yet the size and scope of their coming multifront offensive could well exhaust much of this reserve in a scant two months, so it was imperative that the shipments continue unabated. The U.S. Navy would see to it that they did.

But what the Japanese couldn't do the coming winter—close the La Perousse Strait—would, and possibly as early as mid-October, make the Soviet supply situation a dangerously "close-run" thing. Marshall knew this question was coming. He had cautioned the Soviet leaders at the previous Tripartite Military Meeting that conducting operations in the southern Tsushima-Korea straits "would seriously expose our shipping to Japanese suicide attack by air and surface vessels until we had completely destroyed enemy air strength in southern Korea and until certain portions of the Japanese homeland had been brought completely under our control."[32]

Speaking for the other U.S. chiefs sitting at his side, Marshall explained the following to his new Pacific Allies:

> He appreciated the urgent necessity to the Russian Chiefs of Staff of opening the southern route and said that we would do all in our power to clear the straits as early as possible. . . . It would be necessary, of course, for our mine-sweepers to have adequate air cover during their operations in clearing the straits of mines.

The time required to establish the necessary airfields would depend to a large degree on Japanese resistance in Kyushu and the straits might not be opened until after the middle of December or about six weeks after the first landing on Kyushu.

He pointed out that we would make every effort to expedite the operation for the benefit of our forces as well as for the benefit to the Russians.[33]

General Marshall "wanted to make this point clear since he desired to avoid any misunderstanding as to our capabilities in clearing Tsushima Strait for traffic to Vladivostok."[34] At this time, neither the Soviet nor U.S. commands believed that they would have land forces in the vicinity of, let alone on, the Tsushima-Korea straits. The Soviets' secondary assault to seize Japanese Karafuto on Sakhalin Island was the next highest priority after the seizure of Manchuria and, in fact, Antonov at the meeting two days earlier had asked if American forces could "operate against the shores of Korea," only to be told that, because of limited resources, any amphibious operations against Korea would have to wait. As for the Kyushu side of the straits, MacArthur's plans called for the U.S. Sixth Army to establish and defend a "stop line" only a third of the way up the massive island and more than a hundred miles to the south.[35]

Convoys through the southern straits with supplies for the Red armies slugging it out with the Japanese in Manchuria would be protected by the U.S. Pacific Fleet and the U.S. Army's Fifth Air Force, but there would inevitably be losses. The U.S Joint Chiefs believed that they would likely be heavy. Ships transiting channels constricted by unswept mines and extensive shore batteries on the long Korean and Japanese coastlines—and Tsushima Island in between—would be inviting targets. Moreover, hidden Kamikazes flying from fields and roadways away from established airfields would never be completely suppressed and could easily attack at very low level with very little warning. The United States, however, was now fully committed to supporting Soviet operations and would do whatever was in its power, as General Marshall stated, "for the benefit of our forces as well as for the benefit to the Russians."[36]

Upon the Soviet Union's declaration of war against Imperial Japan on August 8, 1945, orders were issued for a modified version of Operation Keelblocks 4 (also referred to as OpPlan 4), which included no amphibious operations. Instead, the purely naval force was to:

Establish and maintain a line of communications from the ALEUTIANS across the SEA OF OKHOTSK.

Neutralize Japanese bases threatening this line of communications.

Provide protection of convoys against hostile air, surface and submarine attacks between the ALEUTIANS and escort turn around points in the SEA OF OKHOTSK.[37]

As for the potentially far more costly operation in the Tsushima-Korea straits when the northern waters froze over, that military commitment made at the Potsdam Conference ultimately did not have to be carried out. After Japan announced that it accepted the Potsdam Declaration's terms on August 15, 1945, it was immediately apparent to the Soviets, who had invaded Manchuria almost a week earlier, that much of the Imperial Army in Manchuria was indeed following Emperor Hirohito's orders to lay down its arms. For the first time in history, many Japanese formations were agreeing to surrender, and the Soviets were harvesting unprecedentedly large numbers of prisoners instead of having to fight them literally to the death.

This unique and unanticipated situation resulted in at least 594,000 Japanese military personnel being taken prisoner during and after the Soviet offensive.[38] This event was immediately followed by American and British forces experiencing the same thing as some 6,397,000 uniformed military personnel throughout the former empire (excluding Soviet controlled areas) were formally demobilized with few incidents.[39]

This sudden capitulation of Japan forces from the Dutch East

Indies to China and Manchuria and the Home Islands meant that there would be no invasion of Japan—and no young American sailors and airmen putting their lives on the line to force supply convoys through the dangerous waters between Korea and Japan to support the Soviet offensive in Manchuria.

DOC. 12. (*opposite right*) Lieutenant William M. Rigdon, USN, *Log of the President's Trip to the Berlin Conference, July 6, 1945 to August 7, 1945* (Washington: Office of the President, 1945), 23. Extracts from the log are also printed in U.S. Department of State, *Foreign Relations of the United States, Diplomatic Papers: The Conference of Berlin (The Potsdam Conference), 1945* (Washington: Government Printing Office, 1960), 2:4–28. See also Naval Aide Files, HSTML.

APPENDIX R

Extract from the Log of the President's Trip to the Berlin Conference, July 18, 1945

Extract referencing President Truman's meeting with the "Secretary of State and a number of his advisors in the forenoon" on the atomic bomb.

flew over the main entrance to the Palace.

Cecilienhof had been used as a hospital during the war by both the Germans and the Soviets and had been stripped of all its furnishings. The Russians performed a marvelous job in refitting it for the conference, however. It was, perhaps, furnished even better during the conference than originally. Its furniture and furnishings had been brought in from Moscow.

At Cecilienhof President Truman, Mr. Churchill, and the Generalissimo each had a suite, and each delegation had a retiring room and offices.

Wednesday, July 18th:

Sergeant Truman had breakfast with the President this morning.

The President conferred with the Secretary of State and a number of his advisers during the forenoon.

At 1315 the President, accompanied by Mr. Ross, General Vaughan, and Captain Vardaman, left the Little White House by foot for the Prime Minister's quarters. There the President lunched privately with the Prime Minister while Mr. Ross, General Vaughan, and Captain Vardaman had lunch with Junior Commander Mary Churchill and some other members of the Prime Minister's personal staff.

At 1450 the President, together with the Prime Minister and Miss Churchill, left the Prime Minister's residence and walked down the street to Mr. Eden's quarters where they met Mr. Eden and Secretary Byrnes. The party then returned to the Prime Minister's house. The President's party assembled at the Prime Minister's and left with him for Generalissimo Stalin's quarters so that the President could return Marshal Stalin's earlier call.

At 1500 a pouch with mail for the White House was dispatched to Washington.

1504: The President and his party arrived at the Generalissimo's quarters. The President was met as he alighted from his car by Mr. Molotov who escorted him and his party inside where Mr. Stalin awaited. Although most of our party had just left the luncheon table, we were ushered to a large dining table where a buffet lunch was served us. After lunch with attending toasts, the President talked briefly with the Generalissimo. Then they posed for still and motion pictures. The President and party left the Generalissimo's house at 1600 for Cecilienhof. We arrived at the Palace at 1608.

At 1615 the second meeting of the Berlin Conference was convened. The meeting adjourned at 1800, and the President and his party left im-

NOTES

Prologue

Epigraph: Henry L. Stimson, "The Decision to Use the Atomic Bomb," *Harper's Magazine*, February 1947, 102–4.

1. *United States Strategic Bombing Survey* [USSBS], *Pacific: Final Report Covering Air-Raid Protection and Allied Subjects in Japan*, no. 62 [hereafter USSBS: *Air-Raid Protection*] (Tokyo: Civilian Defense Division, 1947), 197.

2. Robert P. Newman, *Enola Gay and the Court of History* (New York: Peter Lang, 2004), 134–48. Newman arrived at this monthly average by extrapolating from the conservative figure of twenty million Chinese deaths from the *Report of the Working Group for Asia and the Far East of the Temporary Sub Commission on the Economic Reconstitution of Devastated Areas* published by the United Nations Economic and Social Council in 1948 (the Chinese government maintains that the figure was closer to thirty million) plus figures for hard-hit Indonesia and elsewhere. He notes that this is buttressed by recent scholarship such as Seiitsu Tachibana, "The Quest for a Peace Culture: The A-Bomb Survivor's Long Struggle and the New Movement for Redressing Foreign Victims of Japan's War," in Michael J. Hogan, ed., *Hiroshima in History and Memory* (Cambridge UK: Cambridge University Press, 1996), 184; Toshio Iritani, *Group Psychology of the Japanese in Wartime* (London: Kegan Paul, 1991), 237; and Gavan Daws, *Prisoners of the Japanese* (New York: Morrow, 1994), 363. An extensive examination of this subject can be found in Werner Gruhl's *Imperial Japan's World War II: 1931–1945* (New Brunswick NJ: Transaction Publishers, 2007). Gruhl is a former chief of the National Aeronautics and Space Administration's Cost and Economic Analysis Branch.

3. Repeated American requests that civilians be allowed to leave—radioed in the clear and on Japanese frequencies—were ignored by Japanese commanders (*Reports*, vol. 1, bk. 1, 275). A partial list of body counts (from five hundred to seven thousand dead by location) from the February massacres compiled by Philippine government's 1951 Quirino Presidential Committee of Secretary of Economic Coordination, Salvador Araneta, can be found in Richard Connaughton, John Pimlott, and Duncan Anderson, *The Battle for Manila* (London: Bloomsbury, 1995), 174–75. See also Connaughton, Pimlott, and Anderson, *The Battle for Manila*, 15, 110–11, 107–38, 144–55, 168–69, 195–96; Robert R. Smith, *Triumph in the Philippines, Central Pacific Drive: History of US Marine Corps Operations in World War II* (Washington: Historical Branch G-3 Division, Headquarters USMC, 1966), 345.

4. USSBS: *Air-Raid Protection*, 197.

5. James Belote and William Belote, *Typhoon of Steel: The Battle for Okinawa* (New York: Harper & Row, 1970), 279–80, 303, 315; and Joseph D. Harrington, *Yankee Samurai: The Secret Role of Nisei in America's Pacific Victory* (Detroit: Pettigrew Enterprises, 1979), 245.

6. William B. Shockley to Edward L. Bowles, July 21, 1945, War Department Study "Proposal for Increasing the Scope of Casualties Studies," with attached paper "Historical Study of Casualties," by Quincy Wright, in Edward L. Bowles Papers, box 34, Library of Congress, Washington DC.

7. USSBS: *Air-Raid Protection*, 197.

8. Vice Chief of the Naval General Staff Onishi Tikijiro in Robert J. C. Butow, *Japan's Decision to Surrender* (Stanford CA: Stanford University Press, 1954), 204–5; and Lord Keeper of the Privy Seal Marquis Kido Koichi in Newman, "The Trashing of Henry Stimson," in *Hiroshima in History: The Myths of Revisionism*, ed. Robert James Maddox (Columbia: University of Missouri Press, 2007), 152.

9. Battle casualties amounting to 28,666 on Iwo Jima are detailed in Samuel Eliot Morison, USN, *History of United States Naval Operations in World War II*, vol. 14, *Victory in the Pacific, 1945* (Boston: Little, Brown, 1960), 14:69. Battle casualties on Okinawa stand at 39,262, with figures frequently stated for ground force "losses" running from 65,631 to 72,000 when including the addition of 26,211 to 33,096 nonbattle casualties. *US Tenth Army Action Report, Ryukyus, 26 March to 30 June 1945*, vol. 1, chap. 11, sec. I:12; and G-1 *Periodic Reports*, no. 13, 1–3, in Thomas M. Huber, *Japan's Battle for Okinawa, April–June 1945* (Fort Leavenworth KS: Combat Studies Institute, U.S. Army Command and General Staff College, 1990), 119–20.

10. Larry I. Bland and Sharon Ritenour Stevens, eds., *The Papers of George Catlett Marshall* (Baltimore: Johns Hopkins University Press, 1996), 5:220–27, esp. 223, from a Marshall-edited transcript made by the Maryland Historical Society. It was published as "Some Lessons of History," *Maryland Historical Magazine*, 40 (September 1945): 175–84.

11. "Roosevelt Urges Work-or-Fight Bill to Back Offensives," *New York Times*, January 18, 1945, 1.

12. The original copy of Hoover's "Memorandum on Ending the Japanese War" (memo 4 of 4, May 30, 1945) with Truman's notation, the White House retypes/carbon copies of this document, and the subsequent exchange of memos among Truman, Grew, Cordell Hull, Stimson, and Vinson are under State Dept., WWII in box 43 of the White House Confidential File (WHCF), Harry S. Truman Library and Museum (HSTLM). The memorandum had been modified substantially in form, but not content, from the document that Hoover sent to Stimson after their May 13, 1945, meeting. Both versions of the memorandum are well-known, and the May 30, 1945, version is frequently cited. After locating the original annotated copy and the subsequent exchange between Truman and his senior civilian advisers, I supplied copies to numerous scholars such as Robert Ferrell and Robert Newman as well as to various institutions.

13. Leahy to Joint Chiefs of Staff (JCS) members Marshall, Henry H. Arnold, and Ernest J. King; Secretary of War Stimson; and Secretary of the Navy James Forrestal, memo SM-2141, June 14, 1945, in *The Entry of the Soviet Union into the War against Japan: Military Plans, 1941–1945* (Washington DC: Department of Defense, 1955), 76 (hereafter *Soviet Entry*).

14. Marshall's figure of 766,700 differs only slightly from that of MacArthur's headquarters, which gave 766,986 as the number of men to be landed within a month and a half of the invasion in "Staff Study, 'Olympic,' Operations in Southern Kyushu," May 28,

1945, appendix B, annex 4, Commander in Chief, Army Forces, Pacific, call nos. N11619 and N11619-B, copy in the Combined Arms Research Library, U.S. Army Command and General Staff College, Fort Leavenworth KS (hereafter CARL).

15. June 18, 1945, meeting in Joint Chiefs of Staff Corrigendum to JCS 1388, "Details of the Campaign against Japan," Records of the Joint Chiefs of Staff: Part 1, 1942–1943: The Pacific Theater, reel 2, CARL. For the text and a detailed analysis of the June 18, 1945, meeting and exchange between Generals Marshall and MacArthur beforehand, see D. M. Giangreco, "Casualty Projections for the U.S. Invasions of Japan, 1945–1946: Planning and Policy Implications," *Journal of Military History* 61 (July 1997): 521–81. For an analysis of the Pentagon staff work on Hoover's memo 4 and the June 18 meeting, see Giangreco, "'A Score of Bloody Okinawas and Iwo Jimas': President Truman and Casualty Estimates for the Invasion of Japan," *Pacific Historical Review* 72 (February 2003): 93–132.

16. "JCS Corrigendum," 4–5.

17. James Jones, *WWII: A Chronicle of Soldiering* (New York: Ballantine, 1975), 230.

18. Jones, *WWII*, 222.

19. Stanley Weintraub, *The Last Great Victory* (New York: Penguin, 1995), 229. In Dudley's previous assignment with the Manhattan Project, he had been a key figure in the site selection for the Los Alamos National Laboratory, New Mexico, and he later retired as a brigadier general.

20. Major Mark P. Arens, Marine Corps Intelligence Activity, USMCR, *V [Marine] Amphibious Corps Planning for Operation Olympic and the Role of Intelligence in Support of Planning* (Quantico VA: Marine Corps Command and Staff College, 1996), 81.

21. Arens, *V [Marine] Amphibious Corps Planning*, 81.

22. Extract from a letter written by James Michener, October 20, 1995, in D. M. Giangreco, *Hell to Pay: Operation Downfall and the Invasion of Japan, 1945–1947*, rev. ed. (Naval Institute Press: Annapolis, 2017), 291.

23. Martin Harwit, *An Exhibit Denied: Lobbying the History of the Enola Gay* (New York: Copernicus/Springer-Verlag, 1996), viii, 426.

24. Harwit, *An Exhibit Denied*, viii, 426.

25. Stewart Alsop, "The President and His Enemies," *Washington Post*, September 1, 1973, A14.

26. James Michener letter in Giangreco, *Hell to Pay*, 291.

27. James Michener letter in Giangreco, *Hell to Pay*, 291.

28. Laura Hein, "Remembering the Bomb: The Fiftieth Anniversary in the United States and Japan," *Bulletin of Concerned Asian Scholars*, 27 (April–June, 1995): esp. 4, 12.

29. Barton J. Bernstein, "A Postwar Myth: 500,000 Lives Saved," *Bulletin of the Atomic Scientists* 42 (June–July 1986): 38–40.

30. Robert P. Newman, *Truman and the Hiroshima Cult* (Lansing: Michigan State University Press, 1995); Maddox, *Weapons for Victory: The Hiroshima Decision Fifty Years Later* (Columbia: University of Missouri Press, 1995); Edward J. Drea, *MacArthur's ULTRA: Codebreaking and the War Against Japan, 1942–1945* (Lawrence: University Press of Kansas, 1992); Weintraub, *The Last Great Victory*; Thomas B. Allen and Norman Polmar, *Code-Name Downfall: The Secret Plan to Invade Japan and Why Truman Dropped the Bomb* (New York: Simon & Schuster, 1995).

31. Giangreco, "Casualty Projections," 521–81.

32. Giangreco, *Hell to Pay*, xxiv.

33. Arthur Schlesinger Jr. quote from a letter to the author, used with permission in *Wilson Quarterly* (Spring 2003): 92, and the *Journal of Military History* (January 2004): 334.

34. USSBS *Summary Report* (Tokyo: Civilian Defense Division, 1947), 26.

35. Robert P. Newman, *Enola Gay and the Court of History* (New York: Peter Lang, 2004), 31–43.

36. Alvin D. Coox, "Japanese Military Intelligence in the Pacific: Its Non-Revolutionary Nature," in *The Intelligence Revolution: A Historical Perspective*, ed. Walter Theodore Hitchcock (Washington DC, 1991), 200; and Drea, *MacArthur's ULTRA*, 202–25. See also Drea, "Previews of Hell: Intelligence, the Bomb, and the Invasion of Japan," *Military History Quarterly* 7 (Spring 1995): 74–81, which was published with extensive endnotes in Drea's *In the Service of the Emperor: Essays on the Imperial Japanese Army* (Lincoln: University of Nebraska Press, 1998) [hereafter *Emperor*] as chapter 11, "Intelligence Forecasting for the Invasion of Japan: Previews of Hell," 154–68. Also available in Maddox, *Hiroshima in History*, 59–75.

37. For a comprehensive examination of the issues involving Emperor Hirohito and the end of the Pacific War, see Herbert P. Bix, *Hirohito and the Making of Modern Japan* (New York: HarperCollins, 2000), 487–530. See also Sadao Asada, "The Shock of the Atomic Bomb and Japan's Decision to Surrender—A Reconsideration," *Pacific Historical Review* 67 (November 1998): 477–512.

38. Bix, *Hirohito and the Making of Modern Japan*, 487–530; Asada, "The Shock of the Atomic Bomb," 477–512; Richard B. Frank, *Downfall: The End of the Imperial Japanese Empire* (New York: Random House, 1999), 288–99.

39. The title of Barton J. Bernstein's article—which appears in *Pacific Historical Review* 68 (November 1999): 561–609—is self-explanatory: "The Alarming Japanese Buildup on Southern Kyushu, Growing US Fears, and Counterfactual Analysis: Would the Planned November 1945 Invasion of Southern Kyushu Have Occurred?" The Robert James Maddox response—in *Pacific Historical Review* 69 (May 2000): 349–50—notes that Bernstein's assertions are made "without any evidence" and that "he lards his prose instead with 'probably,' 'most probably,' and the like."

40. The notion that Truman no longer wanted Soviet participation in the war against Japan, obscurely posited by P. M. S. Blackett in the late 1940s and more famously by Gar Alperovitz in the 1960s, first appeared in the August 9, 1945, *New York Times* in the August 8 datelined article, "French Surprised by Russian Action." Speculation within the unbylined article filed in Paris is cited to unnamed "informed Frenchmen" and "French observers." It was published on page 5 of the edition that was put to bed after the Soviet declaration of war, yet before news had arrived that the Soviets had already invaded Manchuria.

41. Tsuyoshi Hasegawa, *Racing the Enemy: Stalin, Truman, and the Surrender of Japan* (Cambridge MA: Harvard University Press, 2005).

42. Robert H. Ferrell, from panel discussion "What Did They Know and When Did They Know It? Intelligence Assumptions before the Invasion of Japan," at the annual meeting of the Society for Military History, Pennsylvania State University, April 16, 1999. Ferrell's paper from this conference, "Intelligence Assessments and Assumptions: The View from Washington," is available in slightly modified form in his *Harry S. Truman and the Cold War Revisionists* (Columbia: University of Missouri Press, 2006) as chapter 2, "The Bomb—The View from Washington," 37–43.

43. Robert Maddox statement opening the Ferrell panel discussion.

44. Ferrell to author, September 10, 2002, memo; and telephone conversation circa March–April 2004. Ferrell was particularly aghast that a decades-old and long-refuted contention of Truman critic Gar Alperovitz in an October 29, 1988, letter to the *New York Times* that "dropping the atomic bomb was seen by analysts at the time as militarily unnecessary" continued to be widely referenced. Presented in the Alperovitz letter is an interesting collection of cherry-picked quotes from a variety of diary entries and memos by contemporaries of Truman, such as Dwight D. Eisenhower. All are outtakes and have been long rebutted, presented in their actual contexts, or found to be simply made-up stories. A chagrined Ferrell further pointed out that none of the "analysts" advised against using the bombs *before* their use.

45. Stanley Falk quoted in Giangreco, Pritzker Military Museum presentation, "Down the Memory Hole: America's Hidden Role in the Soviet Invasion of Manchuria," Chicago IL, June 14, 2018. Transcript available from History News Network, https://history-newsnetwork.org/article/169567.

46. Kai Bird, "The Curators Cave In," *New York Times*, October 9, 1994, sect. 4, 15.

47. "Roosevelt Urges Work-or-Fight Bill to Back Offensives," *New York Times*, January 18, 1945, sect. 1:1, 13; and "Letters on the Pressing Manpower Problem," sect. 1:13.

48. Kai Bird, "Retribution: The Battle for Japan, 1944–45," *Washington Post Book World*, April 20, 2008; and Zoom press briefing by Kai Bird with Gar Alperovitz and Martin Sherwin, "What Every Journalist Needs to Know About the A-Bombing of Hiroshima and Nagasaki," July 23 and 29, 2020. Links no longer active.

49. Bernstein, letter to author, April 1, 1996.

50. Bland, letter to author, September 19, 1998.

51. "JCS Corrigendum," 4–5.

1. The Manhattan Project

1. Merle Miller, *Plain Speaking: An Oral Biography of Harry S. Truman* (New York: Berkley, 1973, 1974), 165.

2. Robert H. Ferrell, *Harry S. Truman: A Life* (Newtown CT: American Political Biography Press, 2008), 155–61; Alonzo L. Hamby, *Man of the People: A Life of Harry S. Truman* (New York: Oxford University Press, 1995), 248–60; David McCullough, *Truman* (New York: Simon and Schuster, 1992), 256–91.

3. Giangreco and Kathryn Moore, *Dear Harry . . . Truman's Mailroom, 1945–1953: The Truman Administration Through Correspondence with "Everyday Americans"* (Mechanicsburg PA, 1999), 280–83, 289–93.

4. Giangreco and Moore, *Dear Harry*, 280.

5. Major General Frank Lowe to Brigadier General Harry Vaughn, December 2, 1950, restricted to "between you, The Boss [Truman], and me," President's Secretary's File, box 245, HSTLM.

6. Truman, diary entry, December 2, 1950, in Giangreco and Moore, *Dear Harry*, 474: "Now [MacArthur's] in serious trouble. We must get him out of it if we can. The conference [with Dean Acheson and Omar Bradley] was the most solemn one I've had since the Atomic Bomb conference in Berlin. We continue it in the morning. It looks very bad."

7. Memo to Mildred Dryden, December 2, 1943, HST Senate Papers, HSTLM.

8. Elmer Thomas, *Forty Years a Legislator* (Norman: University of Oklahoma Press, 2007), 127.

9. *Manhattan District History*, Book 1—General, vol. 4, Auxiliary Activities, chapter 1, "Legislative Contacts of Manhattan District" (Washington DC: U.S. Army Corps of Engineers, 1946), 2.6.

10. *Manhattan District History*, Book 1—General, vol. 4, 1.3.

11. *Manhattan District History*, Book 1—General, vol. 4, 2.5–6; Leslie R. Groves, *Now It Can Be Told: The Story of the Manhattan Project* (New York: Harper, 1962), 359–60.

12. Truman to Stimson, March 10, 1944, HSTLM.

13. Truman to Stimson, March 10, 1944, HSTLM.

14. Truman to Stimson, March 10, 1944, HSTLM.

15. Stimson to Truman, March 13, 1944, George C. Marshall Library (GCML), Lexington VA.

16. Groves, *Now It Can Be Told*, 365.

17. Thomas, *Forty Years a Legislator*, 127.

18. Thomas, *Forty Years a Legislator*, 129.

19. Stimson diary, March 13, 1944, Yale University Library. Truman had referenced their earlier telephone exchange in his letter and, unlike the stinging diary entry, Stimson's reply to Truman, when mentioning the call, displayed a much different tone: "I remember very well my pleasant talk with you on June 15, 1943, and your ready acquiescence in my request that you trust my assurance as to the character and importance of the Pasco Project, and to not make any investigation into it until this project be accomplished."

20. *Manhattan District History*, 1.2; Vincent C. Jones, *Manhattan: The Army and the Atomic Bomb*, series: *The United States Army in World War II* (hereafter, *USA WWII*) (Washington DC: Center of Military History, 1985), 31, 34, 39.

21. Jones, *Manhattan*, 46, 234.

22. Harry S. Truman, *Memoirs*, vol. 1, *Year of Decisions* (New York: Doubleday, 1955), 10.

23. Truman, *Memoirs*, 1:10–11.

24. Clark Clifford, *Counsel to the President* (New York: Random House, 1991), 57–58.

25. William D. Leahy, August 31, 1949, from interview notes by Jonathan Daniels at HSTLM, 13. The notes taken in preparation for his *The Man from Independence* (Philadelphia: Lippincott, 1950).

26. Truman, November 12, 1949, from interview notes by Jonathan Daniels at HSTLM, 67.

27. Jonathan Daniels Oral History Interview, October 4, 1963, by James R. Fuchs, HSTLM.

28. Lowe to Vaughn, December 2, 1950, HSTLM.

29. Ferrell, phone call to author, circa January 5, 2005, and letter to author, May 10, 2005.

30. Ferrell, letter to author, May 10, 2005.

31. Truman, *Memoirs*, 1:31.

32. James F. Byrnes, *All in One Lifetime* (New York: Harper, 1958), 282.

33. Ferrell, phone call to author, circa January 5, 2005.

2. Projects Milepost and Hula

Epigraph: Henry A. Wallace, *The Price of Vision: The Diary of Henry A. Wallace 1942–1946*, ed. John Morton Blum (Boston: Houghton Mifflin, 1973), 450–51.

1. Grew memorandum, June 14, 1945, *Foreign Relations of the United States* (hereafter *FRUS*), *Diplomatic Papers, 1945*, vol. 7, *The Far East, China* (Washington DC: United States Department of State, GPO, 1960), 901–3.

2. John Snyder, Sam Rosenman, and George Allen to Truman, July 6, 1945, *FRUS: Conference at Berlin*, 1:228.

3. *Truman in the White House: The Diary of Eben A. Ayers*, Robert H. Ferrell, ed. (Columbia: University of Missouri Press, 1991), 62.

4. Truman to Bess Truman, July 18, 1945, in *Dear Bess: The Letters from Harry to Bess Truman, 1910–1959*, ed. Robert H. Ferrell (New York: Norton, 1983), 519.

5. Minutes of meeting with Joint Chiefs and service secretaries, June 18, 1945, *FRUS: Conference at Berlin*, 1:909.

6. John R. Deane, *The Strange Alliance: The Story of Our Efforts at Wartime Cooperation with Russia* (New York: Viking, 1947), 227–28.

7. *Soviet Entry*. See also Robert W. Coakley and Richard M. Leighton, *Global Logistics and Strategy, 1943–1945*, in series *United States Army in World War II* (hereafter cited as *USA WWII*) (Washington DC: Center of Military History, United States Army, 1967), 671–99; and Boris N. Slavinsky, *Soviet Occupation of the Kuril Islands, August–September 1945* (Cambridge MA: Belfer Center for Science and International Affairs, Harvard Kennedy School of Government, 1997), 14–17.

8. *Soviet Entry*, 2; and Slavinsky, *Soviet Occupation*, 14–17. The informal suggestions were made in separate meetings with the ambassador on December 8, 1941, as both men tried to gauge the position of the Soviet government.

9. *Soviet Entry*, 2; Slavinsky, *Soviet Occupation*, 14–17.

10. In September 1941 a correspondent told Solomon Lozovsky that there was an item in the German press saying that their troops could already see Moscow with their binoculars. Lozovsky answered "with a laugh that the Germans would undoubtedly see Moscow, but as prisoners of war." Joshua Rubenstein and Vladimir P. Naumov, eds., *Stalin's Secret Pogrom: The Postwar Inquisition of the Jewish Anti-Fascist Committee* (New Haven: Yale University Press, in association with the United States Holocaust Memorial Museum, 2001), 186. Lozovsky was executed by Stalin in 1952. See also Slavinsky, *Soviet Occupation*, 14.

11. Jacob W. Kipp, *"To Break Japan's Spine" and "Milepost": U.S. Soviet Negotiations over Soviet Entry into the Pacific War, October 1944–February 1945* (Fort Leavenworth KS: Foreign Military Studies Office, 2000), 5, citing "Zaniat'sia Podgotovkoi Budushchego Mira" (Studying preparations for future war), *Istochnik* (The source), no. 4 (1995): 115.

12. Alvin D. Coox, *Nomonhan: Japan Against Russia, 1939*, 2 vols. (Stanford CA: Stanford University Press, 1985), 2:1–62; Coox, *The Year of the Tiger: Japan, 1937–1938* (Tokyo and Philadelphia: Orient/West Press, 1964), 25–65, esp. 27–30, 34–48, 53–54.

13. Edward J. Drea to author, October 27 and 28, 2016, citing Coox translation of Hata Ikuhiko's "The Japanese-Soviet Confrontation, 1935–1939," in *Deterrent Diplomacy: Japan, Germany and the USSR, 1935–1940*, ed. James William Morley (New York: Columbia University Press, 1976), table 1, 131. Soviet troop strength reached 570,000 Soviet troops in 1939. There were about 350,000 Japanese troops at that time.

14. *Soviet Entry*, 20; Hattori Takushiro, ed., *Japanese Special Study on Manchuria* (hereafter *JSSM*), vol. 1, *Japanese Operational Planning Against the USSR* (Tokyo: General Headquarters, U.S. Far East Command, 1955), 23–136; Coox, *The Unfought War: Japan 1941–1942* (San Diego: San Diego State University Press, 1992), 28; and Coox, *The Year of the Tiger*, 38, 150–51.

15. Hattori, *Japanese Special Study on Manchuria*, vol. 1; and Coox, *The Unfought War*, 31–35, 39–41. Drea to author, October 27, 2016, noted that during the 1941 "special maneuvers," Kwantung troop strength had climbed to some 750,000 men. See also Hattori, JSSM, *Strategic Study of Manchuria: Military, Typography and Geography*, vol. 3, part 1, 22–23, and vol. 3, part 4, 57–58. In the early 1940s Japanese planners became greatly concerned at indications that the Soviets were pressing construction of the Baikal-Amur Magistral (BAM) rail line north of the Trans-Siberian and were relieved when it became apparent that work on the BAM had stopped dead in its tracks because of terrain conditions, logistic realities, and manpower limitations (the limited availability of slave labor).

16. Coox, *The Unfought War*, 31–35, 39–41. See also Coox, "Restraints on Air Power in Limited War: Japan vs. USSR at Changkufeng, 1938," *Aerospace Historian* 18, no. 2 (December 1970): 118–26; Coox, "Changkufeng and the Japanese 'Threat' to Vladivostok, 1938," *Journal of Asian History* 5, no. 2 (1971): 119–39. Of particular significance is Coox, "Flawed Perception and Its Effect upon Operational Thinking: The Case of the Japanese Army, 1937–41," in *Intelligence and Military Operations*, Michael I. Handel, ed. (London and Portland: Frank Cass Publishers, 1990), 239–54. During this 1987 lecture, Coox noted that because of weather considerations Imperial General Headquarters "was warning that the point of no return" on a decision to attack the Soviet Union "would be August 10." He then recalled a conversation with Hattori Takashiro who served as its chief of the operations section: "You have all heard of the famous Japanese ability to achieve consensus—it is nowhere to be seen in the summer of 1941. I asked Hattori what his staff believed about going north or south, and he said that they were split 50–50. So I asked him, 'How did you vote?' And he said, 'I took the middle ground. I advocated readiness to go either way, and I didn't vote.'"

17. Deane, *Strange Alliance*, 227–28. See also Slavinsky, *Soviet Occupation*, 14–17.

18. Hattori, JSSM, vol. 1, 38–40, 77, 94–97, 111–28, 162; JSSM, *Typography and Geography*, vol. 3, part 1, 22–23, and vol. 3, part 4, 57–58.

19. October 17, 1944, meeting, FRUS: *Diplomatic Papers, Conversations at Malta and Yalta, 1945* (Washington DC: United States Department of State, GPO, 1955), 370–71; Deane, *Strange Alliance*, 247–48; and memo by second secretary of U.S. embassy Edward Page to Averell Harriman and Deane in Henry Harley Arnold Papers, Military File, 1913–1951, box 225, Manuscript Division, Library of Congress, Washington DC.

20. FRUS: *Malta and Yalta*, 370–71. In his "for the eyes of the President only" message to Roosevelt, Harriman used slightly simpler wording: "Break Japan's spine." Harriman reported: "General Deane and I had a long session this evening with Marshal Stalin and General Antonov on the subject of detailed planning for Soviet participation and cooperation in the Pacific war. Stalin gave us in considerably greater detail the Soviet strategy. . . . He generally approved our Chiefs of Staff's suggestions presented by Deane for Russian role in the war although he placed greater immediate emphasis on the action of his ground forces. . . . [Stalin] spoke emphatically about his determination to assist in ending the war quickly and said 'Break Japan's spine.'" See also Jacob W. Kipp and General Makhmut Akhmetevich Gareev, "'To Break the Back of Japan,' Soviet-American Cooperation and the War Against Japan: Lend-Lease and the Strategic Build-Up for the Manchurian Offensive of August 1945," presented at the annual meeting of the Society for Military History, Pennsylvania State University, April 16, 1999, 37–40.

21. Bland and Ritenour Stevens, *The Papers of George Catlett Marshall*, 4:568.

22. Page to Harriman and Deane in *Arnold Papers*, Military File, 1913–1951, box 225, Manuscript Division, Library of Congress. See also Kipp and Gareev, "'To Break the Back of Japan,'" 31–37.

23. Harriman to Roosevelt, October 15, 1944, and October 16, 1944, box 32, Map Room, Franklin D. Roosevelt Presidential Library and Museum (RPLM), Hyde Park NY; Kipp and Gareev, "'To Break the Back of Japan,'" 7–40, 52–59.

24. Because of the desperate need for trucks in the grinding battles west of the Urals it is possible, perhaps even probable, that before Milepost the Soviet's Far Eastern armies had even fewer trucks available to them than the five thousand spread throughout the region in 1938. Some four thousand of these were reputedly assigned to labor camps. Coox, "The Lesser of Two Hells: NKVD General G. S. Lyushkov's Defection to Japan, Part II," *Journal of Slavic Military Studies* 2, no. 4 (December 1998): 72–110, esp. 82.

25. Kipp and Gareev "'To Break the Back of Japan,'" 40–41; summary of "US Military Mission, Moscow, Russia, to Joint Chiefs of Staff," October 18, 1944, box 33, Map Room, RPLM.

26. Kipp and Gareev, "'To Break the Back of Japan,'" 39, 77–78, citing "Report by Senior Members of the Joint Planning Staff, Appendix B, Line of Supply to Siberia Via Pacific," 27, box 17, U.S. Military Mission to Moscow, ISC Papers, Record Group (RG) 334, entry 309, National Archives and Records Administration (NARA), College Park MD.

27. Kipp, *"To Break Japan's Spine" and "Milepost,"* 2, citing "Report on War Aid Furnished by the United States to the USSR," prepared by the Protocol and Area Information Staff of the USSR Branch and the Division of Research and Reports, November 28, 1945, 6, 14. See also Sergei Matveevich Shtemenko, *The Soviet General Staff at War: 1941–1945*, trans. Robert Daglish (Moscow: Progress Publishers, 1970), 324, 328–29, 336–37. As chief of the Soviet General Staff's Operations Directorate, General Shtemenko had accompanied Stalin to the Tehran Conference and had been responsible before the Moscow Conference for the formulation of the list of what Russia would need from the Americans in order to successfully prosecute the war against Japan. Shtemenko subsequently became one of the principal planners for the invasion of Manchuria and Southern Sakhalin.

28. Molotov to Japanese ambassador Sato Naotake, April 5, 1945, in Slavinsky, *The Japanese-Soviet Neutrality Pact: A Diplomatic History, 1941–1945*, translation and extensive notes by Geoffrey Jukes (New York: Routledge-Curzon, 2003), 152–53, citing *Ivzestia*, April 6, 1945; Shtemenko, *Soviet General Staff*, 336–37.

29. Hattori, *The Complete History of the Greater East Asia War* (Tokyo: Headquarters, 500th Military Intelligence Group, 1954), 4:289–90, translated from Hattori's *Daitoa senso zenshi* (Tokyo: Masu Shobo, 1953), 4:294–96.

30. Drea, "Missing Intentions," 66–73, esp. 68; Coox, *Nomonhan*, 1061–62; Hattori, *Greater East Asia War*, 4:212–14.

31. Drea, "Missing Intentions," 68.

32. JCS 1176, "Russian Participation in the War against Japan," November 23, 1944, and JCS 924/15 "Pacific Strategy" (formerly titled "Operations against Japan Subsequent to Formosa"), April 25, 1945.

33. *Soviet Entry*, 70.

34. JCS 1176, November 23, 1944, and as late as JCS 924/15, April 25, 1945.

35. Memorandum from Brigadier General George A. Lincoln to General George C. Marshall, June 14, 1945, reel 115, item 2656, National Archives Collection, GCML; also available in RG 165, NARA, and Vertical File, HSTLM.

36. Memorandum from General George C. Marshall to Lieutenant General Stanley D. Embick, October 3, 1944, in Bland Ritenour Stevens, *The Papers of George Catlett Marshall*, 4:235–36. See also Kipp and Gareev, "'To Break the Back of Japan,'" 18–19.

37. Message from Harriman to Marshall, November 2, 1943, in Forrest C. Pogue, *George C. Marshall: Organizer of Victory, 1943–1945* (New York: Viking Press, 1973), 291.

38. *Soviet Entry*, 28, 51–52; Colonel Paul L. Freeman Jr., War Department Operations Division, to Marshall, February 13, 1945, provides a summary of a post–Yalta Conference conversation with MacArthur. Similar comments were made to Brigadier General Lincoln from the Operations Division when he met with MacArthur on February 25. Memo, Lincoln to Marshall, March 8, 1945.

39. *Soviet Entry*, Freeman and Lincoln, 28, 51–52.

40. Deane, *Strange Alliance*, 265.

41. Kipp and Gareev, "'To Break the Back of Japan,'" 50, citing "War Game Third Phase," 2, box 12, U.S. Military Mission to Moscow, October 1943–October 1945, RG 334, entry 309, National Archives.

42. Deane to the Joint Chiefs of Staff, January 15, 1945, box 33, Map Room, RPLM.

43. *Soviet Entry*, 45.

44. Meeting, February 2, 1945, *Argonaut Conference, January–February 1945: Papers and Minutes of Meetings* (Office of the U.S. Secretary of the Combined Chiefs of Staff: Washington DC, 1945), 279–80.

45. Meeting, February 6, 1945, *FRUS: Malta and Yalta*, 839–41. See also *Soviet Entry*, 48–49.

46. Kipp to author, July 8, 2014, and July 19, 2016. This exchange is described in volume 3 of Admiral Kuznetsov's memoirs, *Kurs na podedu* (The course toward victory), in the chapter on Yalta. The distance between the La Perouse Strait and the inner zone of the American lake that the Philippine Sea had become is roughly equivalent to the expanse from New Orleans to Halifax.

47. Richard A. Russell, *Project Hula: Secret Soviet-American Cooperation in the War Against Japan*, no. 4 in *The U.S. Navy in the Modern World Series* (Washington DC: Naval Historical Center, Department of the Navy, 1997), 8–12, 33; Slavinsky, *Soviet Occupation*, 17–18, 52; Kipp and Gareev, "'To Break the Back of Japan,'" 44–47, 71; Budzbon, 23, 40–42, 47.

48. Details on the planning for, then cancellation of the Soviet occupation force and be found in Giangreco, *Hell to Pay*, 250–65.

3. Roosevelt, Stalin, and Poland

Epigraph: Charles E. Bohlen conference minutes, December 1, 1943, *FRUS: Diplomatic Papers, the Conferences at Cairo and Tehran, 1943, December 1, 1942*, doc. 378.

1. Harry S. Truman to Bess Truman, July 18, 1945. See also Ferrell, *Dear Bess*, 519.

2. Hopkins's memorandum of Roosevelt-Eden conversation, March 15, 1943, *FRUS: 1943*, 3:13–18.

3. Robert I. Gannon, *The Cardinal Spellman Story* (New York: Doubleday, 1962), 222–23.

4. Charles E. Bohlen conference minutes, December 1, 1943, *FRUS: Diplomatic Papers, the Conferences at Cairo and Tehran, 1943, December 1, 1942*, doc. 378.

5. Bohlen, *FRUS: The Conferences at Cairo and Tehran*, 378.

6. Kathryn Moore, *The American President* (New York: Sterling, 2018), 377.

7. John Lewis Gaddis, *The United States and the Origins of the Cold War: 1941–1947* (New York: Columbia University Press), 151.

8. Averell Harriman and Elie Abel, *Special Envoy to Churchill and Stalin: 1941–1946* (New York: Random House, 1975), 227.

9. Gannon, *Cardinal Spellman Story*, 222–23.

10. *FRUS: Cairo and Tehran*, December 1, 1942, doc. 378.

11. *FRUS: Cairo and Tehran*, December 1, 1942, doc. 378.

12. Harriman, *Special Envoy*, 345.

13. JCS 924, "Operations against Japan Subsequent to Formosa," June 30, 1944, and JCS 924/2, August 30, 1944, 120.

14. JCS 924/2, "Operations Against Japan Subsequent to Formosa," August 30, 1944, 120. The Saipan ratio was also used to project casualties for other proposed operations. For example, the OPD estimated that an invasion of Formosa would cost 88,600 American casualties, including approximately 16,000 dead, which Marshall rounded out to "approximately 90,000 casualties" in a September 1, 1944, memorandum for the Joint Strategic Survey Committee chief, General Stanley D. Embick. See Bland and Ritenour Stevens, *The Papers of George Catlett Marshall*, 4:567–69.

15. Harriman to Marshall, November 2, 1943, in Pogue, *George C. Marshall*, 291.

16. Harriman, *Special Envoy*, 343.

17. August 25, 1944, in Kimball, ed., *Churchill and Roosevelt: The Complete Correspondence*, vol. 3, *Alliance Declining, February 1994–April 1945* (Princeton NJ, 1984), 283.

18. August 25, 1944, in Kimball, *Churchill and Roosevelt*, 295.

19. Harriman, *Special Envoy*, 342.

20. August 26, 1944, in Kimball, *Churchill and Roosevelt*, 296.

21. August 25, 1944, in Harriman, *Special Envoy*, 344.

22. Memo, September 10, 1944, in Harriman, *Special Envoy*, 343–45. See also Deane, *Strange Alliance*, 241–51.

23. Harriman, *Special Envoy*, 351, September 23, 1944.

24. Deane, *Strange Alliance*, 233–39.

25. Harriman, *Special Envoy*, 351, September 2, 1944.

26. Dean, *Strange Alliance*, 241.

27. Meeting, October 17, 1944, *FRUS: Diplomatic Papers, Conversations at Malta and Yalta*, 370–71; Deane, *Strange Alliance*, 247–48; Harriman to Roosevelt, October 16, 1944, box 32, Map Room, RPLM; and memo by Second Secretary of U.S. Embassy Edward Page to Averell Harriman and Deane, box 225, Henry Harley Arnold Papers, Military File, 1913–1951, Manuscript Division, Library of Congress, Washington DC. In his "for the eyes of the President only" message to Roosevelt, Harriman used slightly simpler wording: "Break Japan's spine." See also Kipp and Gareev, "'To Break the Back of Japan,'" 37–40.

28. *FRUS: Malta and Yalta*, 370–71; Harriman to Roosevelt. October 15, 1944, Roosevelt Presidential Library and Museum (RPLM), Map Room, box 32.

29. Harriman, *Special Envoy*, 351, September 23, 1944, box 32, Map Room, RPLM.

30. October 17, 1944, in Dean, *Strange Alliance*, 248.

31. Harriman, *Special Envoy*, 364.

32. Harriman, *Special Envoy*, 371.

33. Harriman, *Special Envoy*, 371.

34. December 16 and December 19, 1944, in Dean, *Strange Alliance*, 259.

35. Elliot Richardson, conversation with author, spring 1978. Although the former U.S. attorney general and defense secretary was in Europe serving as a 4th Infantry Division combat medic in Belgium and Germany during this period (earning two Purple Hearts and a Bronze Star), his later government service provided him numerous opportunities to examine and discuss decisions being made far from his battalion. Discussions with the author and others that evening were wide ranging and included his soldiers-eye-view of the planned invasion of Japan (which he looked forward to: "I was young, gung-ho, and foolish"), naval matters, and his time as an editor and cartoonist at the *Harvard Lampoon*.

36. Memo, President Roosevelt to the secretary of state, Washington, January 5, 1945, *FRUS*, vol. 5, *1945, Europe*, 861.

37. *FRUS*, vol. 5, *1945, Europe*, 861.

38. Gaddis, *Origins of the Cold War*, 150–51.

39. Gaddis, *Origins of the Cold War*, 136, Hickerson later played role in the establishment of NATO and served as Assistant Sec State during the Korean War.

40. Hickerson memorandum to Stettinius, January 8, 1945, *FRUS: Malta and Yalta*, 94–96.

41. Hickerson to Stettinius, January 8, 1945, *FRUS: Malta and Yalta*, 94–96.

42. Hickerson to Stettinius, January 8, 1945, *FRUS: Malta and Yalta*, 94–96.

43. H. Freeman Matthews notes, 3rd plenary meeting, February 6, 1945, *FRUS: Malta and Yalta*, 677–78.

44. Matthews notes, February 6, 1945, *FRUS: Malta and Yalta*, 677–78.

45. Yalta Conference communiqué, February 12, 1945, *FRUS: Malta and Yalta*, 977–78.

46. Gaddis, *Origins of the Cold War*, 165–66.

47. Gaddis, *Origins of the Cold War*, 165–66.

48. William D. Leahy, *I Was There: The Personal Story of the Chief of Staff to Presidents Roosevelt and Truman Based on His Notes and Diaries Made at the Time* (New York: Whittlesey House, 1950), 315–16.

49. Leahy, *I Was There*, 318; *FRUS: Malta and Yalta*, 984. See also Gaddis, *Origins of the Cold War*, 157–73.

4. A New President

Epigraph: Truman, *Memoirs*, 1:264.

1. Harriman, *Special Envoy*, 452; Leahy, *I Was There*, 315–16.

2. Edward R. Stettinius Jr., *Stettinius, Roosevelt and the Russians: The Yalta Conference* (New York: Doubleday, 1950), 318; Harriman, *Special Envoy*, 400.

3. Leahy, *I Was There*; Elsey, 21, 23, 84–86; Harriman, *Special Envoy*, 399–400, *FRUS: Malta and Yalta*, 984.

4. Wilson D. Miscamble, *From Roosevelt to Truman: Potsdam, Hiroshima, and the Cold War* (New York: Cambridge University Press, 2007), 77–78, 82–85, 90–91; Harriman, *Special Envoy*, 436–41; Gaddis, *Origins of the Cold War*, 92–94, 197.

5. Harriman, *Special Envoy*, 452–53; Miscamble, *Roosevelt to Truman*, 124–27, 139–43.

6. Truman, *Memoirs*, 1:227–28; Miscamble, *Roosevelt to Truman*, 133–35. A dated but still useful look at the state of Lend-Lease aid during this period can be found in George

C. Herring Jr., *Aid to Russia 1941–1946: Strategy, Diplomacy, and Origins of the Cold War* (New York: Columbia University Press, 1973), 214–24.

7. Stettinius to Grew, May 9, 1945, *FRUS: 1945*, 5:998.

8. Charles Robbins, *Last of His Kind: An Informal Portrait of Harry S. Truman* (New York: William Morrow, 1979), 117–18.

9. Stimson, "The Decision to Use the Atomic Bomb," 99.

10. Stimson, "The Decision to Use the Atomic Bomb," 99–100.

11. Stimson, "The Decision to Use the Atomic Bomb," 99–100. Along with Stimson as chairman, future secretary of state James F. "Jimmy" Byrnes acted as Truman's personal representative; George L. Harrison, the president of New York Life and Stimson's special assistant on matters related to "s-1" (a code name for the atom bomb); Under Secretary of the Navy Ralph Bard; Assistant Secretary of State William Clayton; the director of the Office of Scientific Research and Development and president of the Carnegie Institution of Washington, Dr. Vannevar Bush; the chief of the Office of Scientific Research and Development and president of the Massachusetts Institute of Technology, Dr. Karl T. Compton; and Dr. James B. Conant, chairman of the National Defense Research Committee and president of Harvard University. Known as the Interim Committee on s-1, the body also contained a scientific panel made up of four Manhattan Project physicists: Enrico Fermi, Ernest O. Lawrence, Arthur H. Compton, and J. Robert Oppenheimer.

12. Ray S. Cline, *Washington Command Post: The Operations Division, USA WWII* series (Washington DC: Center of Military History, United States Army, 1951), 347; "Artificial Harbor," in "Staff Study Operations, CORONET," annex 4, appendix H; and additional details in Martin Halliwell, "The Projected Assault on Japan," *Royal United Service Institution Journal (RUSI)*, August 1947, 348–51.

13. Cline, *Washington Command Post*, 340.

14. Shelby L. Stanton, *Order of Battle, U.S. Army, World War II* (Novato CA: Presidio Press, 1984), see individual division synopses and the chart on page 603; and Giangreco, *Hell to Pay*, 1–10, 38–42, 51–56.

15. Coakley and Leighton, *Global Logistics and Strategy*, 585, 588.

16. *FRUS: Berlin*, 1:6.

17. *FRUS: Berlin*, 1:8.

18. *FRUS: Europe*, 4:1157–58.

19. *FRUS: Berlin*, 1:10.

20. *FRUS: Berlin*, 1:6. British military casualties by the end of 1944 had surpassed 635,000 with the empire as a whole totaling more than 1,043,000, a figure that surpassed U.S. combat casualties to date, "Casualties," *Yank* 3 (February 2, 1945): 17. See also *United Kingdom, Central Statistical Office, Statistical Digest of the War* (London: HMSO and Longmans Green, 1951), 11, 13.

21. Gaddis, *Origins of the Cold War*, 206.

22. Giangreco, *Hell to Pay*, chapter 4, "The Pacific Build-up and Berlin Decision," 38–50.

23. *FRUS: Berlin*, 1:11.

24. *Army Battle Casualties and Nonbattle Deaths in World War II, Final Report, 7 December 1941–31 December 1946* (Washington DC: Office of the Adjutant General, 1987), 6.

25. Stimson diary, January 11, 1945.

26. "Roosevelt Urges Work-or-Fight Bill to Back Offensives," *New York Times*, January 18, 1945, sect. 1:1, 13; and "Letters on the Pressing Manpower Problem," sect. 1:13.

27. Palmer, Wiley, and Keast, *Procurement and Training of Ground Combat Troops*, 221–25.

28. "How Long Will We Have to Fight the Jap War?" *Yank* 3 (June 8, 1945): 2.

29. JCS 924/2, "Operations against Japan Subsequent to Formosa," August 30, 1944, 120.

30. *Selective Service and Victory: The 4th Report of the Director of Selective Service, July 1, 1944 to December 31, 1945* (Washington DC: Government Printing Office, 1946), 55–56.

31. In addition to newspapers of the day, see also John D. Chappell, *Before the Bomb: How America Approached the End of the Pacific War* (Lexington: University Press of Kentucky, 1997).

32. See Wayne S. Cole, *Charles A. Lindbergh and the Battle against American Intervention in World War II* (New York: Harcourt Brace Jovanovich, 1974); Justus D. Doenecke, *Storm on the Horizon: The Challenge to American Intervention, 1939–1941* (Lanham MD: Rowman and Littlefield, 2000); Manfred Jonas, *Isolationism in America, 1935–1941* (Ithaca NY: Cornell University Press, 1966); and Garet Garrett, *Defend America First: The Antiwar Editorials of the Saturday Evening Post, 1939–1942* (Caldwell ID: Caxton Press, 2003).

33. Maurice Matloff, "The 90-division Gamble," in *Command Decisions, USA WWII* (Washington: 1960), 365–81, esp. 376; and *Provision of Enlisted Replacements*, study no. 7, Historical Section, Army Ground Forces (AGF), 1946, 23–24.

34. Undated and untitled May 15, 1945, memorandum by Hoover and accompanying June 1, 1945, memorandum from Major General Thomas T. Handy to Lieutenant General John E. Hull, item 2656, reel 115, National Archives Collection, GCML. For Hoover's cover letter to the undated and untitled paper, see Hoover to Stimson, May 15, 1945, in Henry Lewis Stimson Papers (microfilm edition, reel 12).

35. Undated and untitled, May 15, 1945, memorandum by Hoover and accompanying June 1, 1945, memorandum from Major General Thomas T. Handy to Lieutenant General John E. Hull, item 2656, reel 115, National Archives Collection, GCML. For Hoover's cover letter to the undated and untitled paper, see Hoover to Stimson, May 15, 1945, in Henry Lewis Stimson Papers (microfilm edition, reel 12). Emphasis in original of General Handy memo.

36. Giangreco, *Hell to Pay*, 62–66.

37. Truman to Bess Wallace, July 14, 1917, HSTLM.

38. Truman to Henry A. Wallace after the May 18 cabinet meeting in Wallace, *The Price of Vision*, 451. This was not discussed in front of other cabinet members, as most of them were not authorized to know about top secret military projects such as Manhattan and Milepost. Even the codenames themselves were not used except when absolutely necessary. For example, among select colleagues and in his diary, Secretary Stimson referred to Manhattan as "S-1." Similarly, Stimson's vague references to Milepost as "the Fourth Protocol," and especially "the Special Russian Project," not only can be found in certain levels of memoranda but even in communications with President Roosevelt.

39. FRUS: Europe, 4:1169–70.

40. "Stimson, Henry L., 1945–1950" and "Truman, Harry S., 1945," Post Presidential Individual File, Hoover Papers, Hoover Library; President's Secretary's Files (PSF), Truman Library. See also Timothy Walch and Dwight M. Miller, eds., *Herbert Hoover and Harry S. Truman: A Documentary History* (Worland WY: High Plains Publishing , 1992), 37.

41. This was described by the British ambassador to Washington as an "acute nervousness in responsible circles and amongst the public generally," and he reported that

"the question was being asked whether Mr. Roosevelt's grand design is not in the process of evaporation." In Miscamble, *From Roosevelt to Truman*, 145; British ambassador to Washington Lord Halifax to Foreign Office, May 23, 1945 (no. 3602), Eden: Foreign Secretaries Papers, Main Library Special Collections, University of Birmingham, UK. See also Gaddis, *Origins of the Cold War*, 206.

42. Harriman, *Special Envoy*, 463. Harriman notes that Davies's "personal record of sympathy for Stalin's Russia was written large in his [1941] book, *Mission to Moscow*, and the motion picture based upon it." Truman himself later wrote that Davies was "at that time a Russophile as most of us were." Truman diary, April 8, 1957.

43. Miscamble, *From Roosevelt to Truman*, 146–53.

44. Harriman, *Special Envoy*, 463.

45. Memo, May 23, 1945, Truman Longhand Notes—Presidential File, box 281, Harry S. Truman Papers: President's Secretary's File, HSTLM.

46. Gaddis, *Origins of the Cold War*, 150–51.

47. Gaddis, *Origins of the Cold War*, 224–30; Miscamble, *From Roosevelt to Truman*, 140–43.

48. JCS 1176, "Russian Participation in the War against Japan," November 23, 1944, and JCS 924/15, "Pacific Strategy" (formerly titled "Operations against Japan Subsequent to Formosa"), April 25, 1945.

49. Harriman, *Special Envoy*, 461–62. In Stimson's letter to Joseph Grew, the secretary of war essentially restated what he had been briefed by the army.

50. Harriman, *Special Envoy*, 464.

51. Harriman, *Special Envoy*, 467.

52. Truman diary, September 28, 1945.

53. Truman, *Memoirs*, 1:264.

5. Truman's White House Meeting

Epigraph: Harry S. Truman to Bess Truman, June 17, 1945, in *Off the Record: The Private Papers of Harry S. Truman*, Robert H. Ferrell, ed. (New York: Harper & Row, 1980), 47.

1. Walch and Miller, *Herbert Hoover and Harry S. Truman*, 35.

2. Giangreco and Moore, *Dear Harry*, 34, 141–44, 400–406, 416–21, 432–33.

3. Walch and Miller, *Herbert Hoover and Harry S. Truman*, 37.

4. Walch and Miller, *Herbert Hoover and Harry S. Truman*, 43–53, esp. 50–53.

5. In addition to Bernstein's "A Postwar Myth," 39, where the author of the memorandum is referred to as a "layman" instead of by name or former occupation, other examples include works from Frank, *Downfall*, 133; Gar Alperovitz, *The Decision to Use the Atomic Bomb and the Architecture of an American Myth* (New York: Alfred A. Knopf, 1995), 43–45, 350–51, 520; and many others.

6. The original copy of Hoover's "Memorandum on Ending the Japanese War" (memo 4 of 4, May 30, 1945) with Truman's notation, the White House retypes/carbon copies of this document, and the subsequent exchange of memos among Truman, Grew, Cordell Hull, Stimson, and Vinson are under State Dept., WWII in box 43 of the White House Confidential File (WHCF), Truman Library.

7. Grew to Rosenman, June 16, 1945, in Stimson Safe File "Japan," RG 107, NA. The lack of a cover letter for the carbon copy of Grew's memo to Rosenman in Stimson's possession suggests that memo 4 was also personally discussed by Stimson and Grew.

8. Stimson diary entry, June 11, 1945, Stimson Diaries (microfilm edition reel 9), Stimson Papers, from microfilm at Truman Library; Grew to Rosenman, Stimson "Safe File."

9. Cordell Hull and Grew memos in WHCF, Truman Library.

10. Grew to Rosenman, Stimson Safe File "Japan."

11. Daily Sheets, May 28, 1945, Truman's Appointments File, PSF, HSTLM; and Joseph C. Grew, *Turbulent Era: A Diplomatic Record of Forty Years, 1904–1945*, 2 vols. (Boston: Houghton Mifflin, 1952), 2:1429.

12. Daily Sheets, June 13, 1945, Truman's Appointments File, PSF, HSTLM.

13. Grace Person Hayes, *The History of the Joint Chiefs of Staff in World War II: The War Against Japan* (Annapolis MD, 1982), 706. This source originated as a classified document generated in 1953 by the Historical Section, JCS.

14. Leahy to JCS members Marshall, Henry H. Arnold, and Ernest J. King; Secretary of War Stimson; and Secretary of the Navy James Forrestal, memo SM-2141, June 14, 1945, in *Soviet Entry*, 76.

15. Leahy to JCS members, *Soviet Entry*, 76.

16. Truman to Stimson, original in Stimson "Safe File," NA; copy in Vertical File, HSTLM.

17. National Archives Collection, reel 115, item 2656, GCML. Also available in RG 165, NA, and Vertical File, HSTLM.

18. Handy to Hull, June 1, 1945, National Archives Collection, GCML. Emphasis in original.

19. Coox, "Japanese Military Intelligence in the Pacific," 200; Drea, *MacArthur's ULTRA*, 202–25. See also Drea, "Previews of Hell," 74–81.

20. "Amendment No. 1 to G-2 Estimate of the Enemy Situation with Respect to Kyushu," G-2, AFPAC, July 29, 1945, call no. N6377, CARL. See also Giangreco, "Casualty Projections," 574–77.

21. Giangreco and Moore, *Dear Harry*, 282–90.

22. Stimson "Safe File" Japan (after 7/41), box 8, Records of the Secretary of War, RG 107, NARA. The full text, minus the cover letter was later published in Stimson, "The Decision to Use the Atomic Bomb." First, second, and final drafts in Stimson "Safe File."

23. *Army Battle Casualties*. The final total of U.S. Army and Army Air Force battle casualties stands at 945,515. Also part of the wartime totals were a minimum of 201,937 battle casualties for members of the U.S. Navy, Marine Corps, Coast Guard, and Merchant Marine. See Giangreco, "Casualty Projections," note on 540.

24. Many scholars who have studied the 1945 invasion planning and related casualty estimates have given undue and misleading emphasis to the plethora of staff comments and briefing papers that had no effect within the army hierarchy or on the War Department's manpower policy for that year. See, for example, John Ray Skates, *The Invasion of Japan: Alternative to the Bomb* (Columbia: University of South Carolina Press, 1994), 77–80; J. Samuel Walker, *Prompt and Utter Destruction: Truman and the Use of Atomic Bombs Against Japan* (Chapel Hill: University of North Carolina Press, 1997), 38–39, n12, 116–19; Rufus E. Miles Jr., "Hiroshima: The Strange Myth of Half a Million Lives Saved," *International Security* 10 (Fall 1985): 121–40, esp. 133–38; Barton Bernstein, "Reconsidering Truman's Claim of 'Half a Million American Lives' Saved by the Atomic Bomb: The Construction and Deconstruction of a Myth," *Journal of Strategic Studies* 22 (March 1999): 54–95, esp. 61–64. Errors in the above are due largely to their authors' lack of understanding of how planning documents are created, connected, and used. One notable exception is Richard B. Frank's *Down-*

fall. Although the author focuses on materials generated long after the relevant manpower decisions were made and implemented, Frank demonstrates a far better grasp of the factors affecting casualty projection analysis than has been displayed in other book-length works.

25. JCS 1388/4, "Details of the Campaign against Japan," July 11, 1945; Marshall's remarks and extracts of the President's meeting with the JCS, Stimson, and Forrestal in the June 18, 1945, "Joint Chiefs of Staff Corrigendum to JCS 1388," Records of the Joint Chiefs of Staff: Part 1, 1942–1943: The Pacific Theater, reel 2, CARL.

26. House Subcommittee on Appropriations, *Hearings on the Military Establishment Appropriations Bill for 1946, conducted 25 May 1945,* 79 Cong., 1 Sess. (1945), 1–18. During the appearances of both Marshall and Stimson, testifying separately before Congress, transcripts indicate that they went off the record when they ventured into this highly charged manpower question. Private discussions of the matter with legislators at the Pentagon and in Stimson's office were also not recorded. Only many years later did references to what was discussed surface in other congressional testimony. Aside from his off-the-record testimony before the House Appropriations Committee during discussion of the "inadvisability of war of attrition" and elsewhere, Marshall spoke of "the terrific losses which we would sustain when we invaded Japan" before the House Military Affairs Committee. See the transcript of Charles E. Bohlen's testimony before the Senate Foreign Relations Committee on March 2, 1953, in Charles E. Bohlen, *Witness to History: 1929–1969* (New York: W.W. Norton, 1973), 317.

27. A much-quoted example is Bernstein, "A Postwar Myth," 38–40. Other versions of this article were published under the titles "The Myth of Lives Saved by A-Bombs," *Los Angeles Times,* July 28, 1985; and "The Bombing Did Not Save Lives," *Nuclear Arms 1985 Supplement* (St. Paul MN, 1986), 139.

28. Leahy to JCS, June 14, 1945.

29. Truman diary entry, June 17, 1945, PSF, HSTLM. See also Ferrell, *Off the Record,* 47.

30. Memorandum for the president in JWPC 369/1, "Details of the Campaign against Japan," June 15, 1945; JCS 1388, "Details of the Campaign against Japan," June 16, 1945, call no. N20903.1, CARL.

31. JWPC 369/1.

32. While the JWPC estimated thirty thousand battle casualties for the first thirty days, the navy's estimate for the same period was forty-nine thousand in "Joint Staff Study: Olympic, Naval and Amphibious Operations, Commander-in-Chief, U.S. Pacific Fleet and Pacific Ocean Areas (CINCPOA)," June 18, 1945, 70, call no. R11623, CARL. Admiral King's effort to get this figure into the detailed outline of invasion plans then being produced for the president's use at the upcoming Potsdam Conference (JCS 1388/4) was rebuffed by Marshall (see JCS 1388/1-/2-/3), who stated that it was "unnecessary and undesirable for the Joint Chiefs of Staff to make estimates which can be at best only speculative." The unused JWPC estimates for total ground-force battle casualties from both operations Olympic and Coronet were 193,500, including 43,500 killed and missing—roughly that of the first four months of American battle casualties in France.

33. Memorandum to Lt. Gen. John E. Hull from Brig. Gen. George A. Lincoln, June 16, 1945, microfilm: "GHQ, SWPA, 1941–1945: Chronological Index and Summary of Communications," University Publications of America, reel 12, courtesy Edward J. Drea.

34. Quote in Gilbert W. Beebe and Michael E. DeBakey, *Battle Casualties: Incidence, Mortality and Logistic Considerations* (Springfield IL: Charles C. Thomas, 1952), 13. Dr.

Michael DeBakey, who would later become well known for his work in cardiovascular and heart surgery, was then an army colonel and the Surgical Branch chief of the Medical Corps' Consultants Division. He and Captain Gilbert W. Beebe, PhD, MD, edited the classified War Department bulletin *Health* and produced the analyses that were the basis of many of the casualty projections then emanating from the Army's Operations Division for the invasion of Japan.

35. This table was derived from the DeBakey and Beebe material in *Health*, May 31, 1945, 15.

36. War Department transmissions w-17477 and w-18528; Commander in Chief, Army Forces, Pacific (CINCAFPAC) transmissions c-19571 and c-19848, box 17, War Department messages no. 1001 to 1095, April 29–August 2, RG 4, MacArthur Memorial Archive, Norfolk VA; and memorandum, Lincoln to John Hull, June 15, 1945, microfilm "GHQ, SWPA," courtesy Edward J. Drea. For a detailed analysis of this exchange, see Giangreco, "Casualty Projections," 545–50.

37. Extracts from the June 18, 1945, meeting here and below are from "JCS Corrigendum to JCS 1388."

38. Memorandum, Lincoln to John Hull, June 18, 1945, microfilm "GHQ, SWPA," courtesy Edward J. Drea. Readers may better grasp the phraseology in this memo as well as the significance of the Marshall-JWPC wording if they know that, although the month-long siege of Manila ended on March 3, 1945, Luzon remained the scene of intense fighting until the surrender of Japan. Further airborne and amphibious operations on Luzon were only days away when Truman met with the JCS and service secretaries. See Rafael Steinberg, *USA WWII, Return to the Philippines* (1979), 176–93.

39. "U.S. Tenth Army Action Report, Ryukyus, 26 March to 30 June 1945," vol. 1, chap. 11, sec. 1, 12, call no. N11432, CARL; Huber, *Japan's Battle for Okinawa*, 119–20. See also Giangreco, "Casualty Projections," 539–40.

40. "JCS Corrigendum," 2.

41. "JCS Corrigendum," 3. The statement that "the problem would be much more difficult than it had been in Germany" is telling. It is supported by the follow-up statement that "the operation would be difficult but not more so than the assault in Normandy," which saw incremental advances through the tangled hedgerow country as American forces positioned themselves for a breakout from the Normandy Peninsula. Excluding the considerable number of "other losses," there were 133,316 American and 92,003 British battle casualties during the Normandy campaign, which took place from June 6 through August 31, 1944. American casualties are from *Army Battle Casualties*, 32; the British total is from L. F. Ellis with A. E. Warhurst et al., *Victory in the West*, United Kingdom Military Series (London: HMSO, 1962), 1:488, 493.

42. "JCS Corrigendum," 4.

43. "U.S. Tenth Army Action Report," vol. 1, chap. 11, sec. 1, 12; Huber, *Japan's Battle for Okinawa*, 119–20; and Giangreco, "Casualty Projections," 539–40.

44. The figure of sixty-three thousand was ultimately adopted by the National Air and Space Museum, at the insistence of Barton Bernstein, as the total number of casualties expected by the U.S. military during the invasion of Japan. Use of this artificially low figure further inflamed veterans' passions during the Enola Gay controversy and contributed directly to Harwit's dismissal. See Harwit, *An Exhibit Denied*, 345–46, 380.

45. Diary entry, June 18, 1945, William D. Leahy Diaries, 1897–1956 (microfilm edition reel 4), interlibrary loan, Naval War College, Newport RI to CARL. See also Leahy, *I Was There*, 384.

46. Marshall's figure of 766,700 differs only slightly from that of MacArthur's headquarters, which gave 766,986 as the number of men to be landed within a month and a half of the invasion in "Staff Study, 'Olympic,' Operations in Southern Kyushu," May 28, 1945, appendix B, annex 4, Commander in Chief, Army Forces, Pacific, call nos. N11619 and N11619-B, CARL.

47. For Leahy's frequent accompaniment of Truman, see George M. Elsey, letter to author, March 30, 1997. See also Elsey's lengthy introduction to "Blueprints for Victory," *National Geographic*, May 1995, 55–77, for information on their visits to the White House Map Room. See also Elsey, *An Unplanned Life: A Memoir by George McKee Elsey* (Columbia: University of Missouri Press, 2005), 80–82, 89, 99. Quote in "JCS Corrigendum," 4.

48. "JCS Corrigendum," 5.

6. "I've Gotten What I Came For"

Epigraph: "Details of the Campaign against Japan," 5, in Joint Chiefs of Staff Corrigendum to JCS 1388.

1. Jones, *Manhattan*, 516–17, based on eyewitness and other reports on the Trinity test.

2. Brigadier General Thomas Farrell report on the Trinity test in Jones, *Manhattan*, 516. This report was included in the Groves to Stimson memorandum of July 18, 1945, that was read by Truman at Potsdam.

3. Truman diary entry, July 17, 1945, PSF, HSTLM. See also Ferrell, *Off the Record*, 53.

4. Truman to Bess, July 18, 1945, Ferrell, *Dear Bess*, 519.

5. Truman diary, June 17, 1945. See also Ferrell, *Off the Record*, 47.

6. Wesley Frank Craven and James Lea Cate, *The Army Air Forces in World War II* (7 vols., Chicago, 1953), insert between pages in 5:703–32. On the timing for the release of the press statement see Elsey, *An Unplanned Life*, 90. For accounts of the training, forward basing, and mission see Paul W. Tibbits, *Flight of the Enola Gay* (Columbus OH: Mid Coast Publishing, 1997), and Suzanne Simon Dietz, *My True Course: Dutch Van Kirk Northumberland to Hiroshima* (Lawrenceville GA: Red Gremlin Press, 2012). For a comprehensive history on the U.S. Army and Army Air Forces role in the development and use of the atomic bombs see Jones, *Manhattan*.

7. E. B. Potter, *Nimitz* (Annapolis MD: Naval Institute Press, 1976), 382.

8. Truman, *Memoirs*, 1:415.

9. Jones, *Manhattan*, 534.

10. "Statement by the President of the United States, Immediate Release, August 6, 1945," HSTLM.

11. Tominaga Kengo, ed., *Gendaishi shiryo* (Documents on contemporary history), vol. 39, *Taiheiyo senso* (Pacific War), vol. 5 (Tokyo: Misuzu shobo, 1975), 5:756, in Asada, "The Shock of the Atomic Bomb," esp. 491–94. Asada noted that there are forty-five volumes in *Gendaishi shiryo*, of which five are on the Pacific War. See also Frank, *Downfall*, 288–99.

12. Truman, *Memoirs*, 1:314.

13. *Soviet Entry*, 72.

14. *FRUS: The Conference in Berlin*, 2:43–47.

15. Truman, *Memoirs*, 1:411.

16. Wilson D. Miscamble, *The Most Controversial Decision: Truman, the Atomic Bombs, and the Defeat of Japan* (New York: Cambridge University Press, 2011), 54–78, esp. 57–60. Here, Miscamble provides a clear assessment on how these matters were interwoven. He also addresses how, due to the successful Trinity test, Byrnes's thinking regarding the Soviets shifted back and forth at Potsdam. Although by the middle of the conference Byrnes seemed to think that the United States might be able to "get the Japanese affair over before the Russians got in" (*Forrestal Diaries* [Viking Press, 1951], 78), he soon came to the same conclusion that the U.S. Army had been reiterating since the Moscow Conference war games of late 1944: that the Soviets could do virtually anything they wanted (within the limits of their manpower and supplies, the latter constraint being an area that we had just gone a tremendous way toward eliminating through the Milepost Project).

17. Truman, *Memoirs*, 1:411.

18. Shtemenko, *Soviet General Staff*, 347.

19. "JCS Corrigendum," 7.

20. "Army-Navy Central Agreement Concerning the Ketsu-Go Air Operation," in Hattori, *Greater East Asia War* 4:164, 191. For the impact that the formation of Kamikaze units had on readiness in the conventional force "faced in performing their air defense mission [due to] taskings that curtailed such operations in order to build up and plan for the expected invasion," see *Japanese Monograph No. 17*, "Homeland Operations Record," (Tokyo: U.S. Army Forces Far East, Military History Section, 1959), 122–26, 160. See also 14, 31–32, 46, 80–81 in *Japanese Monograph No. 17*; and USSBS, no. 72, vol. 2, *Interrogations of Japanese Officials*, Naval Analysis Division, USSBS, Tokyo, 1946, Adm. Soemu Toyoda, 2:318, and Vice Adm. Shigeru Fukudome, 2:504.

21. Memo in Stimson, "The Decision to Use the Atomic Bomb," 102–4.

22. Stimson, "The Decision to Use the Atomic Bomb," 102.

23. In an August 9, 1943, memorandum from Marshall to Handy, Marshall recounted that President Roosevelt had told him that "planners were always conservative and saw all the difficulties, and that more could usually be done than they were willing to admit" (Bland and Stevens, *The Papers of George Catlett Marshall*, 4:85).

24. Oral history interview with Lt. Gen. John E. Hull (no interviewer cited), April 8, 1974, 22, Senior Officer Oral History Program, vol. 2, sect. 7, tape 1, United States Army Military History Institute, Carlisle Barracks PA.

25. Craven and Cate, *The Army Air Forces in World War II*, insert between pages in 5:712–13.

26. Bird, "The Curators Cave In," 15.

27. Barton Bernstein to the editor, *Journal of Military History*, 63 (Jan. 1999): 247; and Bernstein, "Truman and the Bomb: Targeting Noncombatants, Using the Bomb, and Defending the 'Decision,'" in *Journal of Military History*, 62 (July 1998): 552. Emphasis in originals. In a letter to the editor in *Pacific Historical Review* 69 (2000): 352, Bernstein maintains: "There is no reliable evidence that in mid-1945 [Truman] anticipated 500,000 or a million U.S. casualties."

28. Ferrell maintains in "Intelligence Assessments and Assumptions" that, since Truman was presiding officer of the Senate and, presumably, a reader of the *New York Times*, "large military call-ups had to come to [Truman's] attention for they were politically sen-

sitive." See D. M. Giangreco and Kathryn Moore, "Half a Million Purple Hearts," *American Heritage* 51 (Dec. 2000): 81–83.

29. Bernstein, "Truman and the Bomb," 551, 153; Barton Bernstein, "Writing, Righting, or Wronging the Historical Record: President Truman's Letter on His Atomic-Bomb Decision," *Diplomatic History* 16 (1992): 171. Emphasis in originals.

30. Giangreco and Moore, *Dear Harry*, 466–76. The first printing of this book contains an error in the endnotes to these pages. Endnotes 8 to 13 should be renumbered 9 to 14, and the printed endnote 14 removed.

31. William M. Rigdon, "Log of the President's Trip to the Berlin Conference, 6 July 1945 to 7 August 1945," 23, HSTLM.

32. Winston Churchill memorandum of conversation, July 18, 1945, *Documents on British Policies Overseas*, 3 vols. (London: 1984), 1:291. See also Truman diary entry, December 2, 1950. In the midst of China's stunning entry into the Korean War and the grim conflict with MacArthur over the direction of military strategy and foreign policy, the president wrote: "Now [MacArthur's] in serious trouble. We must get him out if we can. The conference [with Dean Acheson and General Omar Bradley] was the most solemn one I've had since the Atomic Bomb conference in Berlin. We continue in the morning. It looks very bad." Giangreco and Moore, *Dear Harry*, 474. This private reference to an A-bomb-related meeting at Potsdam was penned two years before Truman's letter to Professor James Lea Cate who, with Wesley Frank Craven, was writing the multivolume *The Army Air Forces in World War II.*

33. Winston Churchill, *Triumph and Tragedy* (Boston: Houghton Mifflin, 1953), 592–93.

34. Bernstein, "Truman and the Bomb," 553.

35. Robert James Maddox, from "What Did They Know?" See also Maddox, *Weapons for Victory*.

36. In addition to Bernstein, "Truman and the Bomb," see also Bernstein's "The Alarming Japanese Buildup on Southern Kyushu, Growing U.S. Fears, and Counterfactual Analysis"; Bernstein, "Reconsidering 'Invasion Most Costly': Popular History Scholarship, Publishing Standards, and the Claim of High U.S. Casualty Estimates to Help Legitimize the Atomic Bombings," *Peace and Change* 24 (1999): 220–47; Bernstein, "Reconsidering Truman's Claim," 54–95.

37. McCullough, *Truman*, 554. Although this quote can be found in David McCullough's 1992 book on President Truman, it was also orally stated to this author in 1997 when Elsey was writing the foreword for one of my earlier books and reiterated nearly verbatim during a discussion with several attendees of his October 23, 2003, presentation at the Harry S. Truman Library. It is apparent that Elsey had found himself having to steer people back to this fundamental reality of the day so many times that this point had become for him a boilerplate statement.

38. Elsey to author, March 30, 1997. See also Elsey, *An Unplanned Life*, 89–90.

39. Pogue, *George C. Marshall*, 23. From a February 11, 1957, interview for the George C. Marshall Foundation.

40. George F. Kennan to author, October 6, 1997. Kennan is best known for his leading role in the development of Cold War programs and institutions, notably the Marshall Plan and the "containment policy" toward the Soviet Union.

Appendix C

1. Ferrell, *Harry S. Truman and the Cold War Revisionists*, vii.

2. For example, see *The Christian Century LXII*, August 29, 1945, 974–76.

3. Norman Cousins and Thomas K. Finletter, "A Beginning for Sanity," *Saturday Review of Literature*, June 15, 1946, 5–9.

4. P. M. S. Blackett, *Fear, War, and the Bomb: Military and Political Consequences of Atomic Energy* (New York: McGraw-Hill, 1949), 134–39; *U.S. Strategic Bombing Survey, Summary Report (Pacific War)* (Washington DC: Government Printing Office, 1946), 22–26.

5. Karl T. Compton, "If the Atomic Bomb Had Not Been Used," *Atlantic Monthly*, December 1946, 54–56; Stimson, "The Decision to Use the Atomic Bomb," 97–107; Henry L. Stimson and McGeorge Bundy, *On Active Service in War and Peace* (New York: Harper and Brothers), 1948. For the views of Williams and Fleming see William Appleman Williams, *The Tragedy of American Diplomacy* (Cleveland OH: World, 1959) and D. F. Fleming, *The Cold War and Its Origins* (Garden City NY: Doubleday, 1961).

6. Herbert Feis, *Japan Subdued: The Atomic Bomb and the End of the War in the Pacific* (Princeton NJ: Princeton University Press, 1961), 179–81. See also Feis, *The Atomic Bomb and the End of World War II* (Princeton NJ: Princeton University Press, 1966); Butow, *Japan's Decision to Surrender*, 228–33.

7. Gar Alperovitz, *Atomic Diplomacy: Hiroshima and Potsdam* (New York: Vintage, 1965), 179–85, 239, 240.

8. Robert James Maddox, *The New Left and the Origins of the Cold War* (Princeton NJ: Princeton University Press, 1973), 63–78. See also Maddox, "Atomic Diplomacy: A Study in Creative Writing," *Journal of American History* 59 (March 1973): 925–34.

9. Martin Sherwin, *A World Destroyed: The Atomic Bomb and the Grand Alliance* (New York: Vintage Books, 1975), 198.

10. Lisle A. Rose, *Dubious Victory: The Atomic Bomb and the End of the War in the Pacific* (Kent OH: Kent State University Press, 1973), 158–60, 185–87, 215–17, 365–67; Barton J. Bernstein, "Roosevelt, Truman, and the Atomic Bomb: A Reinterpretation," *Political Science Quarterly* 90 (Spring 1975): 23–69; "A Postwar Myth," 38–40; and "Compelling Japan's Surrender without the A-Bomb, Soviet Entry, or Invasions: Reconsidering the US Bombing Survey's Early-Surrender Counterfactual," *Journal of Strategic Studies* 18, no. 2 (June 1995): 138.

11. Drea, *MacArthur's ULTRA*, 202–25.

12. The best overview of the NASM script and scholarship is Newman, *Enola Gay and the Court of History*. For a different viewpoint see Michael Hogan, "The Enola Gay Controversy: History, Memory, and the Politics of Presentation," in Hogan, *Hiroshima in History and Memory*. For the "war of vengeance" quotation see "The Crossroads: The End of World War II, the Atomic Bomb, and the Origins of the Cold War," in *Judgment at the Smithsonian*, ed. Philip Nobile (New York: Marlow, 1995), 3.

13. Ferrell, *Harry S. Truman: A Life*, 198–217; Hamby, *Man of the People*, 312–37; Weintraub, *The Last Great Victory*.

14. Maddox, *Weapons for Victory*; Newman, *Truman and the Hiroshima Cult*, esp. 33–56. See also Newman, "Ending the Pacific War with Japan: Paul Nitze's 'Early Surrender' Counterfactual," *Pacific Historical Review* 64 (May 1995): 167–94. Later that year Barton J. Bernstein wrote that the USSBS's pre–November 1945 surrender case "was not substantiated by the survey in its own work." In 1997 Gian Gentile subjected the USSBS to

further damaging scrutiny. See Bernstein, "Compelling Japan's Surrender," 127–28; Gian Peri Gentile, "Advocacy or Assessment: The United States Strategic Bombing Survey of Germany and Japan," *Pacific Historical Review* 66, no. 1 (February 1997): 53–79. Another important volume published in 1995 supportive of Truman's atomic bomb decision, by military historians Allen and Polmar, is *Code-Name Downfall*.

15. Alperovitz, *The Decision to Use the Atomic Bomb*; Walker, *Prompt and Utter Destruction*, 132.

16. Maddox, "Gar Alperovitz: Godfather of Hiroshima Revisionism," in Maddox, *Hiroshima in History*, 14; Bernstein, "The Interpretive Problems of Japan's 1945 Surrender," in *The End of the Pacific War: Reappraisals*, ed. Tsuyoshi Hasegawa (Stanford CA: Stanford University Press, 2007), 25.

17. For example, see Bernstein, "A Postwar Myth."

18. Giangreco, "Casualty Projections," 521–81. On what Truman knew and how he reacted, see Giangreco, "'A Score of Bloody Okinawas and Iwo Jimas,'" 93–132.

19. Herbert Bix, "Japan's Delayed Surrender: A Reinterpretation," *Diplomatic History* 19, no. 2 (Spring 1995): 223. See also Bix, *Hirohito and the Making of Modern Japan*, 533–79, esp. 560–72.

20. Lawrence Freedman and Saki Dockrill, "Hiroshima: A Strategy of Shock," in *The Second World War in Asia and the Pacific, 1941–1945*, ed. Saki Dockrill (New York: St. Martin's Press, 1994), 191–212; Asada, "The Shock of the Atomic Bomb," 478–511.

21. Bernstein's articles include "The Atomic Bombings Reconsidered," *Foreign Affairs* 74, no. 1 (January–February 1995): 135–52; and "Understanding the Atomic Bomb and the Japanese Surrender: Missed Opportunities, Little Known Near Disasters, and Modern Memory," *Diplomatic History* 19, no. 2 (Spring 1995): 227–73. See also Skates, *The Invasion of Japan*, and Chappell, *Before the Bomb*.

22. J. Samuel Walker, "Bomb! Unbomb!," *New York Times Book Review*, December 12, 1999, 35; Frank, *Downfall*, 360.

23. Hasegawa, *Racing the Enemy*.

24. Michael Kort, "Racing the Enemy: A Critical Look," *Historically Speaking*, January/February 2006, 2224; David Holloway, "Jockeying for Position in the Postwar World: Soviet Entry into the War with Japan in August 1945," in Hasegawa, *The End of the Pacific War*, 145–88; Sadao Asada, review of *Racing the Enemy*, in the *Journal of Strategic Studies* 29, no. 1 (February 2006): 169–71.

25. Miscamble, *From Roosevelt to Truman*, 325. See also Robert J. Maddox, "Give Me That Old Time Revisionism," *Continuity* (Spring 2003): 121–45.

26. Hasegawa, *The End of the Pacific War*; Maddox, *Hiroshima in History*; Michael Kort, *The Columbia Guide to Hiroshima and the Bomb* (New York: Columbia University Press, 2007). For a volume that examines some niche aspects of the Hiroshima debate, see Michael D. Gordin, *Five Days in August: How World War II Became a Nuclear War* (Princeton NJ: Princeton University Press, 2007).

27. Sean L. Malloy, *Atomic Tragedy: Henry L. Stimson and the Decision to Use the Bomb against Japan* (Ithaca NY: Cornell University Press, 2008); Andrew J. Rotter, *Hiroshima: The World's Bomb* (Oxford: Oxford University Press, 2009), esp. 307. About half of a third volume, Campbell Craig and Sergey Radchenko's *The Atomic Bomb and the Origins of the Cold War* (New Haven CT: Yale University Press, 2008), is devoted to the events that led to the bombing of Hiroshima, but the authors rely heavily and uncriti-

cally on bits and pieces of Sherwin, Bernstein, and Hasegawa, adding to that mix little more than unsubstantiated assertions and speculation to produce a discussion that is uninformed and often incoherent.

28. Giangreco, *Hell to Pay*, 204.

29. Miscamble, *The Most Controversial Decision.*

30. Paul Ham, *Hiroshima Nagasaki: The Real Story of the Atomic Bombings and Their Aftermath* (New York: St. Martin's Press, 2011). For Richard Frank's review, see *HistoryNet*, February 14, 2017, https://www.historynet.com/book-review-hiroshima-nagasaki.htm.

31. Giangreco, *Hell to Pay*, xxviii.

32. David Dean Barrett, *140 Days to Hiroshima* (New York: Diversion Books, 2020).

33. Waldo Heinrichs and Marc Gallicchio, *Implacable Foes: War in the Pacific, 1944–1945* (New York: Oxford University Press, 2017), 595.

34. Marc Gallicchio, *Unconditional: The Japanese Surrender in World War II* (New York: Oxford University Press, 2020), 211, 213.

Appendix D

1. Jones, *Manhattan*, 274.

Appendix H

1. Released to the press by the Department of State on February 11, 1946; printed as Department of State Executive Agreement Series no. 498; also in 59 Stat. 1823.

2. I. Stalin.

Appendix K

1. Francis B. Kish, "Citizen-Soldier Harry S. Truman, 1884–1972," *Military Review*, February 1973, 30–44.

2. Kish, "Citizen-Soldier," 30–44.

3. Letter of 11 February 1937 to Bess Truman, in Ferrell, *Dear Bess.*

4. McCullough, *Truman*, 229.

5. Alfred Steinberg, *The Man from Missouri: The Life and Times of Harry S. Truman* (New York: G. P. Putnam's Sons, 1962), 190.

6. Joint Chiefs of Staff Corrigendum to JCS 1388, "Details of the Campaign against Japan," June 18, 1945. It was suggested in Barton J. Bernstein's "Understanding the Bomb and the Japanese Surrender: Missed Opportunities, Little Known Near Disasters, and Modern Memory," *Diplomatic History* 19 (Spring 1995): 233, that Marshall's opening statement was "virtually a lecture to Truman, the former army captain," and that the "insecure" president "received counsel that few men, and certainly not a newcomer, could have resisted." Marshall's statement is characterized as "clear and pungent: Be tough and decisive, endorse the Kyushu operation, and be a true leader." In reality, Marshall's introductory remarks, while certainly to the point, were of a style and format that the president would find extremely familiar after a nearly thirty-year career as an army officer.

7. Keijo and Fusan are the Japanese names for Seoul and Pusan on the Korean Peninsula.

8. The AFPAC kill ratio for this period was actually closer to 22.6 to 1. In a statistical anomaly, the kill ratios of the Leyte and Luzon operations also played out at 22 to 1, although the daily tally of known American and estimated Japanese deaths varied considerably within these campaigns. Aside from the 22 to 1 ratio, taken from *Health*, May

31, 1945, 15, were ratios of 8, 9, and 4 to 1 from Saipan, Guam, and Iwo Jima respectively, which were published in that edition but not used by Marshall at the June 18 meeting.

9. [ADDITIONAL NOTE FOR THIS APPENDIX: Memorandum, Brig. Gen. George A. Lincoln, chief of the Strategy and Policy Group, to Lt. Gen. John Hull, chief of the Operations Division l, June 18, 1945, microfilm "GHQ, SWPA," courtesy Edward J. Drea. Readers may better grasp the phraseology in this memo as well as the significance of the Marshall-JWPC wording if they know that, although the month-long siege of Manila ended on March 3, 1945, Luzon remained the scene of intense fighting until the surrender of Japan. For example, from April through late May the U.S. 25th and 32nd Infantry Divisions lost 1,510 killed and 4,250 wounded to secure a series of northern Luzon passes. Their troops also suffered an excessively large number of psychiatric breakdowns—the inevitable result of inadequate numbers of troops committed to a lengthy operation. The 6th Infantry Division battling for the critical dams east of the capital in April saw fully three soldiers lost to psychosis or disease for *each* of its 1,335 killed or wounded. Further airborne and amphibious operations on Luzon were only days away when Truman met with the JCS and service secretaries. See Rafael Steinberg, *Return to the Philippines* in *The United States Army in World War II* (Alexandria VA, 1979), 176–93.]

10. For monthly U.S. combat losses in Northwest Europe, see *Army Battle Casualties*, 32. U.S. Army battle casualties for June (three-plus weeks) and July–September 1944 (four-plus weeks each) were 39,367; 51,424; 42,525; and 42,183, respectively. The monthly European theater average from November 1944 through January 1945 was 65,760, and 44,660 from February through April 1945. U.S. Army average monthly casualties in the Mediterranean Theater through this time frame were 7,884, p. 34. British total (ground force including Canadian and Polish elements) is from *War Diary, 21st Army Group, 'A' Section, SITREP, 29 August 1944* and (Royal Air Force) from Ellis and Warhurst, *Victory in the West*, 1:488. See also *United Kingdom, Central Statistical Office, Statistical Digest of the War* (London: HMSO and Longmans Green, 1951), 11, 13.

11. For an analysis of the weather's critical impact on the timing of the two invasion operations, see D. M. Giangreco, "Operation Downfall: The Devil Was in the Details," *Joint Force Quarterly*, Autumn 1995, 86–94.

12. "Staff Study, 'Olympic,' Operations in Southern Kyushu," May 28, 1944, appendix B, annex 4, CINCAFPAC, CARL. What this figure does not include is the land, sea, and air forces operating in direct combat support of the Kyushu invasion from the Philippines, Okinawa, Iwo Jima, the Marianas, Ulithi, or the sea, nor does it include combat divisions and other units involved in garrison duty, formations specifically earmarked for employment in the follow-up invasion on Honshu, or the support infrastructure at bases further to the rear such as those in Hawaii, the ports of embarkation, and other locations. It also does not count the combat division in "strategic reserve" on Okinawa but does include the one held in "floating reserve" during the landings since it was slated to be committed at the discretion of the Sixth Army commander.

13. Huber, *Japan's Battle for Okinawa*, 119–20. Extrapolated from *10th Army, G-1 Periodic Reports*, no. 13, 1–3.

14. Harry S. Truman diary, June 1, 1945, HSTLM.

15. John J. McCloy, *The Challenge to American Foreign Policy* (Cambridge MA: Harvard University Press, 1953), 42–43.

1. The meeting was held at Truman's quarters, 2 Kaiserstrasse, Babelsberg. Stalin and his party called on Truman at noon and stayed for luncheon. Information as to time and participants other than Vyshinsky from the Log (ante, 12). Vyshinsky's presence is mentioned in a diary entry by Truman dated July 19, printed in William Hillman, *Mr. President: The First Publication From the Personal Diaries, Private Letters, Papers and Revealing Interviews of Harry S. Truman* (New York: Farrar, Straus and Young, 1952), 123.

2. Leahy apparently joined the meeting when the luncheon was served. See Leahy, *I Was There*, 396–97.

3. Transcribed for this volume from longhand notes in pencil. In interviews with Department of State historians on July 11, 1955, January 25, 1960, and February 8, 1960, Bohlen expressed certainty (since at earlier conferences of heads of government it had been his practice, without exception, to transcribe his notes into minutes or memoranda of conversation) that he transcribed these notes into a memorandum of conversation shortly after the meeting took place. Because of Stalin's reference to the entry of the Soviet Union into the war against Japan, it is possible that such a memorandum would have been given special security handling, but a search of the department's various file collections and of the Truman and Byrnes Papers has failed to bring such a memorandum to light. A literal transcription of the original notes is therefore printed here. For a fuller reconstruction of the first Truman-Stalin conversation, prepared by Bohlen in March 1960 on the basis of these notes and from memory, see document no. 1418, post., 1582–90.

For other accounts of this meeting, see Hillman, *Mr. President*, 123; Truman, *Year of Decisions*, 341–42; Leahy, *I Was There*, 396–97; James F. Byrnes, *Speaking Frankly* (New York: Harper & Brothers, 1947), 68, 205; Byrnes, *All in One Lifetime*, 290–91. Byrnes's second account (the account printed in *All in One Lifetime*) erroneously ascribes to this meeting one subject—a peace feeler from Japan—that Truman and Stalin actually discussed on the following day, July 18. See post, p. 87.

Both Byrnes and Leahy mention the fact that Stalin discussed the death or disappearance of Hitler—a subject not mentioned in the Bohlen notes. Since Leahy apparently did not join the meeting until luncheon was served, it is probable that this subject was discussed during luncheon and that the Bohlen notes cover only the conversation before luncheon.

Stimson's diary for July 17 includes the following entry relating to the Truman-Stalin meeting of that date: "The President, however, told me briefly of his first meeting with Stalin and said he thought that he had clinched the Open Door in Manchuria."

4. Marshal Stalin. Although Stalin had been raised to the rank of generalissimo on June 27, he was frequently referred to at the Berlin Conference as "Marshal Stalin" or "the Marshal."

5. Molotov.

6. Possibly an abbreviation for Arciszewski.

7. See document no. 1417, post, section vi.

8. San Francisco; i.e., at the United Nations Conference on International Organization. Concerning the "regime of trusteeship," see chapters xi–xiii of the Charter of the United Nations, signed at San Francisco, June 26, 1945 (Treaty Series no. 993; 59 Stat. [2] 1031).

9. Byrnes.

10. See also memorandum by the president, post, p. 183.

11. Possibly an abbreviation for Americans.

12. Winston Churchill.

13. Roosevelt.

14. Prime minister, i.e., Churchill.

15. Versus, i.e., against.

16. Outer Mongolia.

17. Negotiations.

18. Port Arthur.

19. Concerning the Stalin-Soong conversations referred to here, see *FRUS: Conference at Berlin*, 1:857.

20. See Truman, *Memoirs*, 268–70.

21. The word "assurance" is an interlineation.

22. Manchuria.

23. The reference is to the Soviet-Czechoslovak Treaty of Friendship, Mutual Assistance, and Post-War Cooperation, signed at Moscow, December 12, 1943, which was to remain in force for twenty years. For text, see Department of State, Documents and State Papers, 1:228.

24. See, for example, the agreement regarding entry of the Soviet Union into the war against Japan, signed February 11, 1945. For text, see Executive Agreement Series no. 498; 59 Stat. (2) 1823; *Foreign Relations, The Conferences at Malta and Yalta*, 1945, 984.

25. For a description of and citations to the treaties referred to, see post, 1231.

26. Majority.

Appendix P

1. The papers of the Joint Chiefs of Staff indicate, "These minutes were transcribed from notes taken by the United States Secretaries."

2. See *FRUS: Conference at Berlin*, 2:352.

3. Document no. 1279, post.

4. Document no. 1278, post.

5. Not printed.

6. Not printed.

7. Not printed.

8. Not printed.

9. Not printed.

10. In conformity with Marshall's statement, a copy of the minutes of this meeting was transmitted to the Soviet Chiefs of Staff the next day, July 27, under a memorandum that repeated the observation that in the absence of comment by the Soviet Chiefs of Staff their approval would be assumed. There is no evidence that any reply was made.

11. Not printed.

Appendix Q

1. CCS [Combined Chiefs of Staff], 239/1, note by the secretaries, subject: Operations in the Pacific and Far East in 1943–44, May 23, 1943 (copy for info to CINC, SWPA [General MacArthur], in *Soviet Entry*, 19).

2. Soviet forces in the Far East were plagued by extreme materiel shortages. A telling example of this was their lack of motor transport. Because of the grinding battles west of the Urals it is possible, perhaps even probable, that before Milepost the Soviet's Far

Eastern armies had even fewer trucks available to them than the five thousand spread throughout the region in 1938. Some four thousand of these were reputedly assigned to labor camps. Alvin D. Coox, "The Lesser of Two Hells," 72–110, esp. 82.

3. Deane, *The Strange Alliance*, 255–57.

4. Deane, *The Strange Alliance*, 262–65; Jacob W. Kipp and General Makhmut Akhmetevich Gareev, "'To Break the Back of Japan,'" 31–35, 42–44, 58–62.

5. Kipp and Gareev, "'To Break the Back of Japan,'" 50, citing "War Game Third Phase," 2, box 12, U.S. Military Mission to Moscow, October 1943–October 1945, RG 334, entry 309, NARA.

6. "War Game Third Phase," 9–10, box 12, U.S. Military Mission to Moscow, October 1943–October 1945, RG 334, entry 309, NARA.

7. JCS 1176, report by Joint Planning Staff, subject: "Russian Participation in the War against Japan," November 23, 1944. Copy for info to Commander in Chief (CINC), Southwest Pacific Area.

8. Meeting, February 6, 1945, *Argonaut Conference, January–February 1945: Papers and Minutes of Meetings* (Office of the U.S. Secretary of the Combined Chiefs of Staff: Washington DC, 1945), 279–80. See also *FRUS: Malta and Yalta, 1945* (Washington DC: United States Department of State, GPO, 1955), 651.

9. February 6, 1945, meeting, *FRUS: Malta and Yalta*, 839–41. See also *Soviet Entry*, 48–49.

10. Kipp to author: July 8, 2014, and July 19, 2016. This exchange is described in volume 3 of Admiral Kuznetsov's memoirs, *Kurs na podedu* (The course toward victory) in the chapter on Yalta.

11. In *FRUS: Malta and Yalta*, see Admiral King statement (835), referencing his memorandum (761–62) covering the February 8, 1945, agreement establishing Project Hula: "Admiral King stated that his discussion with Admiral Kuznetsov was an adequate reply to our question concerning the La Perouse Strait."

12. Russell, *Project Hula*, 8–12, 33; *FRUS: Malta and Yalta*, 760–62, 835; Slavinsky, *Soviet Occupation*, 17–18, 52; Kipp and Gareev, "'To Break the Back of Japan,'" 44–47, 71; Budzbon, 23, 40–42, 47.

13. Meetings, February 6 and 9, 1945, *FRUS: Malta and Yalta*, 759.

14. CINCPAC Command Summary [CCS], King to Nimitz, February 20, 1945, bk. 6, 3022.

15. CCS, King to Nimitz, March 24, 1945, bk. 6, 3022.

16. CCS, King to Nimitz, March 24, 1945, bk. 6, 3059.

17. CCS, Nimitz to King, March 29, 1945, bk. 6, 3061.

18. CCS, Nimitz to King, March 29, 1945, bk. 6, 3061.

19. CCS, Nimitz to King, April 5, 1945, bk. 6, 3078; Nimitz to King, May 1, 1945, 3221; and Nimitz to King, info Halsey and Fletcher, May 21, 1945, 3230.

20. This was a very sensitive issue. The Soviets claimed to have lost eight ships to American submarines from the northern reaches of the Philippine Sea through to the shipping lane east of the Kamchatka Peninsula and Paramushiro Island. The first instance in the Sea of Japan occurred with the sinking of oceanographic vessel *Siener* N20 by the USS *Permit* on July 9, 1943. The U.S. later reported only two other major incidents and several close calls and maintained that each time the Russian ships had been running without proper identification and illumination. See Nathaniel Patch, "Friendly Fire in the 'Emperor's Bathtub,'" *Naval History*, August 2022, 26–33, citing *Attacks on Russian Shipping, Submarine Operational History, World War II*, vol. 4, Commander, Submarine Force, U.S. Pacific Fleet,

World War II Command Files, RG 38, NARA; and Alla Paperno, "The Unknown World War II in the North Pacific," translated from her lecture at the International Scientific and Practical Conference "Results of the World War II and Mission on Secure Peace in the XXI Century," St. Petersburg, Russia, House of Friendship and Peace, April 27–28, 2000.

21. CCS, Nimitz to multiple commands, April 5, 1945, bk. 6, 3071; Morison, *History of United States Naval Operations in World War II*, 14:101, 133, 186.

22. CCS, Nimitz to King and King to Nimitz, June 13, 1945, bk. 6, 3247–48.

23. *FRUS: The Conference in Berlin* (Washington DC: Government Printing Office, 1960), 2:351. See also CCS, "Joint Chiefs of Staff to CINCAFPAC (MacArthur), CINCPAC (Nimitz), USSTAFPAC (Spaatz), AGWAR (Adjutant General, War Department)," July 27, 1945, bk. 7, 3415.

24. CCS, Nimitz to King, May 3, 1945, bk. 6, 3222; Nimitz to Commander, Cruiser Division 5 and other relevant commands, July 25, 1945, bk. 7, 3407; Nimitz to Vice Adm. John H. Towers, July 25, 1945, bk. 7, 3496.

25. CCS, Nimitz to Towers; and Nimitz to Vice Adm. Frank J. Fletcher and copied to King, July 28, 1945, 3498–99. See also Allen and Polmar, *Code-Name Downfall*, 151. Adm. Martin would later command the U.S. Seventh Fleet during the Korean War.

26. Appendix P—Potsdam: The Second Tripartite Military Meeting, Thursday, July 26, 1945, from *Foreign Relations of the United States: The Conference in Berlin* (Washington DC: Government Printing Office, 1960), 2:344–353; also CCS, "Joint Chiefs of Staff to CINCAFPAC (MacArthur), CINGPAC (Nimitz), USSTAFPAC (Spaatz), AGWAR," July 27, 1945, bk. 7, 3415.

27. Appendix P—Potsdam; and CCS, 3415–16.

28. Appendix P—Potsdam; and CCS, 3411, 3416.

29. Appendix P—Potsdam; and CCS, 3411.

30. Appendix P—Potsdam; and CCS, 3411.

31. Appendix P—Potsdam; and CCS, 3411; and *FRUS: Berlin*, 2:414–15.

32. *FRUS: Berlin*, 2:351.

33. Appendix P—Potsdam; CCS, 3411, *FRUS: Berlin*, 2:415.

34. CCS, 3411.

35. Giangreco, *Hell to Pay*, 64, 206, 214, 235. On air base development, see 206; "Operations Against Kyushu," ASF-P-SL-2, December 18, 1944, 5, in "History of Planning Division, Army Service Forces," Planning Division, Army Service Forces, Washington DC, 1946, vol. 7, appendix 9-R, 16; *Engineers of the Southwest Pacific, 1941–1945* (Tokyo: Office of the Chief Engineer, General Headquarters, Army Forces, Pacific, 1950), 1:319–20; and Karl C. Dod, *The Corps of Engineers: The War Against Japan* (Washington DC: Center of Military History, United States Army, 1966), 672–73. See also "Report on Operation 'Olympic' and Japanese Counter-Measures," Combined Operations Headquarters, August 1, 1946, pt. 4, CINCPAC table "Appendix 43, Air Base Development." See also *Staff Study, Operations, "Coronet,"* General Headquarters, AFPAC, August 15, 1945, Annex 4, Appendix C.

36. Appendix P—Potsdam; CCS, 3111; and *FRUS: Berlin*, 2:415.

37. CCS, Nimitz to Fletcher and copied to King, July 28, 1945, 3498, and August 8, 1945, bk. 7, 3435.

38. Coox, *Nomonhan*, 1176.

39. *Reports of General MacArthur* (Tokyo: General Headquarters, Supreme Allied Command, Pacific, 1950), vol. 1, supplement, 130.

INDEX

Acheson, Dean, 235n32

Air Force Association, 129

Alaska, xii, 54, 76, 199, 201; training of
Soviet sailors in, xii, 54, 76, 202. *See also*
Hula, Project

Aleutian Islands, 199–200, 211

Alexandrovsk, 194, 208

Allday, Martin, 9

Allen, Thomas B., 11, 217n30, 236–37n14

Alperovitz, Gar, 125–27, 131–32, 134–35,
218n40, 219n44, 219n48

Amberg, Julius, 28

America First movement, 82

American Red Cross, 114

Amur River, 40, 42, 194, 208, 222n15

Anami Korechika, xiii, xiv, 106

Antonov, Alexei E., 66–67; at Moscow Conference, 45, 64, 222n20; at Potsdam Conference, 108, 183, 187–98, 205–10; at Yalta
Conference, 53, 202

Arnold, Henry H., 164, 173, 187, 192, 194–
95, 198

Asada, Sadao, 13, 16–17, 133, 134

Atlantic Charter, 40, 56, 58, 69–70

atomic bomb, 1–2, 4–5, 35, 129, 131–34, 174–
76, 213; authorization of, 104–5, 114, 177,
178; congressional inquiries on, 24–31, 83,
104, 124; debate over use of, 2, 8, 10, 13, 15–
16, 18, 20, 75, 109, 111, 114, 121–23, 130–40,
141–46, 219n44, 230n24; Interim Committee and, 75–76, 227n11; and Japanese leadership, 15, 105–6, 132; shock strategy and,
4, 15–16, 102, 105, 114–15, 132–33, 174; targeted cities of, 105; Trinity nuclear test
of, 76, 105, 111–13, 174; Truman's knowledge of, 20, 22, 24–35, 114, 147, 150, 235n32.
See also Hiroshima; Manhattan Project;
Nagasaki

Atomic diplomacy, 37, 124–27, 130–32, 135.
See also Cold War

Austria, 85

Baltic States, 40, 57–58. *See also* Estonia;
Latvia; Lithuania

Barkley, Alben W., 145

Barney, Operation, 205

Barrett, David Dean, 137

Bering Sea, 190–91, 194, 207–8

Berlin, 78, 83, 104

Berlin Conference, 112–13, 182, 187, 213,
219n6, 235n32, 240n4. *See also* Potsdam
Conference

Bernstein, Barton J., 13, 112, 127, 131, 133,
136, 230n24, 231n27, 232n44, 234n27, 236–
37n14, 237–38n27

Bessell, William W., Jr., 94

Bird, Kai, 19, 112, 135, 219n48

Bix, Herbert, 15, 132

Blackett, P. M. S., 123, 218n40

Black Sea, 40

Bland, Larry, 20–21, 67

Bohlen, Charles E., 182, 231n26, 240n3

Bougainville, 5

Bowles, Edward R., 93, 159

Bradley, Omar, 235n32

Brewster, Oswald C., 92

Bridges, Styles, 145

Bulgaria, 85

Bush, Vannevar, 26, 31, 76, 141, 143, 145, 227

Butow, Robert J. C., 124

Iwo Jima, 2, 80, 92, 97, 110, 167, 216n9, 239n12

Japan: air forces and air power, 109, 175, 196, 204; casualties by prefecture, 117; casualties during war, 1–2, 4, 9, 12, 102, 109, 117, 173; casualties in Okinawa Prefecture, 2; determination to continue war, xii, xiv, 14–16, 47–48, 50, 105–6, 128–29, 131, 133, 139; Kamikaze operations, 109, 210, 234n20; Manila, 2, 215n3; military preparations for war against Soviet Union, 40–42, 47–48; projected casualties, 2; surrender, xiv, 105–6, 139, 211, 218n37. *See also* Imperial Japanese Army; Kwantung Army
Japanese-Soviet Neutrality Pact, 15, 47–48, 50
JCS 924, 49, 83, 86, 92
Jennings, John, 142
Johnson, Max S., 95
Joint Chiefs of Staff, 36, 49, 51–52, 64–66, 71, 88, 109; Joint Planning Staff, 49, 66, 94, 201; Joint War Plan Committee, 94–96, 98, 167, 231n32, 232n38, 239n9; meeting with President Truman, 3–4, 87, 91–93, 102, 103–4, 109, 113–14, 132, 164–65, 172–75, 231n32; meeting with Soviet chiefs of staff, 187–98, 206, 208; Strategy and Policy Group, 50, 92–96, 239n9; Strategy Section, 95
Jones, James, 5

Kagoshima, 5
Kamchatka Peninsula, 52, 194, 199, 201, 206–8, 242n20
Karafuto, Japanese, 49, 201, 205, 210. *See also* Sakhalin Island
Kawabe Torashirō, 47
Keelblocks 4, Operation, xii, 206–7, 211; planning of, 199, 204; Potsdam Conference orders to implement, 211
King, Ernest J., xiv, 3, 19–20, 80, 199, 201–6, 231n32; fleet movement plans and orders, 203–11; and Keelblocks 4, 211; meeting with President Truman, 94, 99–100, 164, 169, 171–72; at Potsdam Conference, xii, 187, 189, 191, 195–98, 205–9; at Yalta Conference, 53–54, 71, 242n11
Kipp, Jacob, 16, 45–46, 53, 222n20, 223n46
Kissinger, Henry, 9

Komandorskie Islands, 199
Konoye Fumimaro, 14
Korea, 25, 38, 43–44, 49–50, 86, 96, 165–66, 190–91, 196, 204–5, 207, 209–12
Korean War, 147, 235n32
Korea Strait, 204–5, 209–11. *See also* Tsushima Strait
Kort, Michael, 121
Kurile Islands, 86, 191, 195–96, 199–207, 209–10
Kuznetsov, Nikolai Gerasimovich, 53–54, 187, 191, 201–2, 206, 242n11
Kwantung Army, 40–44, 50–51, 53, 61, 64, 222n15. *See also* Imperial Japanese Army
Kyle, William H., 146
Kyushu, xiii–xiv, 4, 6–7, 44, 77, 92, 95–100, 102, 103–4, 109, 128–29, 165–66, 168–75, 180, 195–97, 216–17n14, 238n6, 239n13

Lake Baikal, 41, 222n15
Lake Khanka, 42
La Pérouse Strait, 40, 53–54, 202–5, 224n46, 242n11
Latvia, 58, 85. *See also* Baltic States
League of Nations, 58, 68, 85
Leahy, William D., 10, 33, 115, 182, 240n3; on Declaration of Liberated Europe, 70, 72–73; meeting with President Truman and Joint Chiefs, 3, 90–91, 94, 98, 100–101, 164, 170, 172; at Yalta, 70–71
LeMay, Curtis, xi
Lend-Lease, xii, 37, 41, 44, 46, 52, 54, 65–68, 74–75, 78, 84, 200, 222n20
Leyte Island, battle of, 95, 97, 167, 238–39n8, 239n9
Lincoln, George A., 50, 92–93, 95–96, 98, 167, 239n9
Lithuania, 85. *See also* Baltic States
Litvinov, Maxim, 39
Lowe, Frank, 24–25, 28–29, 33, 75, 95, 147–48
Lozovsky, Solomon, 39–40, 221n10
Luzon Island, battle of, 2, 97–98, 167–68, 232n38, 238–39n8, 239n9

MacArthur, Douglas, 77, 93, 96–97, 99, 128, 165, 166–69, 171, 193, 206, 208, 210; on atomic bomb, 105; informed of U.S.-Soviet agreements at Potsdam, 206, 208; on Soviet entry into the war, 39, 50–51

Maddox, Robert James, 11, 15, 17–18, 113, 125–26, 130–31, 135, 177

MAGIC, 50, 128, 131–32, 139. *See also* ULTRA

Mahon, George H., 146

Malloy, Sean, 136

Manchuko, 40, 44. *See also* Manchuria

Manchuria, xiii, xiv, 1, 16, 37, 42–44, 46–51; coordination with U.S. forces, 54, 55, 109, 188–98, 205–12; Japanese control of, 40, 42–43, 46–48, 50, 61, 77, 86, 96; Potsdam, second Tripartite Military Meeting in, 187–98; Soviet invasion plans for, 44–53, 55, 77, 86–87, 107, 185; Truman meeting in, 94, 166; U.S. support for invasion of, 37–38, 43–54, 61, 64–65, 72, 76–77, 86, 96, 107, 138, 205–12; Yalta Agreement and, 153–54. *See also* Milepost, Project; Trans-Siberian Railroad

Manhattan Project, xii, 24–33, 75–77, 92, 141–46, 227n11, 228n38; at Clinton Engineer Works, 141–42, 146; expansion and congressional investigations of, 141–46; at Hanford Engineer Works, 24, 26, 33, 142–46; at Los Alamos laboratory, 141, 143; at Oak Ridge laboratory, 33, 141, 143, 145; and Top Policy Group, 31

Manila, 50, 96; battle of, 2

Mariana Islands, xi, 239n12

Marshall, George C., xiv, 10, 20, 115; on American casualties, 2–3, 19, 80, 82–84, 90–92, 94–99, 101–2, 110, 111, 115; discussing casualties with Truman, 83–84, 94–99, 101–2, 110, 114, 166–68, 171–72; on invasion of Japan, 4, 165–66, 168–69; and Manhattan Project, 26–27, 31–32; at Potsdam Conference, 112, 187–98, 206; on Potsdam Conference objective, 96, 166; and Potsdam Conference Tripartite Military Meeting, 187–98, 199, 206–11; and Soviet entry into Pacific War, 39, 43, 50–51, 74, 96, 102, 166, 170; at Yalta Conference, 53, 71, 201

Martin, Joseph W., 85

May, Andrew J., 136, 142

McCloy, John J., 164, 176

McCormack, John W., 143

Messer, Robert L., 127

Michener, James, 6, 8–9

Mikolajczyk, Stanisław, 70

Milepost, Project, xii, 37–39, 44–48, 53–54, 66–68, 74–76, 83, 86, 107, 138, 200–203, 209, 228n38, 234n16, 241n2; deliveries of, 46–47; and reflagging of U.S. ships, 37, 46, 76; and Soviet requests, 45–46

Miscamble, Wilson D., 13, 135, 137, 234n16

Molotov, Vyacheslav, 40, 72, 74–75, 182

Mongolia, 153–54, 191, 207, 241

Morison, Samuel Eliot, 124

Morton, Louis, 124

Moscow, 14–15, 38, 40, 42–44, 51–52, 61, 64, 66, 72–73, 83–84, 86, 87, 106, 125, 131, 193, 200, 205, 207–8

Moscow Conference, 63–66; Soviets renege on basing agreement of, 66–67, 107. *See also* Milepost, Project

Murmansk, 37, 189

Nagasaki, xiii, 1, 6–7, 15, 105–6, 122–25, 131, 134, 137–39

National Air and Space Museum, 8–10, 12, 19, 129, 130, 134

Nazi government. *See* Germany

Nazi-Soviet Pact, 40

Neutrality Pact. *See* Japanese-Soviet Neutrality Pact

Newman, Robert P., 11, 13, 131, 134, 215n2, 216n12, 236n12

New York Times, 3, 19–20, 80, 218n40, 219n44, 234n28

Nikolaevsk, 194, 208

Nimitz, Chester W., 52, 105, 165, 193, 199–200; on atomic bomb, 105; planning and orders for fleet movements, 203–6, 208. *See also* Halsey, William F.

Normandy, 77, 97, 99, 167, 169, 232n41

Norstad, Lauris, 187, 198

North Atlantic Treaty Organization, 69

Oak Ridge laboratory TN, 141. *See also* Manhattan Project

Oder River, 55

Office of Scientific Research and Development, 26, 31, 76, 141, 227n11

Okhotsk Sea, 53, 190–91, 193–94, 201, 203–4, 207–8, 211

Truman, Harry S. (*cont.*)

Conference objective, 36–37, 55–56, 63, 83–84, 102, 107–8; preconference meeting with Stalin at Potsdam, 37–38, 104, 107, 182–86; as Russophile, 229n42; and Soviet Lend-Lease cut off, 74–75, 84; and Stalin, 37–38, 73, 79, 84–85, 87, 104, 107–8, 126, 182–86; and Trinity nuclear test, 104; Vyacheslav Molotov, White House meeting with, 74–75; White House war council with Joint Chiefs and service secretaries, 3–4, 36, 96–102, 103–4, 109, 113–14, 132, 163–76; Winston Churchill's "iron curtain" and "third world war" warnings to, 78–79, 81, 83–84, 184; World War I, 83, 163. *See also* atomic bomb; Senate Special Committee to Investigate the National Defense Program

Truman, Ralph, 163

Truman-Grew-Hull-Stimson-Vinson exchange, 3, 11, 18, 89–90, 93, 112, 216n12

Tsushima Strait, 44, 54, 195–97, 204–5, 208–11. *See also* Korea Strait

ULTRA, 128–29, 139. *See also* MAGIC

Umezu Yoshijirō, 47

United Nations, 60, 68–69, 79, 85, 108, 126, 215n2; UN Charter, 85, 108, 140n8

Ural Mountains, 41, 47, 223n24, 241n2

U.S. Congress, xii, 69, 82, 94, 231n26; drafting women nurses, 82; Lend-Lease, 67–68, 100; Manhattan Project, 24, 27, 30–31, 141–46; and Senate, xii–xiii, 13, 23, 27–28, 68, 85, 108, 130, 145, 163; and Senate Special Committee to Investigate the National Defense Program, 23–31, 33, 35, 75–76, 80, 82, 94, 104–5, 142–46, 147, 163–64

U.S. elections, 57, 59, 68; Catholic voters and, 57–58, 68, 70; and public opinion, 58–59, 68–70, 84–85, 87, 123

U.S. Military Mission to Moscow, 38, 42, 52, 200

U.S. State Department, 68, 72–73, 74

U.S. Strategic Bombing Survey, 13, 117, 123–24, 131, 134

Ussuri River, 40, 42

Vassilievski, Aleksandr, 193

Vaughan, Harry, 25, 28, 33, 163

Vietnam, 20, 124; protest movement, 8, 124. *See also* Cold War

Vinson, Fred M., 3, 11, 18, 90–91, 93, 112, 216n12

Vladivostok, 38, 41–43, 45–46, 54, 65, 193–97, 201–2, 205, 208, 210

Walker, J. Samuel, 131, 133, 136, 230n24

Wallace, Henry A., 31, 32, 36, 83, 228n38

Wallgren, Monrad, 26, 144

War Department, 2, 11, 24–25, 27–29, 49, 61, 66, 76, 96, 142–45, 147, 166, 200, 232n36. *See also* Pentagon

Warsaw, 50, 59, 61–63

Weintraub, Stanley, 11, 130

White, Wallace H., 145

Williams, William Appleman, 123

Wright, Quincy, 93, 159

Yalta Conference, 34, 38, 44, 49, 52, 55–57, 61, 64, 66, 68–69, 70, 77, 83, 85, 138, 200–201, 203; agreement on the entry of the Soviet Union into war, 71, 72–73, 86–87, 107, 153–54, 183, 185–86; Declaration of Liberated Europe, 70, 72–73; Truman-Stalin pledges to abide by agreements of, 37, 182–86

Yemashev, Ivan, 193, 208

Yugoslavia, 85